ROUTLEDGE LIBRARY EDITIONS:
ENERGY

Volume 7

THE GEOGRAPHY
OF ENERGY

THE GEOGRAPHY
OF ENERGY

GERALD MANNERS

Routledge
Taylor & Francis Group

LONDON AND NEW YORK

First published in 1964 by Hutchinson

This edition first published in 2019
by Routledge
2 Park Square, Milton Park, Abingdon, Oxon OX14 4RN

and by Routledge
52 Vanderbilt Avenue, New York, NY 10017

Routledge is an imprint of the Taylor & Francis Group, an informa business

British Library Cataloguing in Publication Data
A catalogue record for this book is available from the British Library

ISBN: 978-0-367-21122-6 (Set)
ISBN: 978-0-429-26565-5 (Set) (ebk)
ISBN: 978-0-367-21118-9 (Volume 7) (hbk)
ISBN: 978-0-429-26561-7 (Volume 7) (ebk)

Publisher's Note
The publisher has gone to great lengths to ensure the quality of this reprint but points out that some imperfections in the original copies may be apparent.

Disclaimer
The publisher has made every effort to trace copyright holders and would welcome correspondence from those they have been unable to trace.

THE GEOGRAPHY
OF ENERGY

Gerald Manners
Reader in Geography
University College London

HUTCHINSON UNIVERSITY LIBRARY
LONDON

HUTCHINSON & CO (*Publishers*) LTD
3 Fitzroy Square, London W1

London Melbourne Sydney Auckland
Wellington Johannesburg Cape Town
and agencies throughout the world

First published 1964
Reprinted 1966, 1968 and 1970
2nd, revised, edition 1971

*The photograph on the cover of the paperback
edition is reproduced by courtesy of Shell International Petroleum Company Ltd*

*This book has been set in Times type, printed in Great Britain
on smooth wove paper by Anchor Press, and
bound by Wm. Brendon, both of Tiptree, Essex*
ISBN 0 09 110380 0 (cased)
0 09 110381 9 (paper)

TO MY PARENTS

CONTENTS

FIGURES

TABLES

PREFACE

Parts of the first draft of this book were improved by the comments of Mr R. Priddle, Mr D. Thompson and Dr K. Warren, and for their help I am grateful. I also owe a considerable debt to Mr M. Chisholm without whose constructive criticism the book would have been the poorer, and to my wife for her interest, encouragement and assistance in the preparation of the manuscript.

The figures for this second edition were prepared by Miss Margaret E. Thomas in the Cartographic Unit of the Department of Geography at University College London.

G.M.

I

INTRODUCTION

L'architecture économique et politique du monde est conditionnée par les aptitudes inégales des collectivités humains à organiser la production, et, parmi les aptitudes, la mobilisation de l'énergie est une donnée fondamentale (George, 1950, 9).

The nature and the speed of economic development is intimately related to the control and the use of energy, and this relationship has a geographical expression. A low level of energy consumption in an economy is a certain indication of underdevelopment—for economic growth consists essentially of increasing the average productivity of a labour force, and this in turn is directly influenced by the quantity of energy which can be incorporated within the production process. The economic development of a country or region, therefore, hinges upon either the harnessing of its indigenous energy resources or the transport of energy supplies to it. A shortage of energy in an economy presents one of the most difficult barriers to economic progress. If the investment of capital in the energy sector lags, and the supply of energy becomes inelastic, parts of any productive investment are liable to remain idle. Indeed, the availability of energy to an economy is more important than its cost, for whilst energy constitutes an indispensable factor of production, its expense is frequently only a relatively small part of the total costs of manufacture. The importance of energy in economic development, therefore, is very much more than the modest contribution which the producer supplier industries make to the gross national product or its cost to that economy; serving as a catalyst as well as a fundamental input, it has both a qualitative as well as quantitative role in economic growth.

As a consequence of the close relationship between the use of energy and economic development, there is a high degree of positive

correlation between the consumption of energy and the standard
of living in a country. Table 1 shows income and energy consumption per head in several countries, and the close relationship between
the two, a relationship which pertains equally to the several regions
within a country. As Davis put it in 1957 (13): 'Most economies, as
they have developed, have devoted a smaller and smaller proportion
of their national income to the purchase of raw materials. Energy,
however, being required at all stages—primary, secondary and
tertiary—has moved upward more or less in line with and sometimes
ahead of each nation's total output of goods and services.' In
fact, research has shown the existence of such a close relationship,
both historical and geographical, between energy consumption and
the degree of economic activity that it has become common practice
to use the one to estimate the other (Guyol, 1960, 68–70).

Table 1

GROSS NATIONAL PRODUCT PER HEAD, ENERGY
PRODUCTION AND ENERGY CONSUMPTION IN
SELECTED COUNTRIES, 1965

Country	GNP per capita ($)	Energy production (million tons coal equivalent)	Energy consumption per capita (Kg coal equivalent)	Energy consumption per $1 of GNP (Kg coal equivalent)
United States	3,515	1,633	9,671	2·75
Canada	2,658	134	8,077	3·04
Denmark	2,333	1	4,149	1·78
Switzerland	2,331	3	2,699	1·16
West Germany	2,197	184	4,625	2·11
France	2,104	70	3,309	1·57
United Kingdom	1,992	194	5,307	2·66
New Zealand	1,970	3	2,603	1·32
Australia	1,910	38	4,697	2·46
Czechoslovakia	1,561	74	5,870	3·76
USSR	1,340	925	3,819	2·85
Japan	2,122	62	1,926	1·58
Venezuela	882	247	3,246	3·68
Cyprus	702	—	927	1·32
Libya	542	76	613	1·13
Chile	497	7	1,119	2·25

Source: Darmstadter et al. (in press) *passim; United Nations Statistical
Year Book.*

The correlation between energy consumption and the standard of living in countries and regions is, of course, far from perfect (see Fig. 1). Several explanations can be found for this. One is the nature of production and the stage of economic development. Certain types of industrial activity, such as steel and electro-chemical manufacture, consume much greater quantities of energy than others, without necessarily yielding a proportionate increment of wealth to the economy in which they are located. Much heavy industry is in this category. When, therefore, a country is passing through that phase of industrialization which involves the building-up of basic or heavy industries, there is a tendency for the amount of energy consumed per unit of national wealth to be greater than before industrialization—or after industrialization when lighter and service industries come to assume a greater importance in the economy. A second explanation of the imperfect correlation between energy consumption and gross national product is the variable efficiency with which fuels are transported and consumed. Solid fuels, for example, are technically more 'difficult' to transport and to use than liquid fuels and gases. A change in the fuel mix of an economy therefore—the fuel mix is the proportions of different energy sources which are combined to satisfy energy demands in a particular place—may imply the greater use of the more efficient fuels and so modify the precise relationship between energy consumption and wealth there. A third explanation is the nature of the physical environment. Technologically advanced economies in the temperate zones employ considerable quantities of energy for space heating both homes and workplaces, but comparable amounts are not required in tropical climes. And a final factor modifying the relationship between energy consumption and living standards is the possibility of input substitution in the production process. The creation of wealth involves the combination of many factors of production and it is often possible to substitute certain inputs—such as labour or capital—in place of energy inputs if the latter happen to be particularly expensive.

From Table 1 another point emerges. Although a high income per head is accompanied by a high level of energy consumption, it is not necessarily accompanied by the production of large quantities of energy within the same national boundaries. Where other factors favourable to industrial and economic growth are present, energy supplies can be and are imported; and when a local supply of energy is exhausted it is normal for an industry or country to scour the world for further supplies, rather than for production to be transferred to an alternative location with a ready source of energy. In fact, a large proportion of the world's fuel reserves are located in less developed

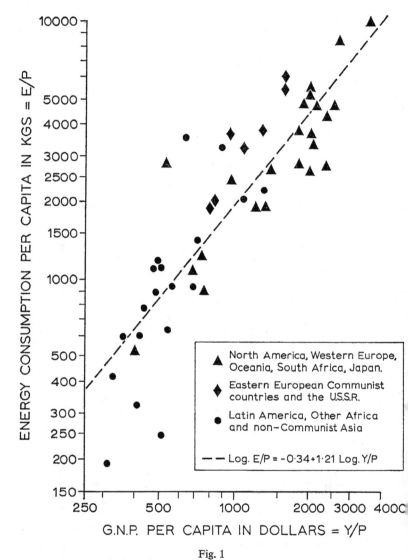

Fig. 1

The relationship between Gross National Product per capita and energy consumption per capita, 1965. (Source: Darmstadter, J. (1970), Energy and the economy, *Energy International*, August, 35)

economies which export the greater part of their present production to Japan, the USA and the highly industrialized countries of Western Europe. Quite clearly, the low levels of energy consumption in these developing countries is no fault of energy supplies, but rather is a consequence of a lack of demand, which in turn is the result of a complex of political, social, historical and economic causes. The same observation can be made at the regional scale. In the United States the two leading States from the point of view of income per head are Connecticut and New York, both of which produce almost no energy, whereas some of the major fuel-producing States have relatively low incomes per head. Only California and Illinois can claim both a high per capita income and a considerable energy production; but there is very little relationship between the two phenomena.

The spatial contrasts between energy production and consumption naturally imply substantial transfers of energy from its sources to its places of consumption. This movement of energy is significant in its own right; but it is the more so for the fact that energy shipments make up a very large proportion of total commodity movements and are a major element in the geography of transport. Just as coal dominated total freight movements by land and sea fifty years ago, so the transfer of oil is by far the largest item of transport by volume throughout the world today. In 1965, some 1,574 million tons of coal equivalent energy entered international trade, and of this 1,395 million tons were liquid fuels.

Energy, therefore, is a critically important factor in three major aspects of economic life. Its use is closely related to the nature and the speed of economic development, to geographical variations in the standard of living, and to some key elements in spatial interaction. In addition, it demands attention in so far as economic growth, and the steady replacement of animate energy with inanimate forms, have led to the expansion of energy production and consumption at an ever-increasing rate in recent decades. World energy consumption rose from 1,485 million coal equivalent tons in 1925 to 2,611 million tons in 1950 and 5,475 million tons in 1965: by 1980 the figure could be 11,195 million tons (Schurr and Homan, 1971, statistical appendix), these figures represent an average annual rate of increase of 2·3 % between 1925 and 1950, of 5·1 % between 1950 and 1965, and of 5·2 % between 1965 and 1980.

Economic geographers seek to understand, by description and analysis, the variable character of economic life over the surface of the earth and the associated spatial interchanges. Yet it is surprising that the study of the energy variable, important though it is, has received comparatively little attention in the past, and still excites only a limited curiosity today. Certainly there have been discussions of, and attempts to measure, the importance of energy in industrial location (Estall and Buchanan, 1961, ch. 3), and in regional economic development (Dales, 1953). But studies of energy *qua* energy have only a relatively small place in the literature of the subject. The work of Odell (1963; 1970) represents an outstanding exception.

In the study of the geography of energy, three sets of questions merit particular attention. The first concerns the production of the energy industries. Where is it located? Why is it located there, and how (and why) does the output of each component producer vary from place to place, and from time to time, in both quantity and quality? Are these production patterns seasonal? Are they changing with time; and if so, what are the significant trends? The second set of questions relates to the transport of energy. From where and to where is energy moved and why? What are the economics and methods of its transport? Are there seasonal characteristics in the energy flows, and what major changes are taking place in these movements? And the third set of questions centres upon the consumption of energy. What changes are taking place in the pattern of energy consumption? What is the energy mix of particular national or regional economies, and is it changing with time? Does the pattern of demand have temporal as well as spatial variations and what are the implications of these market characteristics for the producer and supplier industries?

It is the aim of this book to introduce the reader to some basic ideas which stem from a study of the spatial characteristics of energy production, transport and consumption. One possible approach might have been to examine the geography of each source of energy in turn—that is, to examine the geography of its resources, to discuss the pattern of its production throughout the world, to record the characteristics of its flows to its markets and to list the variety and location of those markets. An alternative approach might have been to study a series of energy economies—to notice the sources of energy consumed there, to examine the nature of energy transport used to satisfy those markets, to observe the substitution of one form of energy for another through time, and to discuss the complexity of the factors influencing the patterns of consumption. Certainly either of these approaches could provide some answers to our basic questions. But they would have several major disadvantages. First, they would tend to be repetitive, for in the case of the 'energy source approach' the factors which influence the geography of one type of energy are often very similar to those which influence another; and in the case of the 'energy economy approach' the critical factors moulding any one energy complex are closely related to those fashioning another, with only differences of emphasis between them. Second, by virtue of being repetitive, in both these approaches it would be virtually impossible to discuss any one of the major factors influencing the geography of energy in sufficient detail to do it justice and to give the study depth. The third, and much the most important, reason is that the pattern of one energy source or region depends in part upon the pattern of all others throughout the world. One cannot, therefore, finally isolate either a type of energy or a particular region without inclining to a misinterpretation of economic and geographical reality.

It is preferable, therefore, to examine the subject from an alternative perspective, avoiding the worst aspects of repetition and building an analytical structure within which the many complexities of the geography of energy might be appreciated at some depth. The approach which has been followed in the succeeding chapters attempts initially to expose something of the basic complexity of the subject by noting the range and the variety of factors which influence the geography of energy in all its facets. Then, in a discussion comprising the greater part of the book, those factors which provide the foundation stones upon which the other, less important, influences rest are singled out for detailed examination. The subsequent analysis thus provides a starting point from which specific questions relating to the geography of energy in particular places and at discrete points in time can be studied; and throughout this essentially suggestive, rather than definitive, approach to the subject, several examples of energy industries, energy flows and energy market complexes are discussed in some detail. In the chapters which follow no attempt is made to describe the contemporary geography of energy. The focus is upon those factors which explain it. In this respect the book stands in contrast to the only other major work with a similar title, Pierre George's *Géographie de l'Energie* (1950), in which the emphasis was upon descriptive rather than analytical understanding.

The approach must be qualified in two respects. First the book is concerned only with the geography of mechanical or inanimate energy. In the writings of the French geographers in particular (George, 1950; Sorre, 1948, 209 ff.), discussions of energy have tended to include some references to the use of animate energy. Important though this is in the nature and the functioning of many local and national economies throughout the world—and especially the less developed world—there is simply not space here for its adequate discussion. The second qualification is partly related to this. Although the examples quoted in the analysis are taken from all over the world, there is a heavy bias towards the literatures of Britain, Western Europe and North America. This results in part from the fact that the greater part of the world's energy is consumed in this North Atlantic region—in 1965 it used nearly 58 % of the world's output. It is also a consequence of the fact that the most detailed energy studies have been conducted and published in these countries. As a result, although the observations and conclusions of this study are generally applicable to the whole world, their relevance to the less developed economies must occasionally be reserved.

A note on measurement

The discussion to this point has referred to energy in a collective sense; but it must be remembered that energy is derived from different fuels and sources of power which present problems of comparative measurement (Warren, 1961). The different physico-chemical and technical characteristics of the several forms of energy, the varying efficiencies with which they are used and the complexities of their modes of consumption present serious and—in the last resort—insurmountable obstacles to the use of a single unit through which the different forms of energy can be *accurately* compared. British Thermal Units, kilocalories and therms can be used to measure heat; horse-power and kilowatts to measure power; coal equivalent tons, oil equivalent barrels and kilowatt hours to measure energy. Yet each of these has the same basic defect that no one numerical total can adequately represent a group of substantially different phenomena being used for quite different purposes. The potential energy of one particular fuel might be every bit as great as another, but the technological means available for their use may be quite different, making one relatively inefficient as a source of energy and capable of less work than the other. Moreover, a given fuel can be utilized for different purposes and the efficiency with which it is put to work can vary enormously. A ton of fuel oil, for example, which represents 10,500 thousand kilocalories of potential heat, could produce about 6,125 thousand kcal of useful space heat, 2,625 thousand kcal of electrical energy but only 875 thousand kcal of locomotive work.

Where electricity is concerned there is an even greater problem, and controversy continues as to whether it should be rated on its thermal value, or on the coal equivalent tonnage of fuels needed to generate it at the current average efficiency of power stations. In past statistical comparisons the conversion factor of 6 coal equivalent tons to 10,000 kWh has tended to be used, representing the amount of fuel which, on average, would be needed to generate that quantity of electrical energy. In 1958, however, the Statistical Office of the United Nations changed the rating of 10,000 kWh of hydro-electricity in its statistics to 1·25 c.e.t., representing the thermal content of that source of energy. Since much hydro-electricity is used as power, this conversion factor obscures the fact that if the electricity were to be generated in thermal power stations over four times as much fuel would be required. This issue exposes the distinction between fuel and power, the importance of which will be noted later (p. 73).

The measurement problem admitted, it is nevertheless useful to be able to make approximate comparisons of total energy production and consumption both within and between countries and over time. The reader must remember, therefore, that many of the statistics which are used in this book are based upon orders of magnitude rather than precise quantities. In order to facilitate comparisons and to reduce the variety of measures quoted, all quantities of energy are expressed in metric units after the practice of the United Nations Statistical Office. Reference to tons, therefore, implies metric tons. (It has to be admitted, however, that the sources of some statistics do not specify whether they are referring to long tons (1,016 kilograms), short tons (907 kg) or metric tons (1,000 kg), and this imprecision has had to be perpetuated; the magnitude of the inaccuracy is fortunately small.) Similarly, distances have been expressed in kilometres and monetary values in United States dollars.

2

THE BASIC COMPLEXITY

The variety of factors influencing the geography of energy

What factors influence which fuel is used in, say, the central heating system of a new house? The choice of the consumer is limited, in the first place, by the range of fuels which are available to him, and is influenced by their relative prices. In some locations only one fuel might be available, but where there is a choice it is highly likely that differences in price will distinguish the alternative fuels. These two factors, availability and price, are of course intimately related, for the geographical distribution of energy resources strongly influences the costs of exploring for, producing and then transporting energy to any given market. The fact that some of the lowest average fuel prices in the United States are in and around Texas, whilst the highest are in New England, is clearly related to the wealth of fossil fuels in the former region and the absence of commercial deposits of fuel in the latter. The price of the different fuels, however, will not conclude the matter for the consumer—for they must be weighed against the capital costs and the efficiency of suitable boilers. Is it better to settle for, say, a relatively expensive gas which burns at a high level of thermal efficiency, or for a coal which is cheaper and demands a less expensive boiler but which burns at a rather lower level of efficiency? And, viewing the matter in a dynamic as well as a static light, what will be the advantages of the different fuels in the near future? Are there liable to be differential trends in their costs; are supplies of all the fuels likely to remain freely available (or is there likely to be a shortage of one of them?); and is it possible that technological advances will alter their present relative advantages?

Nor will the decision of the consumer necessarily rest upon such economic and technological advantages alone. Convenience and service are worth paying for, and he will make some assessment of the merits of the different fuels in this light. Is it worth paying the extra cost of both a fuel and equipment which allow a fully automatic system, as opposed to a combination which requires daily loading? Will one type of boiler require more regular servicing than another? What is likely to be the efficiency of the service offered by the local distributors of the different fuels? Assuming our consumer has previously experienced unsatisfactory service with fuel A, he might be inclined to demote it in his order of preference on this occasion; should a neighbour affirm his confidence in fuel B and its local distributors, then there is a strong likelihood that this fuel will be considered more favourably.

And so one could go on. Even the most casual acquaintance with the factors lying behind the consumption of energy in different places reveals the complexity of the forces which affect the decisions of consumers in their use of fuel. There is a comparable labyrinth of influences moulding the patterns of energy production and transport. These factors—economic and social, political and historical, technical and, at times, fortuitous—are all intimately related to each other; and it is to a discussion of this complexity and interdependence of the factors affecting energy geography that this present chapter is devoted.

What, then, are the major forces which influence the geography of energy? One obvious factor is clearly the distribution of *energy resources* over the face of the globe. The importance of coal in the satisfaction of energy demands in Britain, Poland and South Africa —in 1965, it represented 64%, 92% and 85% respectively of their energy consumption—is obviously closely related to the distribution of that fossil fuel in nature; similarly, the relative importance of hydro-electricity in Canada and Japan—9·2% and 4·7% of the energy used there in 1965—is in part a function of their distinctive geomorphological and hydrological endowments. The geography of the world's oil and natural gas fields, the suitability of sites for the generation of hydro-electricity, and the pattern of the world's coal deposits clearly have a fundamental relevance to the spatial patterns of energy production, trade and consumption. Hartley observed in 1962 that, 'Until lately it was roughly true to say that 90% of the coal reserves of the world and over 80% of the oil reserves lie north of latitude 20° and two-thirds of the water power potential south of it.' Although these figures could be revised in the light of recent discoveries, the general point remains that the world's known supply of energy is distributed in a highly irregular fashion about the face of the globe.

There is, of course, no definitive measure of the world's endowment of energy resources and their distribution. Cost alone prohibits a systematic and comprehensive probing of the earth's crust to produce even an approximate yardstick of resource availabilities. But in any case the interest of society lies mainly in those resources which appear capable of being exploited today or in the near future; and these, of course, change with time as economic circumstances develop and technology advances. Statements concerning the availability and geography of resources, therefore, must always be highly qualified by the constraints of specific economic and technological circumstances, and the limitations of existing knowledge. Within such a set of constraints, it is clear that the *location* of a resource in relation to energy markets—and it is relative rather than absolute location which is clearly important—will strongly influence whether or not it will be exploited, and when (if at all) the exploitation will take place. Given hypothetically, identical occurrences of a particular energy resource in the British Isles and the Falkland Isles, it is fairly safe to predict which of the two would be exploited first, given the present contrasts in the degree of economic development in the two places. On the African continent there are huge potentialities for the generation of hydro-electricity, but their location is such that for many decades they will remain an untapped resource and will have mainly a cartographic value.

The *size* of an energy resource is as important as its location. Oil is found in nearly every country in varying degrees, but the bulk of the world's oil reserves—that is, that part of the resource base which can be economically exploited under existing and immediately prospective conditions—are to be found in the Middle East. A 1968 estimate of British Petroleum put the region's share at nearly 60%. Therefore it is not surprising that, from 3% in 1925, the same region produced nearly 27% of the world's oil forty years later. Although the Middle East is by no means isolated from the major trade routes of the world, its distance from the largest markets for oil is nevertheless considerable. Yet the size and the productivity of the oilfields of that region have out-weighed their relative isolation, to the extent that they have rapidly become one of the major contemporary sources of the world's energy. Similarly, within the context of the energy economy of the United States, the size of the recent oil discoveries in Alaska is clearly outweighing the costs imposed by the severity of physical conditions and the isolation of the resource, and has assured its exploitation.

The significance of the size and the location of energy resources is matched by the importance of their *nature*. With coal, the thickness of seams, the degree of faulting and the carbon content of the rock all affect the potentialities of a deposit for exploitation. In America, for instance, the importance of the northern Pennsylvanian coalfield owes much to the thickness of its seams and the surface outcrops of the coal—both of which lend themselves to a high degree of mechanization. But the Mid-Continent coalfield on the other hand has a large percentage of volatile matter and as a result the range of markets which it can serve is limited; its coals have very little value for the coke ovens of the Chicago-Gary steel industry, for example. Again, oil is not a uniform commodity. It occurs in a variety of forms, some of which are ill-suited to particular markets. Refined Saharan oils from Algeria yield a much lower proportion of fuel oil than Middle East crudes; although the mix would be reasonably well suited to the needs of the United States market (to which it has only limited access as a result of quota limitations, see pp. 179-80), it is not especially well matched to Western European requirements amongst which the market for fuel oil is particularly important. The political posture of the Algerian Government apart, this fact has undoubtedly restrained the rate of development of these North African resources.

The variable nature of potential sites for the generation of hydro-electricity is a major influence in the costs and hence the geography of electricity generation. Some sites, such as that at Niagara, or many in the Swiss and French Alps, are naturally well endowed for the production of power, since either the river régime or a natural lake offers a steady flow of water throughout the year to turn the turbines. Others, however, necessitate the construction of expensive dams in order to store and regulate the flow of water. Generally speaking, the higher the head, and the greater the volume of water, the better are the potentialities of a site for the production of power. Where the regulation of water flow cannot be fully achieved—either because of the nature of the river's régime or through competing demands for water (such as irrigation or navigation)—resort must be made to one of two solutions. The plant can be interlinked with other hydro-electricity stations which have complementary generation characteristics; the Italian linkage of their Alpine power stations (with a peak potential in summer) and their Apennine generators (peak potential in winter) is a good instance. Alternatively stand-by thermal or diesel generating plants can be provided to supplement or replace the hydro-station at certain times of the year; particularly when there are competing uses for water, the stand-by plant may have to be rated at as much as 30% or 40% of the capacity of the hydro-electricity station itself. Such a resort substantially increases the total costs of supply.

An understanding of the location, the size and the nature of energy resources does not, of course, take us very far in accounting for the geography of energy. If a comparison is made between the reserves and the actual production of hydro-electricity power in different Western European countries, there is only a small degree of correlation between them. The generation of hydro-electricity in France, Norway and Sweden is of much the same magnitude, but the potentials of the three countries are of quite different orders of magnitude. In a like manner, the regional hydro-electricity reserves of a country, when examined, are usually found to be quite unevenly developed; the greatest water-power potential in Spain is in Asturias, yet it is in Catalonia that the most exploitation of this energy source has taken place.

The essential role of energy resources in the geography of energy is two-fold. First, it imposes certain physical limitations upon the production of energy—*reductio ad absurdum*, oil can be pumped only from an oil pool. And, second, it powerfully influences the costs of obtaining energy at different places on the earth's surface. The contrasting costs incurred in exploiting the oil resources of different parts of the world admirably illustrates this latter point. Largely as a result of geological contrasts, but also in response to institutional factors which have allowed many more wells to be sunk in the United States than is technically necessary, the average yearly production of each well in that country is only 550 tons, whilst in Venezuela it is 15,000 and in the Middle East 275,000. In turn this means that the average cost of raising a ton of oil in the United States in the early '60s was nearly $11·50, whereas Venezuelan costs were rather more than $6·00 and those of the Middle East less than $1·00. Average costs are, of course, deceptive; there are some American producers with relatively low costs, and the cost of the new Alaskan oil could be as low as $1·65 per ton (Adelman, 1969). Nevertheless, it is easy to see why the price of United States oil is generally so much higher than that of its competitor from the Middle East, even allowing for the taxes and royalties levied there.

The limitations and the costs imposed by energy resources upon their exploitation are by no means fixed, however, for *technical progress* constantly leads to reassessments of their potential value. Besides revising the economics of exploiting existing sources, it reveals the existence of new ones; as a result it changes the nature and the geography of energy production. The invention of the high-speed turbine and the multi-phase motor led to a re-evaluation of water power. The improvement of oil recovery techniques has revitalized many of the older oil fields of the world such as those in Appalachian America, and the development of an off-shore exploration and production technology is transforming the energy resource situation in an increasing number of places around the world. The growing mechanization of coalmining places a premium upon the thicker and the less faulted seams, and emphasizes the advantages of opencast methods of mining. New sources of power are steadily becoming available to man as technology allows him to harness the elements: electricity is now generated from natural geysers in New Zealand and California, in Italy and Mexico; tidal power is being utilized for the generation of electricity in France; solar power is being put to work in the Ararat Valley of Armenia. The Athabaska tar sands—possibly the richest single reserve of oil in the world—may continue temporarily to defy technology in the sense that oil has not yet been *economically* extracted from them; but the steady advance of technical skills suggests that this situation will not continue indefinitely.

Technological competence is, of course, far from uniform the world over. Any appreciation of the role of technology must be qualified as a result by a recognition that it, too, has spatial characteristics. Technical skills are one of the scarcest commodities throughout the world. One of the major barriers to economic advance in the developing countries will for many years be the shortage of skilled technicians to implement their plans for economic development which include the provision of energy facilities. Where skills are generally scarce, it may well be that the availability of a particular skill will influence the nature of energy development; the precocious competence of Soviet engineers in hydro-electric technology before they had fully mastered its thermal counterpart resulted in a certain bias of the early Soviet power plans towards the exploitation of water resources; and this has given Russia some of the largest hydro-electricity projects in the world.

As a consequence of the irregular geographical occurrence of energy resources, plus the growing demand for fuel and power in many parts of the world with only limited (and occasionally an absence of) local supplies of energy, it is obvious that the facilities and the costs of energy *transport* are a matter of increasing importance. Oil, coal, natural gas and electricity have become prominent elements in both national and international trade; and the nature and cost of these flows help to determine the competitive advantage of one fuel against another in the markets for energy. The movement of oil from the Middle East to Japan depends not only upon the availability of large tankers to transport the crude or residual oil, but also upon the low ton/kilometre rates of those vessels which allow the oil to compete against alternative fuels in the Japanese market. Likewise the flow of American coal to Western Europe, albeit in part the result of efficient mining operations in the Appalachian fields, is also a measure of the relatively low costs of hauling coal across the Atlantic. The steady improvement of transport techniques over the last hundred years has not only facilitated a growing volume of energy transfers but by gradually lowering costs has actually encouraged it. At one time the relative inefficiency of both using and transporting fuels meant that there was considerable advantage to be gained from locating industrial activity on or near to sources of wood or coal. But today the much lower level of real transport costs has allowed other factors to play a more important part in industrial location and supplies of energy are transported from all over the earth to the major centres of population and industry. In 1925, some 214 million tons of coal equivalent energy entered international trade (68% of it coal and other solid fuels); by 1950 the total had increased to nearly 500 million (of which 76% was oil and other liquid fuels), and by 1965 some 1,575 million tons of energy was exported, of which about 90% was oil.

The costs of transporting energy vary, then, with technical change. They are also strongly influenced by the markets for energy. The location of a market, for example, has an important bearing upon the costs of transport, since it influences the distance energy has to be transported and the mode of transfer which can be used. Although the cheapest means of moving oil and coal is usually by sea many markets do not have access to this mode of transport; as a consequence, the ton/km costs of meeting their demands are frequently higher than if ocean communications were available. Similarly, it is only where there are large centres of demand that full advantage can be taken of the considerable economies which come with the bulk (production and) transfer of fuel and power. In other words, the size and the location of a market powerfully influence both the types of energy which can be economically sold there, and the costs of their transport.

The *market* for energy, however, is a crucial factor in the geography of energy in its own right. There can be little doubt that the enormous importance of North American and Western European energy demands in the past has left a most decisive impress upon the energy geography of the world. In 1925 together they accounted for over 85% of global demands, and forty years later they still were responsible for 37% and 20% respectively. Already the burgeoning requirements of the Soviet Union and Japan have begun to modify the overall pattern of energy production and transfer, and prospectively they will transform it yet further. Inter-regionally, also, the huge demands of the east coast megalopolis in the United States, and the agglomeration of the British and French economies within the city-regions of London and Paris, have left a clear impress upon the energy geography of their respective countries. Markets, of course, comprise a complex of smaller demands—the energy needs of factories, homes, offices, steelworks, vehicles and the like—and they exhibit enormous variety not only in place and time but also in their precise nature. The Central Electricity Generating Board, for example, can burn coals that are much cheaper, for reasons of both quality and quantity, than those which are available to the ordinary householder—you cannot burn power station smalls or anthracite duff in a domestic grate—with the result that it is in the power station market that British coal can compete most effectively against other fuels. It is very often the precise nature of a market, in association with its size and location, therefore, which contributes substantially to an explanation of the geography of energy.

Transport and market factors, therefore, act and react upon each other, and with the geography of resources to influence the *costs* of providing energy at a particular place. They are yet further related in so far as transport is itself a market for fuel, the location of which is not identical to the location of domestic and industrial consumers. As we shall see later (pp. 69 ff.), the transport sector of energy demands represents a considerable proportion of the total market for energy in some countries. However, the cost of providing energy at a given market is usually impossible to assess with any degree of accuracy or at least agreement. Let us consider, for example, the case of the oil, industry.

The expenses involved in getting crude oil from the ground can be divided into three cardinal elements—exploration, development and extraction. Average American figures suggest that approximately 33% of the costs of producing the fuel are taken up in exploration, 38% in the development of the oilfields and 29% in extraction. In other words, less than one-third of the costs of producing oil are related to current inputs (Adelman, 1962, 3). How, then, can one apportion the other two-thirds of the costs? Exploration involves years of work, mapping, geological survey, land acquisition, research and the like; it involves capital, time, risks and skill. The costs of unsuccessful explorations have to be paid for out of the profits of successful drillings. The industry, in other words, is characterized by joint costs, in which any attempt to decide accurately the cost of a particular ton of oil is full of pitfalls. Further, and especially after refinery operations or when natural gas is found associated with an oil field, the industry is also characterized by joint products where, again, the concept of the average total cost of a single product has virtually no significance. The same problem of how to apportion costs in effect also occurs in the case of trans- porting oil to its market when, say, a vessel or a pipeline are shared by a variety of products. The difficulties are overcome, of course, by adopting a set of *pricing policies* which are as much related to the market opportunities and aspirations of a supply operation as they are to resource production and transport costs.

The case of the oil industry is not unique. Joint costs and products are a feature of coal mining, too. To quote Professor Beacham (1958, 127), writing with reference to the British industry: 'It follows from the nature of the [coal] industry that the price of any particular lot of coal from a particular mine cannot be and never has been very closely connected with the cost of mining it.' Likewise the pro- duction of electricity, when it is combined with schemes for irri- gation, navigation, soil conservation and the like, is in the same situation. The essential point is this. In the *long-run* the total revenue from joint products must cover all costs, and from a single product all joint costs. This requirement does not preclude the possibility that for particular goods produced jointly (or costs incurred jointly) the price is put out of line with the costs. But adjustments in one direc- tion must be compensated by adjustments in another. In the *short- run* the same principles apply, but the divergencies can be—and are —very much greater. Indeed the price can be justified as long as revenue covers working costs and contributes something to over- heads. And in some cases it is even legitimate also to consider any costs which would be incurred by ceasing production; it might be more economic in the short-run to produce at a loss on working expenses rather than incur the costs of closing down an operation.

The short-run allocation of costs and the prices charged for energy can naturally have a decisive impact upon the details of the geography of energy. In Britain, the use of electricity for space heating (one of the least efficient ways of heating homes and buildings, for at best electricity is generated at less than 40% efficiency) has been encouraged by the pricing policies of the electricity industry. It has been suggested that the failure to charge any differential between the several domestic uses to which the energy is put has led to a wasteful pattern of energy consumption (Hawkins, 1952, 155 ff.; Little, 1953, *passim*). Similarly, the failure of both the British electricity and gas industries to charge differential prices between their urban and rural markets—when the latter areas are more expensive to serve—has led to a pattern of secondary energy consumption which is vastly different from that which would have existed had their prices been more closely related to costs.

To some extent pricing policies are related to the nature and influence of *corporate arrangements* in the market. The oil industry provides us with a good example, for outside of the United States and the Communist bloc the market dominance of the seven international 'majors' in that industry is very powerful indeed. Partly in an attempt to reconcile maladjustments in the supply and demand for oil, but also for reasons of profit, the international oil companies for many years agreed upon a basing point system for oil prices which undoubtedly had a conservative influence over the size and geography of the industry. Until 1939 the dominance of the United States in world oil trade led to the creation of a single basing point system, by which Western European buyers of oil had to pay the price of oil in the Gulf of Mexico plus a transport charge from there to Europe, regardless of the source of oil. The growth of oil traffic after 1945, however, meant that this system gave way to a multiple basing point system with the Middle East and Caribbean f.o.b. or 'posted' prices, as well as a Gulf price (Odell, 1970, 98–9). During the late '60s, the rigidity of this system collapsed under pressure from new producer-suppliers in the market (particularly new European companies and the American 'independents') and a continuing surplus of oil supplies in relation to demand. However, for many years the geography of price in the international market contrasted vividly with the situation within the United States; there, the smaller scale of operations, the shorter distances between sources and markets, and a concessions system which does not lend itself to the dominance of large organizations have led to a much more competitive framework for oil operations—within, of course, an increasingly protected market.

Consumers, of course, may not always choose the fuel with the lowest price. First, the efficiency of using alternative sources of energy must be considered. The low cost of mining opencast coal frequently gives it a price advantage at its source, but the fact that it cannot be transported and burned with the same efficiency as natural gas or oil means that the latter two fuels are both highly competitive with coal in many markets. Further, convenience,

B

service and many other non-economic factors are also at a premium
in most energy markets and thereby influence the pattern of fuel
consumption. British oil companies, for example, have on occasions
deliberately set out not so much to offer the lowest priced fuel, but
rather to attract consumers by other means; their approach to the
domestic central heating market, with offers of free technical
advice and credit facilities, is a case in point.

Of increasing consequence in energy geography is the *political
factor*. Trade union influence has limited the amount of opencast
coal mining in Britain, even though this is one of the most profitable
aspects of the National Coal Board's operations. In the United
States, energy industry lobbies seek to influence—and succeed in
influencing—the policies of the Federal Government with regard
to themselves and their competitors; the most effective have
undoubtedly been the smaller domestic producers of oil who have
successfully defended the oil import quota system since 1959, and
so maintained United States' output at a level of perhaps twice or
even three times what it might have been. By such expedients as
import duties, quotas, purchase tax and subsidies, the market for any
particular fuel can be artificially increased or decreased for political
reasons. Likewise, a government or its agency can ensure that a
particular medium of transport is either subsidized, or is allowed
to offer rates in such a way as to support a particular type and
flow of energy. With reference to the American coal industry and
railways, for example, Campbell (1954, 44) observed that 'The
coming of effective rate regulation by the Interstate Commerce
Commission shifted competition away from price to competition for
pressure and influence before the Commission.' It is additionally
important that an increasing proportion of the energy industries
in the mixed economies are wholly or partly owned by governments,
and that within the global framework the demands and production of
the fully planned or command economies are tending to become
tively more important.

Commonly, therefore, such matters as the supply of capital or
the role of an industry in a national energy pattern are judged by
political as much as economic criteria. In the case of the British
coal industry, nationalized and with a contracting share of the
nation's energy market, the fact that its prices are frequently too
high to compete with substitute fuels presents financial, economic
and social problems to be sure, but a political dilemma above all.
The only long term remedy for the health of the industry is to find
a speedy means of contracting back upon its limited number of low
cost pits and profitable market outlets, and possibly to turn to

importing coal. But in so far as the Department of Trade and Industry has authority to shape the broad policy of the industry and to determine whether or not imports shall be allowed, and in so far as the rapid contraction of the coal industry in Britain would pose complex problems and substantial costs of public importance, political decisions will critically—and legitimately—influence the future shape of the industry and the part which it will play in satisfying the nation's energy demands.

Many other factors also affect the geography of energy. Although in the past coal industries the world over have tended to attract a labour force to their mining villages and towns, and although the availability of *labour* might appear at first sight to be an insignificant factor in the distribution of solid fuel production, examples of its influence can easily be found. In Britain since 1945, shortages of labour have limited the output of different mining areas, and in the plans of the National Coal Board for the closure and the modernization of its pits, the need to try to retain an already existing labour force has had to be borne in mind. One of the explanations for the distribution of the new 'master' collieries throughout the anthracite coalfield of South Wales was the need to maximize the accessibility of these new production facilities to already mature mining communities.

Also important in shaping the geography of energy is the *legacy of history*, which expresses itself in many ways. In the first place there is the desire of any enterprise to utilize to the full any of its existing and productive capital equipment. In the case of coalfields, once mines are sunk and capital invested in washeries, railways and ancillary plant at a particular time and under a particular set of technical and economic circumstances, this investment leaves its impress upon the geography of production for many years. Inevitably there is a desire to continue using it for the rest of its useful life, even though subsequent advances in technology and changed market or competitive circumstances make the investment a relatively poor one. Were the Western European coal industry, for example, to be given the opportunity of starting once again *ab initio* with modern knowledge, techniques and demands, the number and scale of mining operations and their distribution throughout the continent would be very different from the reality of today. A further aspect of the legacy of history is the early utilization of the most accessible (and occasionally most profitable) known supplies of energy; the exhaustion of the richest, surface seams of coal and the utilization of the most easily exploited hydro-electricity sites is offset, of course, by the occasional discovery of new low cost resources.

Just as the patterns of energy production are influenced by the past, so too is the distribution of demand. At any given moment in time, the consumption of the several types of energy is not necessarily related to the current prices of the different fuels. Consumers have invested considerable sums of money in capital equipment which generally can only utilize one type of fuel, and this investment is not one to be lightly discarded. The influence of the past upon patterns of energy demand also makes itself felt in another way. The contrasting histories of industrial development in Britain and the United States demonstrate how the timing of the first major industrialization of a country strongly influences its geography of energy demands. In Britain the first major industrialization came before the development of efficient railways and at a time when fuel was used extravagantly by subsequent standards. The result was that it was expensive to move coal, and industry located on or near to the country's coalfields. In the United States, in contrast, the first major industrialization came after the railways had become reasonably inexpensive carriers, and fuel had come to be used with some degree of efficiency. The result was that although there was a certain amount of industrial development on the American coalfields, most manufacturing and population in the United States came to be situated away from them. With the passage of time, new fuels were discovered and came to compete for the energy markets in both Britain and the United States. Quite apart from the fact that the latter country was able to harness a much greater variety of domestic fuels, the existence of a significant proportion of British industry on or near to its coalfields has meant that the National Coal Board has a valuable proximity to many industrial markets, a proximity which serves to its competitive advantage but which is denied to its American counterpart.

Yet a further important factor in the geography of energy is the availability and the cost of *capital*. Energy production has always been, and is becoming more, capital intensive. If capital is not forthcoming—or if it is especially expensive—for the development of a particular energy resource, its exploitation will be impossible. This is an important matter in many developing countries, which frequently have to rely upon imports of energy until such a time as capital becomes available to exploit their domestic energy supplies. Only too often these countries have resources, such as the hydro-electricity potential at Aswan or on the Volta River in West Africa, which will yield only to massive injections of capital. The demands for capital for the energy industries in South America through the decade 1955–65 were forecast at a level equivalent to over 10% of the gross domestic capital formation of that continent, assuming a $2\frac{1}{2}\%$ rate of growth in the gross product annually (United Nations, 1957); it is small wonder, therefore, that deficiencies in the energy supplies of many countries in South America are all too frequent. The scarcity and the cost of capital influences not only *whether* a resource will be exploited but very often it helps to decide *which* resource will be developed. In Nigeria, for example, there is a hydro-electricity potential and there are several natural gas deposits; one of the advantages of the latter is that the capital required for their exploitation is much less than it is for building dams and generating hydro-electricity.

There are, of course, many other influences upon the geography of energy besides those which have been mentioned. Variations in the weather can seriously modify both the level and the spatial characteristics of fuel demand in a country such as Britain. Consider-ations of scenic amenity can materially influence the distribution of hydro-electricity production, the routes and hence the costs of electricity transmission and production, witness the extreme care with which the North of Scotland Hydro-Electricity Board must always tread in the Glens. But to recite all the many factors which can influence the geography of energy is less valuable than to stress their complex interrelationships. Something of this has been seen already, and the role of technology reinforces the point. Technologi-cal developments allow reassessments to be made of the value of natural resources; they change the economics of energy production, and they permit improvements to be made in the modes and hence the costs of energy transport. With changing techniques, new markets are created, and, through the abruptness of the changes which they so often bring, political action is frequently required for social and other reasons. In turn, technologists are challenged by the nature of natural resources, by the inefficiencies and problems of energy production, and by the inadequacies of transport facilities; and their researches and development programmes are influenced by the needs of particular markets and by political objectives.

The location of nuclear power stations in Britain illustrates con-cisely something of the variety of influences upon the geography of energy. After 1945 advances in atomic technology caused a great deal of interest, excitement and speculation, and in particular they suggested the eventual possibility of producing cheap electricity. The economics of generation by nuclear reaction are still a matter for discussion and even at times bitter debate (George, 1960; Schurr, 1963). The costs of atomic power are largely capital costs, and hence the unit costs of production are very much dependent upon assumptions about interest rates, the load factor and the period of time over which the capital is amortized. This problem recognized, the fundamental point about the British programme of nuclear generation is that it rests largely upon a political decision. In the middle years of the 1950s it appeared that Britain was about to face a period of shortage in the supply of domestic fuels. The National Coal Board could not see its way to guaranteeing the electricity industry all the coal that it would require in the foreseeable future, and there was at the time a strategic—perhaps irrational—reluctance to allow the country to become too heavily dependent upon oil imports. Some coal-fired power stations were converted to burn oil—but only as a short term measure. The long term solution, it was decided, should be sought in the development of nuclear power technology. In the White Paper of February 1955, therefore, it was announced that a programme of nuclear power station construction would be started with the object of building twelve stations by 1965, their combined capacity being some 2,000 Megawatts. It is interesting to reflect that, ambitious though the programme was in its day, this capacity is equalled by a single modern power station such as Pembroke or Fawley. Two years later came the Suez crisis, and a panic over the temporary interruption of oil supplies led the Government to revise its earlier plans and to expand the programme nearly three-fold. There were yet third thoughts on the scale of the programme in 1960 when, with falling costs of conventional power, nuclear power plans were rescheduled to a slower pace of building. It was then expected that no more than 5% of British electricity would be generated in nuclear plants by 1965, whereas 1957 plans had envisaged 20–25%. This first nuclear power programme exploited the Magnox reactor. A second programme, announced first in 1964, is based initially upon the Advanced Gas Cooled reactor, and the intention is to commission one new reactor each year during the period 1970–5, to add a further 8,000 MW to the system and thus have some 13,000 MW of nuclear generating capacity by 1975.

The initial motivations behind this British nuclear power programme were by no means simple. There was certainly a strategic element in it, rooted in the desire that the country—traditionally an exporter of energy—should not become too heavily dependent upon oil and other energy imports. There was also a military motive, for the power stations were designed to produce plutonium as a by-product; this was at a time when its price was very high on world markets (subsequently it became much cheaper). It could in fact be argued that the programme has its origin in the decision to build British-made atomic weapons. And finally, there was a long term commercial aspect to the programme—the hope that the experience provided by these relatively expensive stations would give British firms some advantage in a potentially huge export market. The hope has never really been fulfilled.

Within the country, the nuclear power stations have a distinctive geography. Two major factors and three subsidiary ones are most relevant to its explanation (Mounfield, 1961, 1967). The first point to note is the relative mobility of nuclear power generation. The reason for this is simply that the transport costs on the raw material used in generation are very small indeed, for one ton of uranium produces electricity equivalent to approximately 10,000 tons of coal. As a consequence transport expenses on materials can be ignored in location decisions, and other factors become decisive. It is in fact the market which has been primarily responsible for the location of production. During the years when the Central Electricity Generating Board was making location decisions for the first nuclear power programme, England and Wales could broadly be divided into either coal-surplus areas or coal-deficit areas, depending upon the amount of coal which was locally available for the generation of electricity; the two major coal-deficit areas were in southern and north-west England (Fig. 2). It was natural, therefore, that the first nuclear power stations should be located within these two areas which were without adequate supplies of local fossil fuels, and in which the delivered price of coal was relatively high. Six of the eight sites are to be found south of a line drawn between Gloucester and Norwich, a region within which a large share of the country's energy requirements are to be found. Although their power might be consumed in almost any part of the Board's system as a result of inter-regional super-grid transfers, the Sizewell and Bradwell stations are conveniently adjacent to the Greater London market, the Dungeness plant serves the south-east of England, and the Hinkley Point, Berkeley and Oldbury generators are able to meet demands in the south and south-west. The coal-deficient north-west is served by the two nuclear power plants in North Wales at Trawsfynydd and at Wylfa on Anglesey, whilst the South of Scotland Electricity Board built the ninth station at Hunterston to serve the requirements of Glasgow and the Clyde Valley.

The same locational characteristics have continued to apply to the second nuclear power programme, but with two significant differences. In the south of England, second generation reactors are being (or are to be) built alongside the existing Magnox plants at Dungeness, Hinkley, Oldbury and Sizewell; and in the north-west new sites have been found at Heysham and Connah's Quay. In

Scotland, the site at Hunterston is to have a second station, and a proposal exists for the construction of another plant on the Moray Firth. The new locational features of the second programme are, first, the attempted move to the West Midlands market with a station at Stourport, a proposal that was later withdrawn; and second, the move into the higher-cost coalfield regions of South Wales and North-east England, where stations are to be built at Portskewett and Hartlepool. These latter reactors represent the declining availability

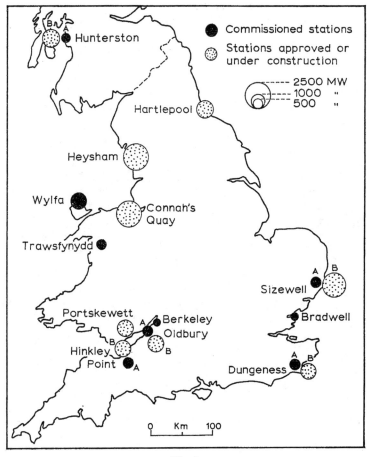

Fig. 2

Nuclear power stations in Britain, 1970. (Source: CEGB)

and the weakening competitive position of coal in those parts of the country.

Whilst British nuclear power stations may be orientated towards their markets, they are clearly not located central to them. The explanation lies in three additional siting requirements which have to be met. The first is the need for water for cooling and other purposes. The requirements of nuclear power plants are such that it is usually only coastal or estuarine sites which can offer water in sufficient quantities—the Trawsfynydd and proposed Stourport stations are exceptional in that they are completely dependent upon inland sources of water. The second requirement is that these power plants should be situated some distance from large centres of population as a safety precaution. To quote the 1955 White Paper: 'The reactors that will be built for the commercial production of electricity will present no more danger to people living nearby than many existing industrial works. Nevertheless, the first stations, even though they will be of inherently safe design, will not be built in heavily built up areas.' The criterion which was originally used by the Joint Location Panel of the Central Electricity Generating Board and the Atomic Energy Authority was that approved sites should be at least five miles from urban centres with more than 10,000 people. With time and the good safety record of the industry, however, these principles came gradually to be relaxed during the second programme, and the stations were allowed to encroach nearer to larger centres of population.

The final siting requirement for the nuclear power stations is that they should impair rural amenities as little as possible. As the proportion of Britain which is either a National Park, an Area of Outstanding Natural Beauty or a Nature Reserve increases, so does it become more difficult to meet all the other location and siting requirements and still not infringe public amenities in some way. The arguments over the siting of some of the stations need not be examined here—all have necessitated a public enquiry—but the point to be noted is that repeatedly considerations of amenity have undoubtedly influenced the siting and pattern of the nuclear generation of electricity.

In sum, therefore, political, resource, economic, technological and social factors have all played some part in the existence, the location and the siting of the nuclear power industry in Britain. Only through an understanding of the variety and interplay of these factors can the geography of the industry be understood.

In order to come to a fuller understanding of the complexity of the many interdependent influences moulding the geography of energy, it is necessary to cut into the system at some point and to examine some of the factors in detail. Only in this way can the forces at work be better perceived. Although the nature of the subject is such that it is impossible to present logical or quantitative evidence to show which of the many factors are most important, experience suggests that three in particular stand out above all others. These are the market factor, the transport factor and the political factor. The greater part of this book therefore is devoted to an examination of them, and it is with the first of the three that the next chapter is concerned.

3

THE MARKET (I)

The size of the market – permanent, cyclical, seasonal and daily changes

In the previous chapter something of the variety and the interdependence of the factors affecting the geography of energy were outlined. By cutting into this web of interrelationships at the point of the market, and discussing its three major aspects—its size, its location and its nature—a valuable set of insights can be gained into one of the most important influences underlying the geography of energy.

The size of the market
In 1965 the United States consumed 1,882 million tons of coal equivalent energy—over one-third of the total world consumption of energy in that year. Such a huge energy market inevitably leaves its mark upon the geography of energy production and transport, and it is no coincidence that simultaneously nearly one-third of the world's energy was produced in the United States. In 1965, America produced 63% of the world's natural gas, 27% of its oil, 22% of its coal and 22% of its hydro-electricity. Similarly, in the same year the USSR provided an energy market of 881 million coal equivalent tons, just over 16% of the world total. In response, that country produced nearly 18% of the world's energy—20% of its coal, 19% of its natural gas, 16% of its oil and 9% of its hydro-electricity. Such obvious international relationships, however, provide only a starting point for our enquiry.

Within a given distribution of energy resources, the size of the market for energy is a major factor in deciding whether and how, when and on what scale, the exploitation of those resources will take place. The effects of market size upon energy geography are felt principally through the costs of energy production and transport, which in turn are affected by the economies of scale. By influencing the scale of production, the size of a market strongly affects the costs of exploiting a resource—and hence its competitive position in the market. The very size of American and Soviet energy demands, for instance, permits a scale of coalmining operations and low unit costs of production, that are denied the mines of, say, West Africa or Latin America. Indeed, modern techniques frequently demand that a market should at least be a minimum size before an energy resource can be economically exploited: the vast amount of capital required to sink a deep coal shaft, or to open up a new oilfield, alone requires this. Although there are large oilfields in the central plateau area of Iran, the Tehran region still gets its oil products by rail and pipeline from Abadan. Moreover, the physical nature of some resources demands exploitation on a large scale and thereby necessitates a considerable local or regional market. Such was the case with the River Volta, where the generation of hydro-electricity at Akosombo had to await the arrival of a substantial demand in the form of an aluminium smelting plant.

In the processing of energy, whether it is the washing, sorting and general preparation of coal, or the conversion of a primary fuel into secondary energy such as electricity or town gas, economies of scale are all too apparent. In oil refining, for example, the unit costs of the investment required fall considerably with the larger plants; British data suggest that, compared with a 1 million tons per year plant, the investment per ton required for a 5 million tons refinery is 35% lower, and that for a 10 million tons complex 45% lower. Comparable economies are also available in the operating costs of larger refineries (Pratten and Dean, 1965, 83 ff.). And to both of these is often added the savings of hauling the crude oil and the products to and from the refinery in larger units of transport.

The economies of scale in transporting energy are in fact of outstanding importance amongst the effects of market size. *Ceteris paribus*, the larger the market, the greater are the potential economies of bulk energy transport, and the lower are the costs there of fuel and power. The nature and magnitude of these economies are discussed in Chapters 5 and 6. An immediate contrast is provided by two works, one large and the other small, located adjacent to tidewater and to each other. The former, for example a Thames-side power station or cement works using coal brought by collier from the Tyne or

Humber, is able to afford its own jetty and import its own coal in bulk; from the jetty the coal can be moved quickly and economically by conveyor belt or pipe to a storage area before use. In such a situation the ton/km costs of transport and handling are very low indeed. But for the smaller market, which might be a domestic consumer or a factory needing to raise steam, the direct import of coal is not feasible. Instead, the consumer has to buy this fuel from a factor importing through a jetty some distance away. In this case, the expense of port handling charges, sorting, a journey by rail or road and a middleman's commission must be added to the cost of collier transport. As a result, the ton/km expenses and the total cost of the coal to the small consumer are inevitably higher than they are to the adjacent large consumer. In fact, it is quite possible that the factory or domestic consumer will decide to use an alternative fuel on the grounds of both economy and convenience, even though energy from coal is cheaper for the adjacent power station or cement works.

The critical importance of the size of markets in the location of the secondary energy industries is discussed in Chapter 7. The problem of supplying gas and electricity to small markets, however, can be explored at this point. Both are transported by continuous media, the cost structure of which is best suited to bulk and regular energy transfers. They both require a minimum size of market therefore before they can be economically distributed. In most technically advanced countries rural supplies of secondary energy are in fact frequently subsidized, either directly or indirectly, since markets there are generally too small and diffuse to be economically served. In Britain, the Area Electricity Boards have no rural-urban differential in their tariffs (in spite of substantial geographical differences in the costs of providing their services); in effect therefore they cause the urban consumer to subsidize his rural counterpart. In the early '60s government subsidies to rural electrification in Europe ranged from 2·2% in the Netherlands to 40% in Sweden and 100% in Czechoslovakia; and in the United States the Rural Electrification Administration provides loans of Federal funds to rural electrification schemes at low rates of interest. Such subsidies are, in fact, a piece of good farming fortune, for the application of electricity to such operations as machine milking, milk cooling, grass and corn drying and grinding do offer considerable economies and advantages to the farmer, and have helped to raise rural living standards.

Where such hidden or open subsidies are not available, market size and transport economies combine to limit the extent of rural electrification. The major exception occurs in those rural areas bordering upon centres of heavier demand where, although the cost of distributing energy is still relatively high, the rural market added to the urban one permits additional scale economies in generation. In addition, where a rural–urban differential in the diurnal and seasonal pattern of consumption exists, a higher utilization factor of the plant is often possible. In circumstances such as these, it is in fact sometimes profitable to extend electricity supply into the low density rural markets immediately around cities and towns.

The interaction of market size, transport economies and pricing policies has had a comparable impact upon the geography of the British gas industry, especially before the exploitation of North Sea natural gas when the industry was essentially a producer of secondary energy. Rural and country town markets, where they are not left completely unsatisfied by the Area Gas Boards, were traditionally served by small and high cost production units. More recently they have been supplied either from larger gas works or from the methane grid, by means of small diameter, high-pressure pipelines. In both cases, however, the Boards were reluctant to introduce an urban–rural price differential with the result that, once again, these smaller markets were supplied with energy partly at the expense of the urban consumer. But in the case of gas, the size of a market can influence not only whether or not its demand can be economically met, but also the best means of doing so, for there exists an alternative to the pipeline for the transport of gas to small markets. This is the pressurized container with liquefied petroleum gas which can be supplied by a discontinuous means of transport. Gas carried in this way is ideally suited to meeting small, irregular and scattered demands, and many of the rural markets of Britain and continental Western Europe are served by this means. The success of Camping Gaz for the small and highly mobile user is well known.

The geography of secondary energy in many developing countries is frequently affected by the limited size of their markets. For instance, since electricity grids are economic only in regions having a considerable demand, the bulk of the inhabited parts of the world have to be served by independent power stations. While, in a heavily populated area with a considerable demand for power, increasing demands for electricity may in a relatively short period of time lead to the interconnection of production facilities, it is highly unlikely that a grid system will ever be introduced into many extensive and thinly populated regions around the globe. The Brazilian grid, for example, is eventually expected to serve only 12% of the territory with 60% of the population, whilst other markets in that country will have to be satisfied by independent stations. Market size also influences the technology with which electricity is generated, for it is generally felt that for units with a capacity of less than about 1,000 kW the factors in favour of diesel as opposed to gas turbine or steam generation are overwhelming. Consequently, diesel units are frequently used in growing markets until they are large enough to justify first a gas turbine, and then a steam plant (or, alternatively, a transmission line). As the developing economies 'take off' and their energy markets expand, so will their energy geography change with emerging opportunities to exploit scale economies in both production and transport. Such economies will permit the real costs of energy to fall, which in turn will encourage the markets there to grow yet further.

These and other changes in the size of the market warrant further consideration. Some changes are permanent and stem from economic and technical development; others are of a cyclical nature, having their origins in the nature of economic growth; yet a third set of changes are seasonal or diurnal and have their roots in the nature of demand. Each of these three types of change will be examined in turn.

Permanent change in the size of markets

Unprecedented changes in the world's geography of energy during the last forty or so years have been a response to many influences —the discovery of new and the exhaustion of old resources, the advance in technological skills for the exploitation, transport and consumption of energy, and the emergence of entirely new centres of demand. But overshadowing them all has been simply the rapid growth of the world energy demand, at an annual average rate of growth of 2·3% between 1925 and 1950, and a rate of 5·1% between 1950 and 1965. The geography of the world's energy needs, however, has shifted substantially during the same period. Whereas in 1925 the USSR and its Middle European satellites consumed only 5·4% of the world's energy, by 1965 they used 23·4%. Asian needs rose from 5·7% to nearly 13 % during the same period. Meanwhile the relative importance of North America and Western Europe declined—although their annual energy use more than doubled. Even more startling has been the changing demands for particular fuels. The consumption of natural gas in North America, for example, increased from 43 to 732 million c.e.t. between 1925 and 1965, and its share of the market increased from 6% to over one-third. During the same period oil consumption in Western Europe rose from less than 17 million c.e.t. to 463 million tons, and its share of the market increased from rather more than 3% to over 50% in 1965.

As a consequence of these changes in the market for both total energy and individual fuels, the United States, once self-sufficient in her energy needs and for many years the world's leading source of petroleum exports, is now a net importer of energy, buying considerable quantities of crude and fuel oils (about 20% of the country's consumption in 1965) from the Caribbean, the Middle East and Canada. There was also a time when California exported considerable quantities of oil products to the Far East; but with the growth of that State's demands (particularly in the south), her domestic resources became increasingly inadequate, exports ceased, and oil came to be imported from Texas and the Far East, from the Middle East and Canada, and (prospectively) from Alaska. In Western Europe, too, the growth of energy demands has radically transformed the energy map. In 1925 the net imports of the region were a mere 10 million c.e.t. energy, whereas by 1965 the figure had reached 591 million tons. More than anything else these figures represent the dramatic growth in the region's energy demands beyond the capacity of its own supplies. But in addition, of course, they reflect the parallel process of a steady substitution of domestic coal by imported oil. This in turn has occasioned the construction of many refineries throughout the whole Continent (see pp. 193 ff.) and a change in the nature of oil imports. Whereas in 1925 Western European imports of oil consisted of only 22% crude and 78% refined products, by the 1965 proportions had been reversed to 77% crude and 23% products.

The growth of oil markets in both the USA and Western Europe has naturally considerably modified the world pattern of oil traffic. Between 1900 and 1939 the flow of oil in international trade was essentially characterized by the transfer of crude oil, and more especially refined products, out of the Western Hemisphere. Up to 1930 it was mainly American oil which was shipped to Europe; and between 1930 and 1939 (with the growth of markets in the United States), it was particularly Venezuelan and other Caribbean sources which supplied Western Europe's needs. The expansion of American and Western European markets after 1945, however, caused an even more dramatic change in the flow of oil, a change contingent upon the development of the oilfields in the Middle East and North Africa. In the last twenty-five years, Caribbean oils have been drawn more and more towards the United States and away from Western Europe until by 1965 less than 10% of the latter's oils originated in the Western Hemisphere—compared with 66% in 1929. Meanwhile, Middle Eastern and North African oils, which had supplied only 13% of Western Europe's needs in 1929, had come to satisfy over 82% of its oil demands by 1965.

The rapid growth of energy markets has not been confined to North America and Western Europe, of course. Indeed, one of the fastest growing and most important energy markets in the world is in the Far East—Japan. As recently as 1957, its consumption of oil was less than 15 million tons. By 1969, demand had increased tenfold to about 150 million tons, and Japan had become the second largest national oil market in the non-communist world, and the most important oil importer. With the country's domestic economy continuing to grow at a brisk pace, and oil demands increasing at about 20% per annum, forecasts suggesting a Japanese requirement for some 600 million tons of oil by 1985 do not seem to be inflated. In response to this growth, Japan initially relied upon the resources of the major international oil companies and quickly became heavily dependent upon the Middle East for about 80% of her supplies. Subsequently, however, efforts have been made to reduce the role of the international industry, to allow Japanese interests to play a greater part in the transport of the crude, to promote the exploration and development of overseas resources in which Japanese capital and control is at least predominant, and thereby to produce by 1985 a situation in which about 30% of the country's oil needs will originate from Japanese-developed sources. The 'yen-oil' trail has already been successfully blazed in the Middle East and North Sumatra; and with characteristic vigour the Japanese Petroleum Development Corporation has invested in a growing variety of oil exploration projects in Abu Dhabi, Alaska, New Guinea, West Canada, Sumatra and Kalimantan; in addition survey work has been supported in the Japan Sea off Kyushu and Hokkaido. The generator of all these developments, it should not be overlooked, is the persistent expansion of energy demands in Japan.

Although a major feature of the geography of energy is the steady expansion of aggregate energy demands, the contraction of particular markets for particular fuels is not uncommon, and is illustrated by the coal industries of both Western Europe and North America. Once the major source of energy the world over, by 1965 coal supplied only 42% of the world's energy needs. Inter-fuel substitutions have left the industry with a steadily smaller share of the market in some economies, and an absolutely smaller market in others. For example, in spite of subsidy and protection (see p. 184) the British industry's output has fallen from about 290 million tons in 1913 to less than 150 million tons in 1970. Its present geography is radically different from that of the early part of the century; the contraction of output has meant that the less efficient mines have been closed down, with a consequent localization of economic and social distress, and the industry has come increasingly to be concentrated upon the lower cost of pits of the East Midlands and South Yorkshire. In turn this has reduced the spatial extent of the industry's effective competition and so encouraged the further substitution of other sources of energy in the British market. The American coal industry has similarly been forced to accept a smaller share of its country's energy market, and in certain of its activities contract its production decisively. Anthracite mining has been particularly affected by the narrowing market opportunities for solid fuel. Its peak output was during the second decade of the century when consumption reached nearly 100 million tons; but with occasional pauses, and brief recoveries, its market position has declined steadily ever since. The high cost of the mining operations, and its replacement first by bituminous coal and then by oil and natural gas in its domestic and industrial heating markets, explain its decline. By 1965 output was less than 15 million tons and represented less than 1 % of the United States' total energy consumption. In contrast, the market record of the bituminous coal industry has at least been one of long term stability. Despite fluctuations between 300 and 600 million tons during the present century, consumption in 1965 at 512 million tons was just about equal to the arithmetic mean of production over the previous fifty-six years. In a steadily expanding national economy, however, this performance represented an industry failing to hold its own in certain sectors and certain regions of the American energy market; and this lack of growth in turn imposed constraints upon the ability of the coal industry to introduce innovations, which naturally affected its competitive position. As recently as 1940 coal and other solid fuels held over half of the American energy market. By 1965, that share had been reduced to less than 24%.

Cyclical change in the size of markets

Many types of cyclical fluctuation in the economic activity of industrially advanced countries have been recognized by economists. They range from a fifty-four-year commodity price cycle to a sixteen-year construction cycle and a two- to four-year variation in the size of inventories. Although it would appear from post-1945 experience that the violence of these fluctuations can be reduced by government action, in muted form they still persist and continue to have a bearing upon the size and the role of different energy industries. The Energy Advisory Commission of the Organization for European Economic Cooperation observed in its 1960 (59) *Report* that one of the major problems in the near future would be 'how the . . . West European energy economy should adapt itself to the fluctuations of demand, which, even if substantially less than before the war, continue to make themselves felt at intervals'.

There are several elements in this problem. In the first place there are some energy industries which are relatively inflexible in their reactions to temporary changes in demand. With the partial exception of strip mining—which is characterized by some degree of flexibility since much of its equipment can easily and quickly be removed to other sites and uses, and employs only a small labour force—the coal industry is an outstanding example. Its nature and techniques are such that its output is relatively inelastic in the short-run. Ten to fifteen years are normally required between an investment decision and its full realization, and between twenty and forty years are sometimes needed fully to amortize the capital investment; and in addition the industry has to assemble a considerable labour force, which cannot always be achieved overnight. Consequently, longer term planning is perhaps more essential for this industry than for many of its competitors; and, in order to meet cyclical changes in demand, it is necessary both to provide for the storage of coal in the short-run, and to consider putting some of its mines (or parts of its mines) on a care and maintenance basis at periodic intervals. Either or both of these courses of action increase the cost of coal considerably. Thus, the most attractive markets for this fuel are those which are relatively stable. There are occasions, naturally, when the market for coal temporarily contracts to such an extent that further stocks can no longer be economically carried, and the least efficient mines have to be closed. This can lead to a permanent loss of the coal resources (through the flooding of workings and the inability subsequently to reopen them), and the possibility of an irreparable dispersal of the labour force. In 1969–70, for example, the (British) National Coal Board was unable to respond to a temporary upswing in the Western European demand for coal; although for over a decade it had been concerned about its steady loss of markets, and had been engaged in the deliberate contraction of its facilities and labour force, once it had run down its substantial surface stocks it could not avoid the galling experience of seeing domestic and overseas' demands remain unsatisfied. In the contrasting cases of oil and natural gas, on the other hand, the turn of a valve can save a resource indefinitely, and their small, skilled and thus highly mobile labour force is easily replaced. The result is that, in contrast to coal, it is not normal for a cyclical contraction of energy demand for hydro-carbons to result in any significant waste of oil and gas resources and these two industries, can respond much more readily to temporary fluctuations in demand. As a further result, when the oil and natural gas industries are in competition with coal, their flexibility often allows them to gain markets after a down-swing of economic activity.

A second set of problems which stem from cyclical variations in the demand for energy occur when a large percentage of the total cost of providing energy at a market comprises—or might comprise —capital costs. In such circumstances, the magnitude of the fluctuations have a bearing upon the way in which, and the costs at which, those demands can be satisfied. For example, where there is a demand for electrical energy, and nuclear technology is both available and apparently the cheapest means of supplying the base load, it is important to plan that the nuclear station will be of a size appropriate to supply energy approximately equivalent to the lowest point in the demand cycle—otherwise the load factor of the plant is liable to fall below its optimum, and the economics of the investment might be undermined. Although this factor is offset to some degree by steadily rising energy demands in most markets, it cannot be ignored, in the planning of small production–supply systems above all.

In the long run, cyclical fluctuations in the total demand for energy are closely linked with fluctuations in economic activity. But in the shorter period the relationship between the two is more complicated. Quite apart from the effect of changes in the efficiency of energy use, there are times when there is a negative correlation between total energy demand and measures of economic activity, and particularly between the demand for a particular source of energy and economic activity in general. For example, in the United Kingdom between the years 1956 and 1958 the Gross Domestic Product increased by 0·7%, but the consumption of energy fell by 5%; and whilst the market for coal contracted by 14% that for oil increased by 47%. Such variations are by no means unique and at their heart, as Priddle (1961) has demonstrated, is the behaviour of economic activity in those sectors of an economy where a particular fuel is the principal source of energy. Of the three sectors of industrial, transport and domestic demand, the most violent economic fluctuations are to be found in the industrial sector. In the British recession of 1956–8, for example, industrial production accounted for less than half of national energy demand and yet was responsible for nearly three-quarters of the total shortfall of demand below the medium-run trend. A fuel, therefore, which primarily serves the industrial sector of an economy, is obviously liable to much greater variations in demand than one which serves the transport or domestic sectors. With the loss of its railway and steamship outlets, and with the contraction of its gasworks and domestic demands, the British coal industry (like its counterpart in the United States) has come to rely increasingly for its prosperity upon sales to the power station, coke oven and industrial markets. Together by 1968 these took up nearly three-quarters of the coal industry's shipments. In contrast, nearly half of the sales of the oil industry are in the transport, domestic and agricultural sectors of the market, all of which are relatively insensitive to fluctuations in the business cycle.

The effect of cyclical fluctuations upon the demand for an energy industry varies, therefore, with the flexibility of its production with the relative importance of capital in its total costs, and with the characteristics of those sectors of demand with which it is principally concerned. But herein lies only part of the story. In certain respects, it is valuable to consider the consumption of a fuel within the context of a 'life sequence' consisting of three phases. The first, or 'substitution' phase, embraces the development and the application of a new fuel in a national energy market. During this phase other fuels are replaced at such a rate that it is this substitution factor (rather than the expansion of aggregate demand) which essentially underlies the increasing sales of the new fuel. An example is provided by the replacement of wood by coal in the industries and houses of the USA during the last century; and fuel oil is playing a similar role in the industrial heating market of Western Europe today. In this first phase, the process of substitution means that cyclical economic fluctuations have relatively little effect upon the demand for the fuel concerned. But in the second, or 'dominant', phase on the other hand these fluctuations are much more important. Then, the fuel concerned satisfies a much larger share of total energy demand than any of its competitors, and there is a tendency for variations in the size of the market as a whole to be the primary determinant of changes in its output. Coal in the British economy (at least until the late '60s) and oil in that of the Argentine, are examples of a fuel in such a dominant phase; stagnation or a fall in the total demand for energy will automatically be reflected in the demand for these fuels.

The final or 'decline' phase of the 'life sequence' of a fuel comes with its replacement by another fuel or fuels. Such a development tends of course to be a long term affair, with the decline of demand being somewhat irregular, slow in times of economic expansion and rapid during periods of recession. The reason for this irregularity is simply that in times of economic growth all fuel-using capital equipment tends to be fully utilized, whilst in a recession it is the older 'marginal' plant, designed to use the once-dominant fuel, which is the first to go out of service. The irregular nature of demand in this third phase is illustrated by the use of coal by American railways in the years after 1945; demand declined every year, but especially rapidly during the periods of economic recession. Similarly, for some time now, natural gas has been gradually if irregularly replacing fuel oil in many of the industrial and domestic heating markets in the United States. The stage in the 'life sequence' of a fuel, therefore, to some extent modifies the effect of cyclical fluctuations upon the demand for, and the geography of, energy.

Seasonal and daily change in the size of markets

Only on rare occasions is the demand for fuel and power regular throughout the day or year (Fig. 3). Patterns of living, variations in the weather, and the nature of industrial processes all make for continuing changes in the volume of energy needs, which in aggregate create variable markets through time as well as in space. These changes present the energy industries with a problem, the solutions to which considerably influence the geography of energy.

The essence of the problem is as follows (and the parallel with the dilemmas of public transport as it seeks to satisfy peak demands is clear). In order to meet the needs of a market which exhibits daily or seasonal variations, it is necessary to provide capital equipment (for the production, consumption and transport of energy) which is in use for only a small proportion of the day or year. The investment in this equipment is considerable, and has to be paid for even when it is unused. The greater the variations in demand, therefore, the less efficient becomes the use of the capital investment, which in turn increases the unit cost of meeting the energy demand. In other words, the greater the seasonal and daily changes in the size of the market, the more difficult it is to take advantage of the economies which stem from an intensive utilization of capital and labour.

The acuteness of this problem varies with different energy industries and the types of transport employed. Contrast the coal and electricity industries in this matter. Coal can be stored either at the mine or at its market, and as a result steady production throughout the year is theoretically possible provided the costs of storage for fluctuating demands can be met. In contrast, with the exception of pumped storage schemes, electricity cannot be stored but must be generated at the time of demand. Again, coal can be transported by boat, train or lorry; with these discontinuous media, many of whose facilities are shared by the coal industry with other goods, seasonal variations in the movement of coal can sometimes be offset by the attraction of other traffics. Electricity, in contrast,

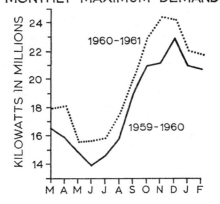

MONTHLY MAXIMUM DEMAND

1960-1961

1959-1960

KILOWATTS IN MILLIONS

24
22
20
18
16
14

M A M J J A S O N D J F

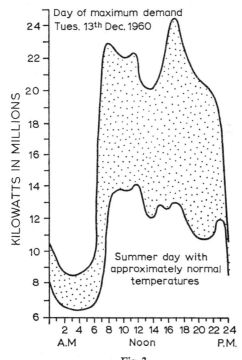

DAILY VARIATIONS IN DEMAND

Day of maximum demand
Tues. 13th Dec. 1960

Summer day with
approximately normal
temperatures

KILOWATTS IN MILLIONS

24
22
20
18
16
14
12
10
8
6

2 4 6 8 10 12 14 16 18 20 22 24
A.M   Noon   P.M.

Fig. 3

Load fluctuations on the Central Electricity
Generating Board system,
1960–61. (Source: CEGB)

must bear all the expenses of its own transmission lines and grid
system, and it has to accept the fact that the capital cost of this
continuous means of transport represents a much greater proportion
of total transport costs than it does in the case of the discontinuous
media (Chapters 5 and 6). The coal industry, therefore, by virtue
of its nature and the economics of its transport media, is much better
able than the electricity industry to adapt itself to seasonal fluctuations in demand. Since it is to the gas and electricity industries that
the problem presents the most difficulties, the rest of the chapter will
be concerned only with them.

Two basic approaches are available to the energy industries as
they seek to intensify their use of capital and labour. The first is to
minimize the cost of that part of their capital equipment which is
used only at peak periods of demand; the other is to devise means
whereby fluctuations in demand can be at least smoothed out. These
approaches underly the following discussion, and have given rise to
four principal means whereby the problem can be lessened, if
not solved. These are the reduction of the capital costs involved in
the production of energy for peak demands; the interlinkage of
market areas to permit the sharing of peak capacity; the storage of
energy; and the use of pricing policies to encourage a more regular
demand through time.

To turn to the first of these, the manufactured gas industry
historically found one solution to the problem created by fluctuating
demands by producing water gas from coke and oil. The expense of
making gas by this method is high; but the capital cost is relatively
small compared with conventional plant, and as a result only a
small amount of investment lies idle for the greater part of the
time. Similarly, the electricity industry uses diesel and gas turbine
generating units for peak load generation. Their running costs
may be relatively high. But with low capital and labour costs, and
the ability to generate at very short notice, these generators can
meet the peak demands of both individual firms and—as with the
remote-controlled gas turbine unit in the heart of south-west England
—quite extensive areas with a small aggregate demand. An unusual
case was the use of the 5,400 kW generators of T2 tankers moored
around the coast of Scandinavia to meet deficiencies of hydro-
electricity supply in 1959 and 1960 following periods of unusually
low rainfall (Pugh, 1962).

The electricity industry has also found a variety of other solutions
to short.term market fluctuations within this general category. The
use of old, less efficient and written-down generating plants to meet
peak demands has already been mentioned. In addition, it is possible

to construct a base load power station which is capable of operating above its normal capacity for a short period of time. Although the efficiency of such a station is temporarily lowered, by reducing the amount of steam extracted for feed-water heating, more electricity can be generated to meet peak demand. Again, by taking advantage of turbine tolerances, for short periods of time pressures can be increased up to about 5% in order to boost electricity output. When these latter two solutions are used, the location of peak generation will be determined by the decision made for the siting of base load production; but where separate peak generating plant are employed, their location will invariably be market orientated.

If hydro-electricity and thermal electricity are both produced and inter-linked within a single production and supply system, by virtue of their relative costs or the nature of river régime one is invariably better suited to peak generation than the other. In Chile and in some parts of Canada the average cost of thermal electricity tends to be higher than that of hydro-electricity, with the result that the latter is usually used for meeting base load demands. Generally, of course, when the two are developed within a single economy, their costs tend to be roughly comparable, otherwise it would not have been economic for both to be developed. Their exact relationship in the supply system, and their particular roles in the satisfaction of different phases in the demand cycle, vary with differences in working (that is, production and transmission) costs from place to place. They also vary with the régime of water flow. In Scotland, for example, the hydrological characteristics of many of the hydro-electricity schemes are such as to favour a low load factor because of their relatively high heads, their limited storage capacity and the fact that their seasonal run-off characteristics are ideally matched with the seasonal nature of electricity demand. The heaviest loads are in winter, and under average conditions the run-off from October to March is nearly twice that of the six 'summer' months (Henderson and Allan, 1960). As a consequence, Scottish hydro-electricity is well suited to serve peak winter demands either directly or through pumped storage schemes. The same is true of the Alpine hydro-electricity resources of France which, formerly used to satisfy only local demands, are now incorporated within the national electricity supply system. The relative costs of hydro and thermal generation, plus the régime of the rivers, have determined that hydro-electricity —in addition to its consumption in the local electro-metallurgical and electro-chemical industries of the Alpine valleys—is best used to meet the peak demands of the Paris market for four hours to each day during the four winter months with maximum electricity demands.

Under present technology and costs, the combination of nuclear with conventional power is most economically assured when the former is used to satisfy the base load demand. This is a direct consequence of the very high capital costs of nuclear power—which imply that a deterioration in the load factor of a nuclear power station considerably increases the unit costs of generation—but its exceedingly low operating costs. George (1960), taking a somewhat optimistic view of nuclear power economics, showed how a fall in the load factor to 40% would increase the unit costs of nuclear power by over 100% whereas the increased cost of conventional generation would be only 35%. British nuclear power stations, therefore, are given priority in the satisfaction of base load demands so that their very high capital costs can be spread over as many kilowatt-hours of electricity as possible. As a corollary of this policy, all new coal-fired power stations in Britain are designed and built *ab initio* for what is known as two-shift running, that is, for an overnight shutdown. The spatial expression of this arrangement and the contrast between winter peak and off-peak electricity flows can be seen in Fig. 4.

The second means of reducing the problem of short term fluctuations in demand is by the interlinkage of market areas to allow the sharing of peak generating capacity. This is feasible at all scales. Within a city the incidence of peak electricity demands varies between the suburbs and the centre. In London, the morning suburban peak demand is between 8 and 8.30, whilst that of the City is an hour later. Consequently, the inter-linkage of the two areas offers certain economies in the provision and use of peak generating plant. The cross-Channel cable between Britain and France, completed in 1962, is in part a political symbol; but its economic justification is nevertheless based upon the same principle. This 200 kV direct current link between Lydd and Le Porte (near Boulogne) is worthwhile because there is a time lag between the daily peak demands in the British and French electricity markets, and part of the peak generating capacity of the two countries can therefore be shared. The North Wales gas grid provides a further example of the same principle: linking the holiday resort markets of the coast with their summer peak and the industrial area of the North Wales coalfield (with its winter peak), economies can once again be obtained from the sharing of peak production plant.

On a continental scale, the long-range plans of the USSR envisage the development of a nationally coordinated and integrated power system, controlled from a single load dispatching centre. Initially

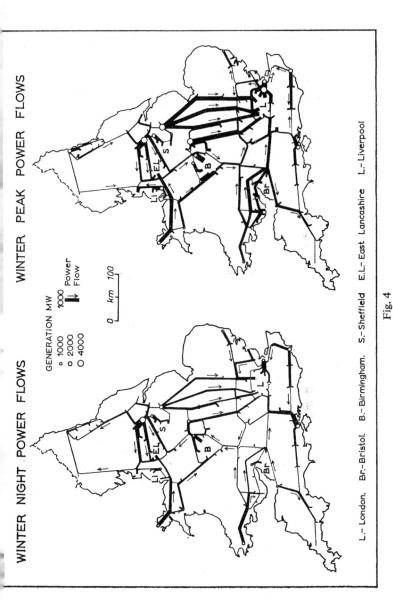

WINTER NIGHT POWER FLOWS   WINTER PEAK POWER FLOWS

GENERATION MW
o 1000
o 2000
O 4000

1000 Power
Flow

0   km   100

L.- London.   Br.- Bristol.   B.- Birmingham.   S.- Sheffield   E.L.- East Lancashire   L.- Liverpool

Fig. 4

Estimated winter power flows on the Central Electricity Generating Board system, 1970-71.
(Source: Booth, 1967, 11)

a number of regional networks have been established, some of whose transmission lines exceed 800 km in length, in both the European and Asian parts of the country. These have been, or are in the process of being, tied together by trunk lines with voltages as high as 1,400 kV; the rationale of these lines is to facilitate the transmission of large blocks of power from east to west, and to take advantage of variations in the incidence of peak loadings in the eleven time zones of the Soviet Union (Sewell, 1964). This rapidly emerging continental network stands in contrast to the situation in the United States. Although the many private and the few public producer-suppliers have come together to form seven broad regional power system groups, and although these are linked together to form a coast to coast system, many of the inter-ties are quite small and the electricity industry is unable to take advantage of the contrasting demand and supply patterns in different parts of the country. The gains to be derived from stronger inter-regional links are widely recognized. Stronger east-west links would permit a sharing of daily peak load plant. Stronger north-south links would allow seasonal energy transfers between the West-South Central region (with a summer peak demand) and the north-east (with a winter peak), or between California (summer peak) and the Pacific north-west (winter peak). However, institutional inertia plus a divergence between the interests of the federal authorities and the private utility companies has delayed the large scale construction of the appropriate inter-ties.

The storage of energy is the third means of overcoming the problems of short term variations in demand. The simplest and the earliest technique used by the gas industry for this purpose was the gas holder located near to the centre of its market. An alternative solution is to enlarge the diameter of a pipeline near to the market and thus facilitate the storage of peak load gas in the pipeline. This technique is used by the El Paso gas pipe to California which, 60 to 66 cm in diameter near the gas fields, is enlarged to 76 cm as it reaches Los Angeles. Useful though they may be to meet daily fluctuations of demand, the gas holder—or its modern counterpart in the form of a battery of high-pressure cylinders—and the enlarged transmission pipe have insufficient capacity, or are too expensive on a large scale, to meet the longer term, seasonal vagaries of the market. An alternative solution which has been found, therefore, is the underground storage of gas. The first such storage area in Britain was an exhausted natural gas field in Scotland at Cousland; much more extensive aquifers have also been prospected for storage in southern England. Similar techniques are also used in continental

Europe, where coke-oven gas is stored near to the Ruhr, and natural gas (for Paris) is kept underground during the summer months near Versailles.

Underground storage is used extensively by the American gas industry which has a considerable problem of seasonal load variations as a result of its widespread use of space heating. To ensure a high load factor in the very extensive network of natural gas transmission pipelines (the length of which exceeds the total kilometres of track operated by the railways), several hundred of these underground gas stores are in use near the largest urban and industrial markets. Both exhausted gas fields, or geological structures not originally containing gas but suitable for storage, are used to hold the gas during the summer months of low demand, after which it is available for the heavy space heating needs of winter. A variation upon this solution is to use a gas field close to a market to meet only its peak demands, whilst base load gas is brought from further afield. In northern California, for example, a dry gas field at Rio Vista is used solely for the peak needs of San Francisco, whilst most of the city's gas is received from out of State (Parsons, 1958).

The conversion of natural gas into a liquid by refrigeration affords yet a further means of storing it. The technique of liquefying methane, which is used extensively for the transport of natural gas by ocean tanker, was first developed to solve some of the problems of peak gas demand in Cleveland (Ohio). The reduction of the volume of the gas in the course of refrigeration to a fraction of that in its gaseous state—one-sixhundredth at minus 160°C—is singularly advantageous of this technology.

Although it is impossible to store electricity, it is nevertheless possible to store water from which electricity can be generated. Increasingly, therefore, pumped storage schemes are being designed whereby surplus electricity generating capacity is used to pump water from a lower to an upper reservoir during off-peak periods; the water in the uper reservoir is then available to generate electricity at periods of peak demand. Although three kilowatt-hours of electricity are needed to pump water equivalent to two kilowatt-hours of potential energy to a higher level, the technique improves the efficiency of a supply system, particularly since it obviates the inefficient stopping and starting of the load base generating sets. This method of 'storing' electricity has been adopted in Britain in association with the nuclear power station at Trawsfynydd in North Wales. There, surplus electricity at times of relatively low demand is used to pump water at Blaenau Ffestiniog a few kilometres away; the scheme thereby allows the nuclear power plant to work at a very high load factor,

and at the same time it makes available some 300 MW of hydro-
electric generating capacity for the West Midlands and south Lancashire at periods of peak demand. Pumped storage is also used to
considerable advantage in Scotland (Fulton, 1962). Rugged terrain
is not necessary, however, for such schemes. The Hamburg Electric
Company has built an artificial lake above the River Elbe for pumped
storage and use in association with its thermal electricity stations.
Most pumped storage schemes are designed essentially to 'shave the
peaks' off daily loads. Others, however, are used to 'store' electricity
between seasons. For example, in Switzerland and Austria, by
means of pumped storage water is conserved in the period after
melt to meet some of the heavier demands of the following
winter.

  The final means of lessening the problems posed by fluctuations
in energy markets involves the use of pricing policies to encourage
a more regular demand. American gas transmission companies, for
example, impose a tariff comprising a flat demand charge (based
upon maximum requirements) and a commodity charge (related to
the actual quantity of gas purchased). At off-peak periods, however,
they are often prepared to transport gas at a rate close to the commodity charge and taking no account of the demand charge. In
other words, they are willing to transport gas at a rate which meets
their running cost and offers them a small profit, but which makes
little or no contribution to the pipeline's capital cost. Such a policy
yields more revenue than if it did not exist, and it is based upon the
same economic principles that prompt railways to run excursion
trains. In return for the low cost off-peak gas, the consumer has to be
prepared to have his supplies cut off as soon as a more remunerative
market becomes available. These sales of interruptible (or 'dump')
gas—which represented about two-fifths of the gas sold to American
industry in the middle '60s—have greatly influenced the geography
of energy in the United States. The largest quantities are consumed in
California; but it is in the Middle West and in the south-eastern States
where they have disrupted the established markets of other fuels,
under-selling all competition and embarrassing the coal industry in
particular. (The coal industry, in turn, has sought recourse to political
action in order to restrain the further extension of these sales; see
p.187). In the long-run, of course, it is in the best interests of the
gas industry to reduce the amount of interruptible gas. Such low
prices to some consumers mean that others have to bear a dispropor-
tionately large share of the capital cost involved in transporting the
energy. This is reflected in the fact that those distribution companies
which have extensive summer storage facilities near to their markets,

and which have come to rely less on interruptible sales to maximize the use of their own (or an associated transmission company's) pipelines, are usually able to quote lower household and commercial rates than those who sell large quantities of interruptible gas in the summer months.

Both general and specific tariff structures are used by the electricity industry to the same end. In Britain, for example, the Central Electricity Generating Board has a two-part tariff consisting of, first, a fixed charge per kilowatt of maximum demand; and, second, a running charge for each unit of electricity consumed. In recent years, in an attempt to reduce its load problem, the Generating Board has increased its fixed charge at the same time as it has reduced its running charge; it has thereby provided an incentive for the regional Area Boards (who distribute and sell electricity) to improve their load factors. This has been achieved to some extent by the latter adopting a comparable rate policy for the sale of electricity to the final consumer. There has in fact been a gradual improvement in the load factor of the British electricity industry in recent years for whereas in 1920 the load factor was as low as 30%, with the nuclear power station at Trawsfynydd in North Wales. There, by 1947–8 it had increased to 43% and the present figure is about 52%. Such a load factor, however, is still below those of other countries where less variable climatic conditions, longer working hours and more shiftwork in industry, or (in a few instances) a higher proportion of heavy and continuous demands from electrochemical or electro-metallurgical industries, make load factors of 55% or over possible. In fact, some of the main systems of the United States electricity industry have load factors over of 60%.

Besides its general rate policies, the electricity industry can also offer specific rates to encourage a more regular consumption of electricity. The industry can offer particularly low rates for thermal storage heaters which are designed to cut-out at peak periods. It can push sales in those activities where the load factor is particularly high, and it can encourage some industries to use electricity at off-peak periods, especially those with semi-automatic operations which can be concentrated in the off-peak hours. Because they have a relatively small labour cost, the use of electric furnaces, electric kilns, pumps in mines and the like can be limited to those times of the day when the rates for power are slightly lower. The same can be said of charging batteries for use in industrial trucks and vehicles, pumping loads in drainage schemes, cold-storage warehouses and ice-making factories, in all of which the cost of power is a sufficiently large item in operating expenses to make some inconvenience

acceptable at a reduced rate. As with other means designed to meet
the problem created by seasonal and daily fluctuations in the size
of the markets for fuel and power, policies such as these leave their
impress upon the geography of energy.

4

THE MARKET (II)

The location of the market – the nature of the market – electricity generation in the United States

The location of the market

All other things being equal, those resources of energy which are nearest to a market will be utilized to satisfy the demands there. The importance of the location of markets in the geography of energy is to this extent self-evident. The demand for coal in the industrial Donbas is satisfied by the local mines, just as the greater part of the energy needs of Venezuela are met from its considerable resources of oil and natural gas. But other things, it cannot be overlooked, rarely are equal. As a consequence, the effect of the location of a market upon the geography of energy frequently becomes attenuated and indirect. In any case, location is always a relative rather than an absolute phenomenon, and the space-relations of a market are highly qualified by its associated transport facilities, their characteristics and their costs. Thus, as will be seen in Chapter 5, for the bulk transport of the fossil fuels, the costs of overcoming the distance between North America and Western Europe are small. Appalachian coking coals can effectively compete with local coking coals in the British market, particularly when spot or term charter rates are low; and the crude oils of the Middle East are highly attractive in the tidewater markets of America's east coast despite their much longer haul than domestic oil. Location in the last resort, in other words, is a measure both of geographical space and of transport opportunities and costs.

C

The striking contrasts between the patterns of energy consumption in different countries are fundamentally rooted in the opportunities afforded by their own natural resources, plus the spatial relationships of those resources to their domestic demands. Partly by virtue of their relative proximity, but also of course in response to political and economic priorities, a country's own supplies of energy tend to be used in preference to imported fuels provided they are available at a reasonable cost and are convenient for use in the domestic market. Thus, the United States and Canada with their considerable wealth and variety of energy resources have complex energy economies, their markets being shared between oil, natural gas, coal, nuclear power and hydro-electricity; in contrast, the much narrower resource range of, say, Poland, East Germany and Iran has encouraged the emergence of economies which rely heavily upon a single source of energy. This does not deny, of course, that some countries with a very narrow resource base are capable of drawing upon a wide range of international energy sources—the case of Japan is especially noteworthy.

Again, the geographical patterns of energy consumption *within* a country are strongly influenced by the regional distribution of energy resources. The use of extra-regional supplies quite obviously involves an expenditure on transport costs which will be avoided, if possible. Thus, quite contrasting patterns of energy use can characterize different regions within a country. Hydro-electricity and oil fuels, for example, play a more important role in the Pacific north-west than they do in America as a whole. Whilst these two sources of energy satisfy approximately 44% of the energy needs of the United States, they represent three-quarters of the fuel and power used in the Pacific north-west. The explanation lies largely in the difference between the average prices of energy in the United States on the one hand, and in Washington and Oregon on the other; and these price differentials, in turn, strongly reflect the location of the north-west's markets with their easy access to low-priced hydro-electricity and relatively inexpensive water-borne oil. Such regional differences in energy consumption within the United States have their counterpart within Britain where the largest markets for oil as a boiler fuel and for nuclear power generation are in the coal-deficient parts of the country, especially south-east England.

A nearby market, in other words, provides a powerful—though by no means certain—stimulus to the exploitation of an energy resource, just as the existence of a considerable distance between a source of energy and a potential market for it frequently leaves the source either temporarily or permanently undeveloped. A lack of nearby markets for Middle East natural gas can be blamed for the slow and modest progress made in its exploitation to date; and the same observation could be made of many other known energy resources elsewhere in the world. There has, for example, for some time been a considerable potential market for low-cost natural gas in Japan, but the distance which separates it from the ample Alaska and Brunei supplies (together with attendant technical difficulties) meant that until recently this demand remained wholly unsatisfied. The importance of the distance between a market and a source of energy naturally varies with each type of energy and its transport economics: the exploitation of a hydro-electricity resource some 1,000 km from a potential market is much less likely than is the tapping of an oilfield situated the same distance away (see p. 90 ff.). The distance between an energy market and the alternative resources available, therefore, influences both the types and the quantities of the energy consumed there.

Further, the spatial relationship of markets to energy transport routes also modifies the geography of energy consumption. Arizona, for example, a State without resources of natural gas, lies between the gas fields of New Mexico and Texas on the one hand, and the huge southern Californian energy market on the other. Largely by virtue of this location, the State has been able to obtain low cost supplies of natural gas, for it has tapped the large diameter pipelines laid to serve Los Angeles's demands. Without these pipes to California it is impossible to assess accurately how much gas Arizona would have imported from its neighbour; but the size of its market would certainly have precluded the use of large diameter pipelines, and would thus have increased the cost of transporting gas away from its source. (A smaller demand for the gas at its source, however, might well have meant that the field price of the gas was compensatingly lower.) The importance of the spatial relationship between energy markets and transport routes is also illustrated by contrasts in the development of the Italian and Scandinavian oil refining industries. The pattern of crude and product prices at Mediterranean and North Atlantic ports makes it generally unprofitable to ship products back towards the Middle East; the result is an excess of capacity and a net export of products by the Italian industry, and a continuing net import of products in the case of the Scandinavian countries (see p. 205).

The importance of the market location is further emphasized by the effects of a change in a market's geography. After World War I coke manufacture in America underwent a radical relocation due to changing technology. Before the war, the older, beehive, method of producing coke invariably took place at or near the mouth of a coal mine, and as a result the industry was highly localized in Pennsylvania. In fact, in 1914 over one-half of the country's coke was produced in the Connellsville District of that State. After 1918, however, the beehive ovens were steadily replaced by the by-product method of coke manufacture, which is usually found in association with integrated iron and steel works. The steel industry, however, was generally located away from the mining districts of Pennsylvania, and an increasing proportion of American coke production came steadily to be located outside that State. As a consequence of this shift in the coke industry, certain geographical changes occurred in the Appalachian coal industry. Most important was the decline of mining in Pennsylvania and the expansion of coal production in West Virginia and Kentucky. Simultaneously new coal flows were established as traffic by rail contracted, and more use was made of the more economic inland waterways to transport coal to its new markets. There were, it is true, other factors which contributed to the changing geography of the Appalachian coal industry at this time. Particularly important was the gradual exhaustion of some of the older Pennsylvanian seams, and a change in railway demand from the low volatile coals of central Pennsylvania to the high volatile coals of the west of the State. But, 'Of all the factors affecting the distribution of Pennsylvania bituminous coal [between 1918 and 1929] the shift from the beehive method to the by-product method of producing coke had the most profound influence' (Fritz and Veenstra, 1935, 139).

The nature of the market

One of the most important factors influencing the geography of energy is undoubtedly the extent to which markets are 'free' or 'planned'. Between the two extremes of a *laissez faire* free-for-all and an all powerful authoritarian control over economic transactions (neither of which exists in reality) lie many varieties of political economies. The degree of political intervention in the market, however, and the way in which it influences investment decisions, taxation policies, the supervision of the energy industries and the pricing of their products clearly has a decisive role in moulding the geography of energy. The evolution of international contrasts in energy consumption cannot be explained, therefore, without full recognition of the planned nature of, say, the Soviet market, and the way in which for so many years demands for energy undervalued the worth of oil and natural gas, and overvalued both coal and hydro-electricity (Campbell, 1968, *passim*); similarly, the 'mixed' nature of Western

European economic life, with its internationally varying styles and degrees of public intervention in the evolution of energy needs, is an important component on the demand side of energy geography. These are points which are followed up in more detail in Chapters 8 and 9.

Energy requirements originate from three sectors of an economy —the domestic, industrial and transport sectors—and the proportions of each varies from region to region and country to country. In Table 2, something of the differences in sector demand in Western Europe, North America and Japan are recorded for the year 1964.

Table 2

ENERGY DEMANDS IN WESTERN EUROPE,
NORTH AMERICA AND JAPAN, 1964
(million tons coal equivalent)

	Western Europe* (%)		North America (%)		Japan (%)	
Final consumption in:						
industry	319	(29·7)	678	(35·4)	73	(38·0)
energy sector†	93	(8·7)			12	(6·3)
transport	170	(15·8)	406	(21·2)	33	(17·2)
domestic and						
miscellaneous	276	(25·7)	488	(25·5)	27	(14·1)
Total final consumption	858	(80·0)	1572	(82·0)	145	(75·5)
Transformation losses and non-energy products‡	215	(20·0)	344	(18·0)	47	(24·5)
Total primary energy consumption	1073	(100·0)	1916	(100·0)	192	(100·0)
of which:						
electricity generation§	264	(24·6)	403	(21·0)	57	(29·7)
coking coal	93	(8·7)	74	(3·9)	20	(10·4)
petroleum products,						
non-competitive	187	(17·4)	494	(25·8)	35	(18·2)

* OECD Europe.
† Coal used in mines, oil used at refineries, transmission losses of electricity and gas.
‡ Especially chemical feedstocks.
§ Nuclear and hydro equivalents included.
Source: Organization for Economic Cooperation and Development 1966, passim.

The relatively large role of transport requirements in the North American market, and the particularly large share of industrial demands in the Japanese market, are two points of immediate contrast. Similarly, the share of the domestic sector in the energy consumption of economies located in temperate and sub-arctic regions tends to be much greater than the same sector in their tropical and sub-tropical counterparts—at least until rising living standards in the latter can afford an extensive use of air conditioning equipment. The industrial sector generates only a very small percentage of total energy demands in the developing world; and the transport sector tends to be responsible for a significantly higher proportion of national energy consumption in those countries with a high average standard of living. These contrasts are important. Where, for example, domestic and industrial space heating needs make up a significant proportion of the total energy market, and where there are considerable seasonal and daily fluctuations in these requirements, the energy industries are particularly faced with the problem discussed in Chapter 3. When demand in the industrial sector dominates total energy requirements, and the economy is subject to phases of buoyant and depressed activity, it is another set of dilemmas which face the producer–supplier industries.

The markets for energy in these three broad sectors are by no means independent, however, for the size of demand in one sector can set limits upon the magnitude of consumption in one of the others. This can be the case with petroleum products, and Indian conditions provide a relevant example. Particularly large demands for kerosene (used for lighting and cooking) and for diesel oil in that country completely dominate the petroleum market. The potential consumption of these products, however, substantially exceeds the quantities which can be obtained from refinery operations within India without creating huge surpluses of other petroleum products—or a high level of kerosene and diesel oil imports plus foreign exchange difficulties. As a consequence, the demands for these products has to remain in part unsatisfied, and the present share of the Indian energy market which is served by the oil industry (23% in 1965) appears unlikely to be significantly increased in the near future, even though the country's energy needs may grow substantially during the next decade. The greater part of this increase seems likely to be met from domestic resources of coal and hydro-electricity.

When a market and a refinery mix cannot be suitably adjusted, and there are no foreign exchange or political constraints upon trade, the two obvious solutions are to import any product deficits from other places and to transfer surplus distillates elsewhere. On the west coast of the United States, the need for residual oil is relatively small and the greater part of petroleum demands are for the top and middle distillates; rather than limit the refining of gasoline in California, therefore, the surplus residual oil is shipped to the industrial markets in the north-east of the country. Such a solution to the problem naturally depends upon the availability of suitable consumers elsewhere to absorb the surplus products, just as the alternative solution would demand the availability of appropriate products from other places. Where such transfers are not feasible, however, the market mechanism through price adjustments forces a shift in the nature of demands.

The pattern of sector demand is also important in another respect. Most energy requirements are general in nature and can be satisfied by two or more alternative fuels. But some energy needs are specific and can be met only by one fuel. Blast furnaces, for example, require coke and automobiles petrol. When a specific energy demand dominates an important sector of an energy economy, therefore, the nature of that demand can strongly influence the geography of energy. For example, in North America the transport sector in 1965 represented over one-quarter of final energy consumption, and non-competitive petroleum products equalled nearly one-third of final demand (see Table 2); in Western Europe, on the other hand, transport demands were less than 20% of final consumption, and the non-competitive petroleum demands only a little over 22%. In consequence, the North American economy was relatively—as well as absolutely—more dependent upon the oil industry than its Western European counterpart. Moreover, in so far as the oil industry produces joint products, a large non-competitive sector with only limited price competition affords the industry a particularly powerful competitive stance in those markets where it faces competition from other sources of energy. Invariably the industry adopts a much more aggressive pricing policy in fuel oil markets than in gasoline markets.

Specific demands can also influence the overall pattern of energy consumption in local and regional markets. Assuming a particular fuel is demanded in a market and is in limited supply, its price will tend to rise and 'inferior' uses will cease to be served; in other words, those demands for which alternative fuels are available and which cannot afford to pay a high price for the fuel in question turn to other sources of energy. The market for, and the supply of, natural gas at times provides an excellent example of just this process. The special advantage of gas in those operations where a clean source of heat is required (for example, in the manufacture of glass) means that it has some 'superior' markets which maintain their demands even when the delivered price of the gas is relatively high. When supplies of gas are limited and demand for them grows rapidly, price changes tend to shift consumption away from 'inferior' uses (say, the electricity utility market where cheap substitute fuels are available) to 'superior' ones. Adelman (1962, *passim*) has shown how in New York State in the '50s, the rate of growth of gas consumption was fastest in the two markets where price increases were the greatest.

In the very short run, of course, all domestic, industrial and transport demands tend to be specific, for most capital plant is capable of using only one type of energy; and once a piece of capital equipment has been bought to use a particular type of fuel there are strong economic incentives to continue using it until replacement is absolutely necessary. In the longer run, however, most energy demands are general rather than specific, and ultimately the greater part of an economy's requirements can be satisfied by one of several sources of energy. Although very few markets are as competitive as the few multiple-fuel power stations which have been designed to burn almost any kind of fossil fuel—the new Porto Corsini power station near Ravenna (1400 MW), for example, is capable of burning coal, heavy or fuel oil, petrol or natural gas—the technical possibility of substituting different sources of energy in most markets implies a high degree of inter-fuel competition in the long run. And, 'When, from a technical point of view, there is a high elasticity of substitution among different forms of energy, the price is the decisive factor determining energy use' (United Nations, 1957c, 39).

In sum, the relative importance of a fuel within an economy depends, first, upon the importance of those uses for which it has special technical advantages, and, second, upon its competitive relationship with other fuels which can be used for the same purposes. This competition is based not only upon criterion of price per unit of energy but also upon other factors such as the efficiency and convenience of the alternative fuels in use, or the quality and the reliability of different supplies. Their sum effect is to generate a constant change and flux in the geography of energy. Take the American case.

One hundred or so years ago, nearly 90 % of American energy needs were met by burning wood. At the turn of the century, coal was assuming an equally commanding position, and by 1910 fuelwood accounted for little more than 10 % of the country's energy consumption. World War II was another turning point. After 1920, oil and natural gas began steadily to increase their share of the market, and by 1946 petroleum was as important as coal. Within another fourteen years oil and gas together were satisfying some 70 % of the country's energy needs, and the contribution of coal had gradually declined to about 28% as its markets were gradually eroded away by more convenient and more economical fuels (Schurr *et al.*, 1960, *passim*, Landsberg and Schurr, 1968, *passim*). These inter-fuel substitutions have produced a radical transformation in the flow of energy from its sources to its markets. In the early part of this century American energy transfers were highly localized in the north-east of the country and spatially the movements were fan-like as the coal was moved by rail and water from its Appalachian sources to the markets in the manufacturing belt. This flow—somewhat reduced in volume—still persists, but superimposed upon it now is the movement of oil and gas in pipelines and tankers. Once again in spatial terms it is fan-shaped, but today the energy transfers are upon a much larger scale, as the oil and the gas of the southern Plains and the Gulf Coast are moved to their nation-wide markets and especially to the manufacturing belt. The dynamic nature of this American energy geography has its roots in the competitive nature of most of the country's energy markets.

One qualification to these generalizations concerning the nature of inter-fuel competition must be noted, however. It involves the distinction between fuel and power. Coal, oil and natural gas are fuels, and generally they can be substituted for each other; they can be used either as a fuel or as a source of power; and the choice between them is largely a matter of the factors which have already been discussed. But falling water and controlled nuclear energy can be used only to generate electricity, and a range of energy markets is thereby denied to them. This distinction between fuels and power has been blurred in the past largely because the greater part of economic development throughout the world until recently has been based upon the use of fossil fuels, which are sources of both fuel and power. But in such regions as central and eastern Canada or Norway, where there are ample hydro-electricity resources but a scarcity of fossil fuels, the distinction is of considerable significance since there are limitations to the value of electric power in many industrial processes. At one time these limits were technical. But today many of the technological weaknesses of electrical power have been removed, and in a certain sense electricity can be regarded as the most desirable form of energy since it can be used for nearly every non-transport use, even the reduction of iron ore. The contemporary limitations to the value of electric power nevertheless remain. Now they are economic rather than technical.

These limits stem from the fact that electrically generated heat is very much more expensive than heat produced by using a fossil fuel.

It is therefore only rarely practicable to use it in industrial heating markets. Exceptions can of course be found: electric furnaces produce some steels and alloys; in the electro-process industries, electricity is used for both electrolytic and heat-producing purposes; a few manufacturing processes use electric heat because of its cleanliness and ease of control; and sometimes surplus electricity is used to raise steam. But these are exceptions. Since heat is needed in almost all industrial processes at some stage, it can be argued with Dales (1953, 181)—although he tends to overstate the case—that 'Fuels provide an energy base for the whole range of modern production, whilst water power alone will be able to support only a very narrow range of industry centred around a few electro-process industries, and those industries which require only a small amount of heat in their production process'. It follows as a corollary, therefore, that the nature of demand determines whether or not local resources are capable of its satisfaction, and hence the characteristics of energy flows when that demand is met.

Just as changes in the location of a market affects the geography of energy, so also do changes in its nature. In Western Europe, for example, an increasing affluence is leading to a greater use of the motor car. It is also reasonable to expect that firms there will grow bigger (per unit of output) and will seek to lower their costs through longer production runs, even though this involves the distribution of their manufactures over greater aggregate distances to their markets. There will, in other words, be a substitution of scale economies for transport economies. Together these trends are likely to increase the relative importance of the Western European energy economy's transport sector, part of which has specific requirements for gasolines. In turn this will increase the continent's dependence upon oil imports, encourage a further expansion of the refining industry and thereby make available other products to compete against coal and natural gas. Technology, convenience, politics and the like will also, of course, play a part in the evolution of Western European energy markets; but the changing nature of demand will have an important role to play also.

Electricity generation in the United States

A review of developments in the geography of electricity generation in the United States (Landsberg and Schurr, 1968, 144 ff.; Federal Power Commission, 1964, *passim*) serves to consolidate the observations of this chapter and the last on the importance of the size, location and nature of the market in the geography of energy. Two aspects of the electricity industry are of fundamental importance in this context. The first is that it is one of the most rapidly expanding markets for primary energy in the country. Between 1950 and 1965 the energy required to generate electricity more than doubled, and in the next fifteen year period up to 1980 some forecasts suggest that there will be a further trebling of primary energy requirements. The reasons for this exceptional growth lie partly in the rapid pace of technological progress in the United States, which is constantly developing new uses for electricity in the home and in business; the rapidly expanding air-conditioning market, for example, is one of the most important of the growing uses of electricity. In addition, industry and commerce increasingly are coming to depend upon electricity utilities for their various energy needs, rather than relying as in the past upon their own boilers and purchases of primary energy. The sum effect of these developments is that electricity consumption per head in America is tending to double every fifteen years.

The second fundamental aspect of the electricity industry is that it provides one of the most competitive markets for primary energy; indeed, in certain respects it is perhaps the nearest approach to a 'perfectly' competitive market. A number of factors account for this. For example, since the units of consumption within the market are very large (a 2,000 MW plant, for instance, represents a market for between 4 and 5 million tons of coal per year), it is invariably worthwhile to construct a railway, a jetty or a pipeline to supply a power station if one is not already available; as a result, no one fuel can monopolize a particular market just because it is the only one for which transport facilities are immediately available. In addition, the various fuels can technically compete on more or less equal terms. The capital costs for gas firing, and to a lesser extent for oil, are rather lower than those for coal but the difference is relatively small; in any case, coal has a small compensating advantage in terms of efficiency since less heat is lost in creating water vapour during combustion, and its exhaust gases can be more easily used to produce additional heat. Further, the cost of installing equipment to burn two or three fuels is not very much more than it is for a single fuel, and the cost of altering a station to burn one fuel rather than another is relatively small. Roughly one out of every three installations for which the Federal Power Commission publishes detailed information has facilities for burning more than one type of fuel. In 1965, 30% of the plants did in fact burn both coal and one or two other primary fuels, and over 10% burned both oil and natural gas. The most frequent combination was in fact coal and natural gas under agreements which allowed the power plants to use (interruptible) low-priced gas during the summer months when the demands for space-heating gas are at a seasonal low. This high degree of competition in the thermal electricity market means that it is the delivered price of the alternative fuels which is especially critical in determining the degree to which any one fuel is used.

For the last forty years, the one consistent feature of the electricity industry has been the declining role of hydro-electricity power in the country as a whole. Responsible for generating 34% of all electricity in 1930, its share had fallen to 29% in 1950, 19% in 1960, and 18% in 1965. Meanwhile the importance of oil and natural gas had increased from 10% in 1930 to 27% in 1965. Their increased use was at the expense of coal until about 1950, by which time it was used for 47% of generation, compared with 56% twenty years earlier. Since 1950, however, coal has been making something of a come-back and by 1965 it was once again the primary fuel for 55% of United States' electricity. The explanation of these trends lies in differential movements in the delivered price of the competing fuels, evaluated in the context of their associated costs such as handling, waste disposal, pollution and the like.

Coal, which is burned to generate roughly two-thirds of the *thermal* electricity in the United States, was able to reduce its delivered prices to the utilities from $1·09 to $0·98 per million kilo calories between 1952 and 1964. This performance, which represented a substantial price decline in real money terms, was a reflection of the steady improvement in the efficiency of the industry. Productivity rose substantially in the mines with the introduction of continuous mining techniques underground, and with a greater concentration of capital resources upon large scale strip mining where efficiency per man-hour is particularly high. In addition considerable progress was made in improving the technology of coal transport (see p. 111) and in the bargaining of lower rates from the railroads. The coal industry was most successful in meeting competition from other fossil fuels in the older industrial states and in the eastern part of the country generally (see Table 3 and Fig. 5). These are very large markets—the East North Central and the Middle Atlantic regions alone accounting for more than 40% of American thermal power generation in 1964—and they were served from the Appalachian and Eastern Interior coalfields, the proximity of which undoubtedly aided the coal industry in its fight against competitive fuels. In the Pacific, Gulf and Mountain states, in contrast, coal made relatively little headway up to 1964. However, the exploitation of low-cost opencast mining technology, improved transport arrangements and the economics of high voltage transmission began to give the

Table 3

REGIONAL THERMAL ELECTRICITY PRODUCTION AND FUEL COSTS IN THE UNITED STATES, 1952 AND 1964

Region	Regional % of US thermal generation 1952	Regional % of US thermal generation 1964	1952 Coal	1952 Oil	1952 Natural gas	1952 Total	1964 Coal	1964 Oil	1964 Natural gas	1964 Total	Fuel costs ($ per mill. kcal) 1952 Coal $	1952 Oil $	1952 Natural gas $	1964 Coal $	1964 Oil $	1964 Natural gas $
New England	4·9	3·9	51	49	—	100	63	33	4	100	1·49	1·44	—	1·35	1·38	1·37
Middle Atlantic	21·8	15·5	84	11	5	100	77	15	8	100	1·16	1·41	1·06	1·04	1·27	1·34
East North Central	29·8	25·0	91	—	9	100	96	—	4	100	1·04	2·32	0·78	0·98	1·93	0·99
West North Central	7·4	7·6	47	2	51	100	50	—	50	100	1·16	1·52	0·81	1·04	2·02	0·97
South Atlantic	14·3	14·6	77	13	10	100	79	11	10	100	1·08	1·34	0·74	1·01	1·36	1·29
East South Central	5·2	10·6	70	—	30	100	92	—	8	100	0·80	—	0·58	0·77	2·00	0·98
West South Central	10·2	11·6	1	—	99	100	—	—	100	100	0·65	1·75	0·37	0·60	1·70	0·78
Mountain	1·8	3·8	29	11	60	100	45	4	51	100	0·91	0·96	0·64	0·77	1·03	1·06
Pacific	4·8	7·6	—	55	45	100	—	17	83	100	—	1·14	0·80	—	1·23	1·29
TOTAL	100·0	100·0	67	10	23	100	65	7	28	100	1·09	1·32	0·58	0·98	1·30	1·01

Source: National Coal Association, Washington, D.C.

industry a new competitive edge in at least the Mountain states, where its share of the market increased from 29% to 45% between 1952 and 1964, and where further large coal-burning plants are being erected or planned in Utah and Nevada.

The firing of power station boilers with natural gas has remained rather more localized than in the case of coal. Natural gas has been able to maintain its monopoly in the power station market of the West South Central region—where Texas and Louisiana alone consume about one-third of all the gas used to generate electricity in the United States—and it continues to play a significant role in the Mountain and Pacific States. The natural gas industry has also reached out and captured markets in the north and the east of the country—pipelines reached New England for the first time in 1954—and has been particularly vigorous in selling its fuel on an 'interruptible' basis. As residential and commercial demands for natural gas decline sharply during the summer months, the gas suppliers are willing to sell their fuel to utilities at particularly attractive prices, taking the view that, since the main expense in delivering gas is the overhead cost of their pipelines, sales at even low prices are better than no sales at all provided they make some contribution to these overhead costs. The prospects for a further growth of gas sales on this basis have been somewhat dimmed in recent years, however, by the steady rise in gas prices generally, and especially the delivered prices to the electricity utilities. Whereas in 1952 the electricity utilities were paying natural gas suppliers on average only about one-half what they were paying for coal (on a heat content basis), twelve years later gas was proving to be a slightly more expensive fuel. The steady rise in the value of gas was a response to the extension of its pipeline system, the widening of its market areas and the growth of new and superior uses for which higher prices could be charged. The emerging premium also stems from mounting pressures upon the utilities in large urban areas especially to reduce their pollution of the atmosphere. In both southern California, where local ordinances prohibit the use of fuel oil during the summer months and during any other time when natural gas is available, and in New York city, where an agreement has been reached to burn gas at in-town power stations, to close down a number of old coal and oil burning plants, and to accelerate the adoption of pumped storage facilities outside of the city, the advantages of natural gas as the cleanest of the fossil fuels has been amply demonstrated.

The electricity generating industry's use of fuel oil is much more localized than its use of the other two primary sources of energy. Florida and California together account for about 40% of utility

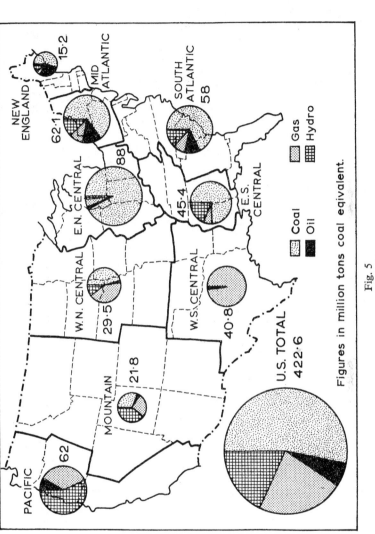

Fig. 5

Sources of electric power generation in the United States, by regions,
1964. (Source: Landsberg and Schurr, 1968, 147)

Figures in million tons coal equivalent.

NEW ENGLAND 15·2

MID ATLANTIC 62·1

SOUTH ATLANTIC 58

E.N. CENTRAL 88

E.S. CENTRAL 45·4

W.N. CENTRAL 29·5

W.S. CENTRAL 40·8

MOUNTAIN 21·8

PACIFIC 62

U.S. TOTAL 422·6

Coal   Gas
Oil   Hydro

demands, and Gottman's east coast Megalopolis for about two-thirds of the rest. Throughout the last twenty years, fuel oil has been generally priced significantly above the level of its competitors; in 1952 it was on average priced 23 cents and 51 cents per million kilo calories more than coal and natural gas respectively, and in 1964 the counterpart figures were 32 cents and 29 cents. It is for this reason that the large-scale use of fuel oil by the utilities has remained limited to what are principally a number of seaboard locations where low transport charges on the oil and access to world-wide sources of supply give it a cost and price advantage. The share of fuel oil in the electricity generating market fell from 10% to 7% between 1952 and 1964. Although it is likely that the decline would have been somewhat less had foreign fuel oils not been denied free access to the United States' market (especially after 1958 when oil prices internationally began to drift downwards), the mounting campaign against sulphur dioxide and other noxious emissions in large urban areas has exposed a new weakness in the fuel's competitive position.

These trends in primary fuel consumption by the thermal electricity industry have certain important implications for the overall geography of energy in the United States. Two-thirds of American thermal electricity is generated in four census regions—East North Central, Middle Atlantic, South Atlantic and East South Central. In these regions, with the exceptions of the States of Mississippi and Florida, not only is coal the major fuel used but (at least until the mid-'60s) it was tending to increase its share of the market. If 'Coal Competitive Zones' are defined as those States in which coal served at least 10% of the electricity utilities, primary fuel demands in 1964, they are responsible for the generation of nearly 80% of American thermal electricity. Defining 'Gas Competitive Zones' on a comparable basis, they account for about 48% of the national utility market. The rather fewer 'Oil Competitive Zones' generate just over 30% of the country's thermal electricity. The fact that coal is most competitive, and in places increasingly competitive, in by far the greater part of the rapidly growing utility market prompts the speculation that the demand for coal from this quarter is inherently strong and is likely to increase steadily in the foreseeable future. The coal industry's recent record of price stability and increasing productivity certainly encourages such a prediction, as does the possibility of lower transport costs through the use of larger unit and integral trains.

This prospect of a continued growth in the demand for solid fuels from the electricity utilities has important implications for the

American coal industry. In recent decades, many of the economic and social problems of this industry have arisen from the stagnation or the contraction of its total sales; shrinking demands from the railroads and for (industrial and domestic) space heating in particular have tended to dominate its mood and overall fate. But the absolute level of demand in these two markets has reached a point where further declines will make very little impact upon the total demand for coal; and, prospectively, the growing needs of the electricity utilities will dominate the industry's market situation. Largely as a result of the multiplying demands for electricity, the American coal industry has entered upon a phase of increasing output once again. This does not mean that its relative importance in all energy markets will necessarily increase; nor does it mean that all the problems of the industry are over—the nature and the location of demand are changing and these will leave their impress upon the geography of coal mining; nor does it overlook the economics of nuclear power, which have begun to challenge the coal industry in many of its largest and traditional markets. Nevertheless, it does imply a much healthier coal industry in the foreseeable future than in the recent past.

Nuclear power does, of course, pose a major problem for the coal producers. After many false hopes in the 1950s, and following the famous 1964 decision of General Electric to issue a standard price list for its atomic power plants, nuclear power came increasingly to be introduced into the United States' generating system. Between 1966 and 1968 utilities ordered new generating plants equal to as much as 56% of the total generating capacity in existence; of these, nuclear plants represent over one-third. There are some forecasts which suggest that by 1980 nuclear power will be as important a source of energy as coal (Winger *et al.*, 1968, 29), and that as a result the share which the latter can hold of the electricity utility market as a whole (that is, including hydro-electricity) will fall from 55% to 35%. The nuclear share in the meantime will grow from less than 1% to 36%. Natural gas, water power and oil together will share the remaining 29% of the 1980 market.

In contrast to coal, natural gas is most competitive as a power station fuel in those parts of the country where the market is much smaller. To be sure, some of the fastest rates of economic growth and of utility expansion are to be found in Florida, in the West Central region and in California. Some forecasts suggest that the Gulf Coast market will treble in size between 1965 and 1980. Natural gas also has the asset of a growing number of pollution conscious communities in urban America. However, it has to compete with a considerable realised hydro-electricity potential in the Pacific and Mountain regions; in 1964 hydro accounted for nearly 60% and 40% respectively of their electricity needs (see Fig. 5). The natural gas industry has also become increasingly concerned by the fact that the ratio of reserves to production (R/P ratio) is steadily falling (Federal Power Commission, 1969). And it cannot be unaware of the growing number of superior uses for which it can obtain higher than utility prices. Against such a background it would be surprising if natural gas did not come to serve a declining share of the thermal electricity market. The future role of oil, on the other hand, is highly uncertain. Whilst the downward trend in the real price of oil on the world market offers the continuing possibility of very inexpensive power station fuel for many east and west coast locations, public policies continue to deny it free access—at least to east coast plants (see p. 180). With the Federal government's attitudes likely to be as important as any other factor in determining the future role of fuel oil in the electricity utility market, speculation concerning its prospects are singularly hazardous.

This discussion of the American electricity industry is not designed, however, primarily to make these points—important though they might be in an understanding of some of the broader aspects and trends of energy geography in the United States—but rather to illustrate in a single industry the importance of the three principal aspects of the market in the geography of energy. These are its size, its location and its nature. The importance of the size of the thermal electricity market and its rapid rate of growth is underlined by the effect which success therein can have upon the long term fortunes of a primary fuel industry. The outstanding success of that same coal industry in capturing the largest share of the utility fuel market in turn reflects the importance of the second aspect of the market, its location. More specifically, it has been seen how the spatial relationships between the major electricity load centres and the sources of the alternative primary fuels have played a decisive role in the evolution of the generating industry in recent years. Finally, with the technology of thermal electricity generation permitting the substitution of one primary fuel for another, the nature of the resultant market is both highly competitive and makes the delivered price of alternative fuels critically important. As a consequence, a considerable regional and sub-regional variety in the use of alternative fuels, and a steady flux in the geography of primary fuel consumption, characterize the industry.

In the course of the discussion, some reference has been made to the economics of energy transport—to the development of unit train technology for the shipment of coal, to the sale of 'interruptible' natural gas in order to improve the economics of pipeline transport, and to low cost water transport for the import of crude oil. It is to a deeper examination of these and other energy transport matters that the next three chapters are devoted.

5

TRANSPORT (I)

Energy transport facilities, costs, and characteristics in general – transport by water – by rail – by road

One of the outstanding characteristics of the energy geography of the world is the rising volume of international and inter-regional energy transfers. This traffic represents the growing divergence of the distribution of energy sources and the geography of energy markets, and it is the purpose of this chapter, and the following two, to expose something of the role of transport facilities and costs in the shaping of energy geography. The questions are relatively simple. Given a demand for energy at a particular place, what role does transport play in determining how that demand will be satisfied? Given a resource of energy at another location, in what ways does transport influence if (and when) it will be used?

In those circumstances where suitable supplies of energy are available at or adjacent to the location of demand, the importance of transport is clearly small. In the late eighteenth and early nineteenth centuries the geographical coincidence of the clayband and blackband iron ores in the coal seams of west Durham and South Wales meant that there was no significant transport problem in the provision of fuel for the manufacture of iron there. Similarly, twenty years ago the demand for oil in southern California could be satisfied from local resources, and the task of supplying Los Angeles County from the fields and the refineries nearby was relatively straightforward. However, it is most unusual to find a geographical coincidence of energy resources and energy markets.

The potential consumer is as a result presented with one of two choices. Either the demand for energy can be transferred to the resources of energy; this occurs occasionally in such activities as the manufacture of coke, the smelting of aluminium, the production of carbon black or the refining of crude oil.

Alternatively the energy is transported to its market. In this case, the provision of transport facilities, if they are not already in existence, is essential in order that energy can be made accessible and available. In nineteenth-century South Wales, the winning of the vast coal wealth of the Rhondda Valley was contingent upon the Taff Vale Railway extending its lines to Treherbert and Maerdy from Ponty-pridd, just as the more recent exploitation of Libyan oil awaited the laying of pipelines from the inland oilfields to the Mediterranean seaports of Marsa el Brega, Ras Sidar, Ras Lanuf and Tobruq plus the provision of tanker berths there for its export to Western Europe and North America. If transport facilities are not made available, on the other hand, the demand for energy will remain unsatisfied, or only partly satisfied. In the recent industrial history of several Latin American countries development projects have been delayed or abandoned as a consequence of inadequate electricity facilities.

In reality, it frequently happens that only a limited range of transport facilities are available within an economy. This can sometimes be a major determinant of how an energy demand is satisfied. Oil from the Prairie Provinces has to be transported either overland, or by a combination of land transport and inland waterways, if it is to be sold in Canada's eastern markets. Competing with it is oil from the Middle East and Venezuela which can be shipped over the greater part of its much longer journey in large tankers with low ton/km freight rates. As a result of these low freight charges, the foreign oils can be sold at attractive prices in Quebec, and the competitive range of domestic oil extends only as far as eastern Ontario. Demands in Montreal, for example, are almost entirely supplied from imported oils. Canadian domestic producers therefore suffer from their inability to use ocean tankers, the cheapest form of oil transport (see Table 4).

It has sometimes been suggested that nuclear power could be highly competitive in those countries where the existing railway system is inadequate to move further quantities of coal (United Nations, 1957a, 14). In such circumstances nuclear energy is made more attractive by the fact that a considerable investment in additional transport capacity would be required to make coal available at the energy markets, particularly those located at a

Table 4

COST OF TRANSPORTING ENERGY TO MONTREAL AND HALIFAX,
circa 1955
($ per coal equivalent ton)

(a) The costs of supplying Montreal:	
(i) Oil—by super-tanker from Aruba to Portland, Me.	
(2,600 km), then by pipeline (385 km)	$1·0–1·5
(ii) Coal—by collier from Sydney, N.S. (1,165 km)	$2·0–2·4
(iii) Oil—by 76 cm pipeline from Edmonton (3,280 km)	$2·0–3·1
(iv) Natural gas—by 86 cm pipeline from Southern Alberta	
(3,520 km)	$6·8–9·9
(v) Coal—by rail from Sydney, N.S. (1,705 km)	$8·2–9·4
(vi) Electricity—by high-tension line from Bersemis River	
(400 km)	$3·7–4·6
(b) The costs of supplying Halifax:	
(i) Coal—by coolier from Sydney, N.S. (394 km)	$0·7–0·8
(ii) Oil—by super-tanker from Aruba (3,200 km)	$1·0–1·5
(iii) Coal—by rail from Sydney, N.S. (362 km)	$1·7–2·0
(iv) Electricity—by high-tension line from mine mouth	
Sydney, N.S. (352 km)	$2·3–2·9

Source: United Nations, 1957a, 45.

considerable distance from the coalfields. For example, the low cost coal of India and South Africa could satisfy most of the existing and potential electricity requirements in those countries if rail— or alternative water—transport facilities were everywhere available. But since they are not (the argument continues), uranium, which has low transport costs and which could be made available without any major extensions to the existing rail network, becomes a highly competitive alternative. The final equation of advantages in this matter, of course, is by no means easy to solve. The extension of rail facilities for coal haulage would normally provide surplus capacity for other purposes, and would be an essential ingredient in the basic infrastructure for economic growth. Further, for countries like India with a problem of endemic underemployment, investment in labour-intensive coal mines has certain advantages over investment in capital-intensive nuclear plant.

The precise nature as well as the range of transport facilities available in an economy can also influence energy geography. In the years after World War II, when there was a severe fuel shortage in Europe, Britain had to import a considerable tonnage of coal from the United States. But the fact that the former had traditionally been a coal-exporting country, and had used only small colliers for coastwise shipments, meant that there were no unloading facilities for ocean-going colliers at British ports. As a result, American coals had to be imported via the Continent, where they were transhipped into smaller vessels. The flow of energy during those years, in other words, was modified by the nature of Western European dock facilities.

Transport facilities are also important since they enlarge the markets capable of being served by particular sources of energy. The building of a new facility to tap an energy resource invariably leads to a chain reaction of events in which a new relationship between energy supply and demand, new prices and hence new competitive positions for the different sources of fuel or power are established. A good illustration of this general point is provided by the American natural gas industry. In the early days of oil production, natural gas was priced as a surplus product. Its value was low simply because there was no market for it within easy reach, and because supply always outstripped demand. With continued oil exploration, further supplies were constantly being made available, yet the markets in Texas and Louisiana remained small. The invariable reaction of the oil producers was to flare off the gas at its source (a practice which is not uncommon still on many of the world's oilfields today). Since the 1930s, however, and especially since 1945, pipelines have been built between the natural gas fields and the largest energy markets in the United States to make this fuel available in nearly every section of the country. In 1946 some 38% of the gas wells of Texas were 'shut in' for lack of a pipeline outlet; by 1951 only 25% remained so; and virtually none are 'shut in' today. At first, when it was frequent for only one pipeline to tap each field, monopsony (i.e. a buyer's monopoly) joined with the relatively low level of demand to keep down the price of gas. But with the growth of market outlets and the subsequent arrival of several companies to tap the resources of each field, monopsony gave way to more competitive conditions in which the price of gas began to rise. With huge potential demands for this fuel existing throughout the United States, and a growing competition for the limited resources which were available, only the action of the Federal Power Commission (see pp. 174 ff.) provided a restraining influence upon field prices. The transformed market and price situation of natural gas, in other words, stems from the investment in pipeline facilities.

Whilst recognizing the fundamental importance of transport facilities, however, it is upon the costs of transport that our discussion must focus, for their direct and indirect influence upon the geography of energy is crucial. The economics and characteristics of the several transport media available to move energy from a given source have a strong bearing upon the price which will be asked of a potential consumer, and thereby influence the extent to which that particular source will be used to meet his needs. Similarly, given an existing or prospective value of energy in a particular market, the costs of energy transport in relationship to the unit costs of exploitation help to determine the likely return for a producer—and hence whether or not it is worth his while to serve that market.

The real costs of transporting energy have fallen dramatically, of course, over the past one hundred years. Although the cost of moving coal from Cardiff in 1871 was up to four times the price of coal there, by 1902 the cost of transport had fallen to less than the price of coal for most destinations; and since the turn of the century the real cost of moving coal over a given distance has fallen still further. The exploitation and the shipment of oil has provided an even cheaper means of transferring energy. The cost of carrying energy by collier is considerably greater than the cost of moving an equivalent quantity of oil by super-tanker (see Tables 4 and 5) —partly because in energy terms one ton of oil is equalled only by $1\frac{1}{2}$ tons of coal, but also as a result of the oil industry's superior transport organization—and the fairly uniform delivered price for oil throughout the world strongly reflects its low transport cost. The trend towards a lower cost of moving energy has been carried a stage further by the arrival of nuclear power, for one ton of uranium will under favourable conditions yield energy equivalent to 10,000 tons of coal—yet its transport cost is negligible. Overland, the cost of transferring energy in the form of uranium is about one-hundredth of that of carrying a comparable quantity of energy as coal, and the comparison with sea transport costs is even more acute. Hartley (1962) has estimated that the cost of transporting fuel elements containing one ton of uranium from Cardiff to west Italy is about $280 and to Japan $560; the cost of moving an equivalent quantity of energy as coal would be $53,200 and $97,000 respectively.

The falling real cost of energy transport does not necessarily mean, however, that transport costs make up a smaller percentage of the total costs of energy at its market. In many instances, the real cost of energy production has also been falling. Indeed, in recent years the ratio of coal transport costs to the mine value of coal in the United States has tended to increase (thereby reversing the previous trend). The cost of transport thus remains a key element in the total cost of energy today. Mined in Bengal and Bihar, Indian coal lies some 2,000 km from its major domestic markets in the east and 3,000 km from those in the south; and, although the price of coking coal ex-pithead was as low as $4 to $4·40 per ton in 1955, transport costs raised the wholesale price in Bombay and Madras to $16 to $17·20 respectively. In Britain, on average 25% to 30% is added to the mine price of coal as a result of haulage charges, and in the United States, where average distances are much greater, the figure is 70% for coal that is moved by rail—and nearly three-quarters of production is still shipped by this means. The transport element in the delivered price of gas and electricity is also considerable. The average costs of transmitting North Sea natural gas to most parts of the country appear likely to add between 40 and 60% to its beach price on the east coast of England, and smaller consumers incur a further distribution expense. The Federal Power Commission (1964, 26) have estimated that transmission and distribution costs represent on average about half of the delivered costs of electricity.

Figures are also available for oil. In the United States the cost of transport generally represents about 25% of the total cost of oil products. Oil transport costs from Aruba in the Netherlands West Indies to Bello Horizonte (Brazil), however, contributes as little as 16% to the retail price, whilst in the West European market freight rates can represent 33% of the price of heavy fuel oil. Clearly, *ceteris paribus*, the nearer a market is to its sources of oil, the smaller will be the share of transport in total costs. In 1956, 45% of the c.i.f. price of crude oil in northern Europe was freight charges, whilst the comparable figure for southern Europe was 38%. But other factors besides distance also enter into this situation; in particular, the medium of transport is very important.

The several means of transporting energy can usefully be divided into two groups. The first group is the so-called 'discontinuous' media—lorries, railways, barges and sea transport. And the second is the 'continuous' media—pipelines and transmission lines. As a generalization, the first group, which is capable of moving coal, oil, gas (in tankers) and nuclear fuel, can be used to transport variable amounts of energy at irregular intervals. The second group, in contrast, provides for the continuous movement of energy at a constant rate; it can be used to transfer gas, oil, coal and electricity. The division is to some extent unreal in so far as lorries can be used to provide a regular flow of coal to a power station, and the volume of gas passing along a pipeline often varies. The distinction between the two groups of transport media must not be pressed too far. Nevertheless, it is worth retaining since the discontinuous forms of transport have a lower proportion of capital expenses in their total costs, the implications of which will shortly become apparent.

In a very crude fashion it is possible generally to compare the costs of moving energy by tankers, high voltage cables, pipelines, colliers, roads, barges and railways by converting their costs to a common unit. In Tables 4 and 5 this unit is cents per coal equivalent ton. Such comparisons must be handled with great care for the actual ton/km cost of any individual transport operation is influenced by a considerable variety of factors. It varies, for example, with distance, with the characteristics of the route, with the scale and the regularity of the energy flow, and with the structure of the medium's freight rates. Further, in these generalized comparisons no note is taken of the efficiency with which the different fuels can be used. As a result, the advantages of transporting coal to satisfy an energy demand appear much more favourable than they are in reality, since no account is taken of the relative inefficiency with which that fuel is often consumed. Nevertheless, these calculations do give a general idea of the magnitude of the differences in the costs of transporting fuels by the alternative means available. On that score alone they are instructive, and from them certain broad conclusions can be drawn.

The estimated costs of transporting several types of energy to the Montreal and Halifax markets from a variety of sources are recorded in Table 4. From these figures it is clear that the cost of moving a ton of coal by collier from the Nova Scotia coalfield to Montreal is as high as—and sometimes higher than—the cost of moving an equivalent quantity of energy as oil from Alberta by pipeline; but it is only about one-third of the cost of transporting the same amount of energy in the form of natural gas from the Prairies. That same gas can be piped to Montreal for slightly less money than carrying coal from Nova Scotia by rail. But the lowest transport cost involved in providing Montreal with energy (at least from these alternatives) is by importing oil from the Caribbean through Portland, Maine, using both modern super-tankers and a large diameter pipeline. On the other hand, the least expensive means of transporting energy to the coastal and much smaller Halifax market is by shipping coal by collier from Nova Scotia. Rather more expensive is the import of oil from the Caribbean. And more costly still is the rail haul of coal from the Maritimes. From both sets of figures it would appear that the most expensive means of moving energy is by the use of transmission line. However, it is necessary to divide the cost of electricity transmission by three in order to obtain a true comparison of delivered energy costs, for it can be used at about 100% efficiency, whereas (as has already been noted) coal is converted into electricity at only about 35–38 % efficiency. In this light the cost of transmitting electrical energy becomes highly competitive with the costs of transporting coal and oil to both the Montreal and the Halifax markets.

The figures of Table 4 refer, of course, to the supply of two geographically distinct energy markets. The satisfaction of their energy demands involves the transport of the several sources of energy over quite contrasting distances. Coal has to be shipped only 1,165 km from Sydney to Montreal, whereas the major source of hydro-electricity quoted is 400 km away. The analysis needs, there-fore, to be carried a stage further by reducing such a set of costs not only to common unit of energy, but also a common distance. Table 5 does just this and lists for each major energy source the cost of

Table 5

COST OF TRANSPORTING CANADIAN ENERGY BY VARIOUS MEDIA, *circa* 1955

Form of energy	Method of transport	Distance (km)	Unit	Cost/100 km (cents)	Cost/coal equivalent ton/100 km (cents)
Oil	Super-tanker	Coastwise	1 Ton	4·4–6·6	3·1–4·6
Oil	76 cm pipe-line	3,200	1 Ton	8·8–13·2	6·3–9·3
Natural gas	86 cm pipe-line	3,200	Th cu m	24·3–35·3	19·3–28·1
Coal	Collier	Coastwise	1 Ton	17·2–20·7	17·2–20·7
Coal	Rail	2,400	1 Ton	48·3–55·1	48·3–55·1
Electrical energy	High-tension line	640	1,000 kwh	25·0–31·0	218·1–272·5

Source: Davis, 1957, 348.

moving one ton of coal equivalent energy over a distance of 100km. It is evident from these figures that, generally speaking, the cheapest means of moving energy is by transporting oil in tankers or through a large diameter pipeline. Coal is considerably more expensive as a result of its high cost of handling, plus its lower calorific value and lower bulk density, which means that it occupies about twice as much space as an equivalent amount of fuel oil. Nevertheless, coal ship-ment by sea tends to be slightly cheaper than is the transport of natural gas by pipeline. The cost of moving coal by rail, on the other hand, is about three times more expensive than its movement by water. Electrical energy once again appears in the Table as the most expensive form of energy transport, and it must be treated with the same qualifications as before. It is noteworthy, in addition, that the figures for high voltage transmission are based upon the cost of transmitting energy over 640 km, a distance at which certain diseconomies have set in. As will be seen in the next chapter, there are many circumstances in which it is more economic to transmit electrical energy than it is to move coal or natural gas overland. The point underlines the caution with which one must approach such a generalized set of figures.

Generalized though they may be, these differences in the costs of energy transport undoubtedly leave a recognizable impress upon the broad patterns of energy geography. The ten-fold growth of oil production, for example, from just over 150 million tons in 1925 to 1,562 million tons forty years later, is undoubtedly related to the ease and the economy with which that fuel can be transported. Thus, whilst exports of solid fuels increased at an annual average rate of 0·2% from 146 to 159 million tons between 1925 and 1965, international trade in oil increased at nearly 8% per annum from 68 million to 1,395 million tons. Whereas solid fuels represented nearly 70% of total energy trade internationally at the beginning of the period, their share had fallen to 10% by the end.

But the attractiveness of a particular means of transport is not solely measured by its cost. Its general characteristics have a considerable importance, too, as can be seen in a comparison of tankers and pipelines for the movement of oil. In addition to their low ton/km expense, tankers have the advantage of being a highly flexible means of transport. They can carry any type of oil. They can be transferred easily from one route to another, even during the course of a single voyage. Since the provision of additional carrying capacity can be made in relatively small increments compared with the total tonnage already in existence, they are ideally suited to a steady growth in demand. And, through the use of storage facilities at both ends of their routes, seasonal variations in demand need not be reflected in a seasonal flow of oil; hence the optimum use can be made of a tanker fleet. These claims concerning the flexibility of tanker traffic need to be qualified by the fact that the largest and most modern vessels can use only a limited number of terminals, and are denied a passage through the Panama and even a reopened Suez canals. Nevertheless, pipelines by comparison are a very rigid means of transport. Although it is widening, the range of oil products which they can carry is limited. They provide for the movement of relatively fixed quantities of energy over predetermined routes, and their capacity can only be marginally increased by the installation of additional pumping equipment. Of course, the capacity of a pipeline can be increased considerably if the initial throughput under-uses the facility and every advantage is taken of extra pumping facilities and looping subsequently; the South European Pipeline from Lavera to Strasbourg and Karlsruhe had an initial capacity of 10 million tons of oil per year, but 30 million tons is now possible without any major alterations to the pipeline. However, this is feasible only by a considerable under-utilization of the pipeline (and the investment) initially. Unlike investments in tankers, therefore, which can be partially based upon the growth of oil traffic in general, the construction of pipelines must be justified by the potential flow of particular types of oil, and the nature of the markets, along a given route.

The other discontinuous means of transport—roads, railways, barges and colliers—have something of the same flexible characteristics as oil tankers; transmission wires share the same inflexibility as pipelines. Such characteristics as these play an important role in determining the means whereby particular energy demands are satisfied, and particular energy resources developed. This will become more apparent as the economics and characteristics of the major forms of energy transport are discussed in more detail. In this chapter the discontinuous modes of transport are considered; an examination of pipelines and transmission lines is deferred until Chapter 6.

Energy transport by water

Ships provide by far the cheapest means of discontinuous transport (see Fig. 7). It has already been noted that oil tankers offer the lowest rates for the long distance, bulk movement of (conventional) energy; and the cheapest means of transporting coal is by bulk carrier, also. It is for this reason that wherever possible the oil products of British refineries are transported to intermediate depots by coastal tanker, and that oil from Texas goes via the Panama Canal to California. Similarly almost all the coal destined for the London power stations and supplied by the Northumberland and Durham coalfield is transported by collier, and many of the power stations of southern England have a coastal location. The advantage of a tidewater route in cutting transport costs similarly attracts many Appalachian coals destined for New York and New England via Newport News and Norfolk; the published rates for

94   The Geography of Energy

hauling coal all the way by rail from West Virginia to Boston
remain almost twice those of the rail and tidewater route.

Table 6

CAPITAL COST OF OIL TRANSPORT MEDIA IN THE
UNITED STATES, *circa* 1955

Equipment	Investment ($ mill.)	Investment per mill. ton/km of capacity ($ th.)
16,000 dwt tanker	5·8	3·8
30,000 dwt tanker	9·3	2·9
45,000 dwt tanker	13·2	2·8
*100,000 dwt tanker	16·0	1·7
Barge (10,000 ton capacity)	1·7	3·9
1,600 km pipeline		
—20 cm diameter	30·0	14·4
—30 cm diameter	38·7	6·2
—40 cm diameter	53·7	5·2
—60 cm diameter	78·7	2·6
10,000 litre rail tank car	0·003	29·1
6,000 litre road tanker	0·005	3·9

* Built in Japan.

Source: Emerson, 1957, 22.

The low costs of sea transport are rooted in the relatively low
ton/km capital costs of ocean-going vessels. It can be seen in Table
6 that the capital required for a 45,000 dwt ton tanker in the United
States about 1955 was $2·8 thousand, whereas a 40 cm (16 in)
pipeline was $5·3 thousand and a railway tank car was $29·1 thousand
per million ton/km of oil carrying capacity. It is true that the cost
of a very large, say 60 cm diameter, pipeline was lower still at $2·6
thousand, but even this was more than the $1·7 thousand of a
100,000 dwt super-tanker built in a Japanese shipyard at the same
time. The differences between the costs of building tankers in the
United States, on the one hand, and in both Japan and Western
Europe on the other—with vessels launched from American yards
costing approximately twice that of their rivals—is but one of the
variables in the capital costs of ocean transport. Two others are
the date of construction and the size of the vessel.

In recent years there has been a vast improvement in the efficiency
with which tankers, and bulk carriers for coal, are built. And Japa-

nese yards have tended to set the pace. With the specifications of tankers changing steadily, it is not easy to quote price falls with any precision; but it is not unreasonable to think in terms of the purchase price of a 30,000 dwt tanker falling by over 50% from about $7·5 million in the early '50s to about $3·5 million fifteen years later. The price of bulk carriers has fallen somewhat slower, since mass construction techniques have not been so vigorously exploited in their case; the savings for the coal trade have nevertheless been considerable. The capital cost of ocean vessels has fallen in another sense, too. In the early '50s, all orders were placed on a 'sliding scale' basis, and purchasers were obliged to meet any increases in ship-building costs between the placing of their order and the delivery of the vessel. A decade later, however, growing competition in the shipbuilding market meant that shipyards were prepared to accept fixed price contracts, and nearly all purchasers were given generous credit facilities, normally an 80% advance at $5\frac{1}{2}$% interest, with repayment spread over eight to ten years.

The changing size of energy carriers has been even more dramatic. In the years immediately after World War II, the largest bulk carriers were about 10,000 dwt, and the largest tankers about twice that size. Since then, the average size of vessel has steadily increased, and the largest afloat have seen an even greater transformation. In the middle '50s came vessels of 40,000 dwt; then 50,000 dwt, 60,000 dwt and so on until by the early '70s vessels of 250,000 dwt were becoming increasingly common and a tanker of 470,000 dwt had been ordered. The effects of this trend upon the capital cost of tankers and bulk carriers have been spectacular. In 1956, a 31,000 dwt tanker might have cost $125 per ton, and a year later a 66,000 dwt vessel $90 per ton; by 1968 tankers of 200,000 dwt were available for $70 per ton and in 1969 ships of 300,000 dwt were being quoted for $67 per ton. To these capital cost economies have been added major savings in operating expenses, once again partly as a consequence of increasing vessel size. Larger vessels are cheaper per ton/km to run than smaller ones. Approximately the same number of men are required to operate a 200,000 dwt tanker as are needed for its 20,000 dwt counterpart. Indeed, by exploiting to the full modern developments in automation, a new super-tanker in the 100,000 dwt range can be crewed with only half or even one-third of the men normally employed on a T2 (16,000 dwt) tanker such as dominated the oil trade in the immediate post-war years. Large vessels have lower insurance costs, repair bills, maintenance charges and administrative costs—per ton/km—than their smaller counterparts. And the total operating expenses per ton of, say, a 15,000 dwt tanker on an 8,000 km haul is likely to be three times greater than its 65,000 dwt counterpart. Operating expenses make up some 55–60% of the total costs of ocean bulk transport. The total costs of tanker operation, and their variations with vessel size, are summarized in Fig. 6; scale economies in dry bulk carriers are quantified in Table 7.

The increasing size of tankers and bulk carriers has been and will continue to be checked by several factors. Clearly, the sources of the energy and also their markets must be large enough to permit the

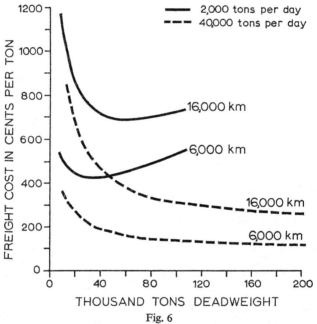

Fig. 6

Scale economies in ocean tanker transport, *c.* 1970.
(Source: Hallett and Randall, 1970, 29)

transfer of the oil or coal in large quantities. In only limited places are they so. To take advantage of an oil tanker carrying 300,000 tons of crude, a very large refinery of, say, 15 million tons per year throughput, or a complex of smaller refineries with the same aggregate capacity, are really required—otherwise the storage facilities required become unjustifiably expensive. The number of refineries of that size and over, however, is very limited indeed. Again, the depth of the Panama, and at one time the Suez, Canal has kept the size of ships

Table 7

SCALE ECONOMIES OF DRY BULK CARRIERS, *circa* 1970

Size: (tons deadweight)	15,000	25,000	40,000	65,000	90,000	120,000	160,000	200,000
Construction cost (per ton*)$	158·4	132·0	117·6	105·6	98·4	91·2	84·0	76·8
Daily running costs (per ship)$								
Fuel	242·4	374·4	556·8	854·4	1108·8	1396·8	1732·8	2040·0
Other	861·6	1041·6	1144·8	1308·0	1466·4	1668·0	1958·4	2244·0
Total	1104·0	1416·0	1701·6	2162·4	2575·2	3064·8	3691·2	4284·0
Daily capital costs† (per thousand tons)	72·5	60·2	53·8	48·2	44·9	41·5	38·4	35·0
Daily running costs (per thousand tons)	73·7	56·6	42·5	33·4	25·9	25·4	22·8	21·4
Total daily cost (per thousand tons)	146·2	116·8	96·3	81·6	70·8	66·9	61·2	56·4

† Based on 10% return + 6% depreciation and a 350 day year.

*Ignoring investment grant of 20% in UK.
Source: Hallett and Randall, 1970, 29

D

using them down to about 65,000 dwt; the continuing importance of this factor is underlined by the decision of a major Japanese shipyard to build a standard *Panamax* bulk carrier (of 65,000–69,000 dwt, depending upon the moulded draught) which is the maximum size capable of negotiating the Panama Canal. And, naturally, there are only a limited number of ports which can readily handle vessels of 100,000 dwt and over.

It is, of course, much easier to provide deep water loading and unloading facilities for tankers than for dry bulk carriers hauling coal. By making use of single-point moorings offshore, and by pumping the oil under water to land, tankers can take advantage of deep water some kilometres off the coast. Alternatively, it is possible to part-unload oil into a smaller vessel whilst both are at sea and nearing their market destination. The Gulf Oil Company has elected to establish a major trunk route for its 276,000 dwt tankers between the Middle East and the natural deep water harbour at Bantry Bay in south-west Eire, where the crude is transhipped into smaller vessels via a tank farm for distribution to the company's Western European and North American refineries. Nevertheless, it remains the case that to some extent the large tankers, but more especially the large dry bulk carriers, cannot possibly share the same flexibility of routes and ports as their smaller counterparts. When the larger vessels are built, therefore, it is usually a response to the opportunities for trade along a particular route—or particular routes—and nearly all are hired out on long term charters.

One further aspect of the economies of ocean bulk transport also imposes a constraint upon the increase in ship size. This is the economics of the length of haul. Since the amount of time which a vessel spends earning at sea increases with the average length of its trips, tapering rates (that is falling ton/km rates with increasing distance) have long been a feature of ocean freights. Assuming that it takes two days both to load and to unload a vessel, and that the line-haul and the return run in ballast take four days each, a vessel can theoretically be at sea and can be earning a return upon the capital invested in it for only one-third of its life. If on the other hand the line-haul and ballast runs each take eighteen days, the potential earning power of the ship increases and it can earn a return on its capital for 45 % of its life, Thus, a 60,000 dwt dry bulk carrier capable of handling coal on a 3,000 km return haul incurs total costs of about 2·9 mills per ton/km; but the same vessel on a 20,000 km return haul has costs of only 2·1 mills (10 mills = 1 cent). As a consequence of these long-haul and scale economies of ocean transport, not only can large vessels on a long run offer similar or lower rates compared with smaller vessels on a shorter run. But also, for any given length of ocean haul, there is in theory an optimum size of carrier. As the length of a haul increases, so does the potential earning power of a vessel increase also; and as the earning power of a vessel increases, so are shipowners generally prepared to invest more capital in the operation. With a larger share of their total costs stemming from capital charges, compared with smaller ships the large bulk carriers are well adapted to the longer hauls. But where shipping distances are short, and the percentage of time which a tanker or a collier must inevitably spend in port is high, there is a natural preference by the shipping industry to substitute working for capital costs and hence to keep down the size of vessel employed.

The economy of ocean bulk transport with its low ton/km costs, therefore, is deeply rooted in a relatively high degree of vessel use. The more revenue ton/km a ship can be worked, the lower become its ton/km capital costs. It was inevitable, therefore, that in the increasingly competitive markets for both shipping and energy raw materials the owners and operators of these bulk carriers should seek to intensify the use which they made of their vessels. To the falling capital costs of bulk carriers, in other words, has been added the further economy of falling capital costs per ton/km. To achieve this, energy shippers have been encouraged to make use of vessels for periods longer than a single voyage by attractive offers of substantial freight discounts on long term charters and contracts of affreightment of anything up to fifteen years. 'Contractual tramping', as these arrangements have come to be known, in large measure has replaced the former 'open' tramp trade. In addition, since a ship in port incurs about 75% of the expenses of a ship at sea, the use of faster loading and unloading equipment—and hence the reduction in port time—has also allowed a fuller use to be made of bulk carriers.

Yet a third way in which the shipping industry has been able to intensify its vessel use has been by seeking suitable return cargoes to raise its 'payload–distance' ratios. A tanker plying between two ports, hauling crude oil in one direction and ballasting back in the other, has a ratio of 50%; a return haul of petroleum products, on the other hand, would raise the ratio to 100%. Trading opportunities for such direct return cargoes, however, are rare. The shipment of Appalachian coals from Hampton Roads to eastern Canada, and then haulage of iron ore back from Sept Isles to Baltimore, is something of an exception. Triangular trades, on the other hand, by which vessels are able to earn some freight revenue on two legs of a three-legged round trip are more frequently possible. For instance, American coal can be shipped to Western Europe, and then Liberian iron ore moved back to the United States, in the same bulk carrier which has only the run from Western Europe to West Africa in ballast. Similarly, bulk carriers hauling coking coal between the United States' east coast ports and Japan are able to pick up Latin American iron ore for the final stage of their return journey.

A fundamental limitation upon the size of these triangular trades are the geographical imbalances in bulk commodity flows. Whereas in 1965 the United States exported 31 million tons of coal by sea and imported 31 million tons of iron ore, both Western Europe and Japan were net importers of both these raw materials (amongst others). Spatial imbalances are less, however, when liquid and dry bulk commodity movements are considered. Consequently, so-called 'OBO' vessels have been designed and built to carry either oil or a dry bulk commodity, and thus to permit an additional set of triangular or even quadrangular trades. Sumatran oil, for example, can be shipped to California in vessels which pick up iron ore for the Japanese iron and steel industry, and then ballast back to Sumatra; likewise, North African oil shipments to Scandinavian refineries can be associated with Swedish ore movements to Rotterdam. The 97,600 dwt *Fukuyama Maru* is engaged on the route from the Persian Gulf (crude oil) to Western Europe (ballast), then to Liberia or Brazil, and (iron ore) to Japan; on the Brazilian run, the round-trip voyage is over 50,000 km, and the payload–distance ratio 66%.

Ocean transport costs are one thing. Ocean freight rates are another. The general level of ocean freights at any one time is influenced by a variety of factors, not least of which is the relationship between the supply of and the demand for shipping capacity of various sorts. The rate settled for any particular voyage(s), in addition, tends to reflect the efficiency with which such a voyage employs the ship, the nature and length of the charter, the size of the vessel, the length of the haul, the ownership of the vessel, the flag being carried, and other such matters. Certainly in the long run a shipowner will expect to make a profit, and therefore his rates will bear some relationship to his long term costs. But in the short run, his rates will be related to his assessment of the quantity of energy needing shipment compared with the tonnage of shipping which he knows is available to transport it—that is, according to his expectations of the market. Water transport rates, therefore, are liable to considerable fluctuations. They may rise to a level where the shipowner is making a large enough profit to cover both his running and capital costs; they are also capable of falling to a level where the return is equal to the running costs of a charter minus the costs of laying the tanker up. They may even fall below this if the vessel is subsidized from the profitable charters of other ships—and this obviously happens in many cases.

Tanker rates, in particular, fluctuate with the supply of and the demand for available tonnage, and with the nature (that is, the length) of the charter. The limited number of alternative uses for tankers means that when traffic is slack they cannot be diverted to carry alternative freights, and results in a large number of vessels looking for only a limited amount of trade. The use of oil tankers for the haulage of grain is an exception and a small palliative, and there nevertheless remain periods when tanker capacity is either under-used or in short supply. As a consequence, tanker rates tend to exhibit rather wider fluctuations than those of many other types of shipping. And, of course, it is the spot or single voyage rates which fluctuate most of all. Therefore, in order to stabilize their costs, energy shippers have increasingly come to charter tankers and bulk carriers for periods of eight, ten or even fifteen years, or have signed contracts of affreightment under which shipping companies take over the responsibility of handling specified tonnages of energy raw materials between particular origins and destinations and for an agreed number of years.

In any discussion of energy transport costs, it is the costs to the user that are ultimately important, and these costs may contain a hidden element of subsidy, or some other form of political distortion. For many years now the Canadian Government has subsidized the transport of coal from Nova Scotia to the Quebec and Ontario markets in order that it might compete there with American coal. Similarly, the coastwise shipment of American oil is more expensive than it need be because, following the 1920 Merchant Marine Act (the so-called Jones Act), only tankers built, registered and crewed in the United States are allowed to bid for the traffic. The high cost of building ships in America has already been noted; the labour costs of United States' crews are about four times and five times those of Britain and Italy respectively (O'Loughlin, 1967, *passim*). These high cost characteristics of United States domestic tanker operations have important implications for the overall transport pattern of American oil, for the relatively high cost of domestic tanker transport means that the break-even point compared with pipeline transport is further than it would be otherwise; and this in turn enhances the competitive position of pipelines (see p. 114 ff.).

The variety of factors influencing the rates of ocean energy transport, then, is all too clear. And most of the difficulties involved in quoting a realistic rate per ton or per ton/km for comparative purposes are repeated in the case of the other transport media. Two generalizations can be proposed with confidence, however. First, variable though they may be, by and large freight rates do approximately reflect ocean freight costs, and the exploitation of scale and long haul economies in bulk shipping during the past twenty years has been mirrored in the rates charged. In the late '50s, for example, crude oil was shipped to Western Europe from the Middle East for about $6·00 per ton; the 1970 rate, using vessels of over 75,000 dwt on long term charter, was less than half that figure. In 1960, coal was shipped from the United States to Rotterdam in tramp vessels of 10,000–15,000 dwt, and the rate fixed varied between about $3·50 and $8·00 per ton. By 1965, the rate for term charters of 20,000 dwt dry bulk carriers had fallen to between $3 and $4 per ton. By 1970, the use of 50,000 and 60,000 dwt bulk carriers reduced the (medium term contract) rate to just over $2 per ton. The immediate effect of these lower freight rates (per ton and per ton/km) has been to give a new flexibility to the procurement of energy raw materials for the industrial economies of the world, especially in times of emergency. The closing of the Suez Canal in 1967 at one time would have imposed intolerable burdens upon the oil supplies of Western Europe. Instead, not only were some alternative supplies readily shipped in from the Caribbean, but Iranian and Far Eastern crudes were diverted around the Cape at quite modest additional costs. Indeed, in spite of the longer Cape route, through the use of 200,000 dwt tankers a freight rate of $2·40 per ton was possible for the Middle East–Western Europe haul, compared with a rate of $3·60 per ton in 50,000 dwt vessels. By 1969 oil movements around the Cape had increased eight-fold over their 1966 level to about 210 million tons, with the closure of the Suez Canal accelerating the change-over to giant carriers. The changing economics of ocean bulk transport has meant that the global pattern of energy flows and resource development has been speedily and significantly altered. The industrially advanced—yet frequently natural resource deficient—economies of Western Europe, the United States and Japan have been able to reach out further afield for their energy supplies. Once constrained by ocean freight rates normally to purchase their imports from sources within, say, 8,000 km or nearer if possible, each of these countries is now able to import its requirements from virtually any country in the world which has the necessary resources and easy access to tidewater.

The second generalization is that a range of ocean freights can be quoted for the transport of energy raw materials over particular distances, and it is instructive to compare these with a range of rates for the other transport media. For the Western European energy market the average cost of transporting oil over, say, 1,500 km by tanker ranges between 0·3 and 1·2 mills per ton/km (for vessels of 150,000 dwt and 10,000 dwt respectively); the comparable figures for barges are 2·4 and 3·6 mills, and for pipelines carrying between 50 and 1 million tons per year the range of costs is from 0·6 up to 7 mills per ton/km. The costs of oil transport by rail and road are yet higher again, and the whole spectrum of transport costs is illustrated in Fig. 7, which is based upon the evidence of Hubbard (1967, *passim*). Comparable data for coal transport are illustrated in Fig. 8, and once again the economies to be gained from the low line-haul costs of water transport are abundantly clear.

However, this advantage of the low ton/km freight rates of water transport has to be qualified by the high terminal costs of this means

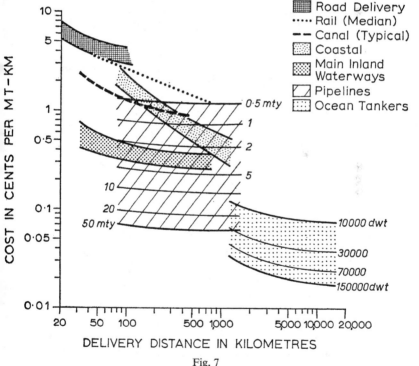

Fig. 7

Comparative costs of oil transport by various media in Western Europe, *c.* 1967. (Source: Hubbard, 1967, 80)

of transport. For example, a terminal charge—loading and unloading rates, port dues, wharfage, pilotage and the like—can add as much as 30% to the cost of a 520 km journey by a small 3,250 dwt tanker, and for a 26,000 dwt ocean-going vessel carrying distillate, terminal costs are largely responsible for the 33% increase in ton/km costs when a journey is reduced from 8,000 to 1,600 km. Further, when a market has no direct access to tidewater the costs of transport are increased not only by the high cost of handling at the break-of-bulk point, but also by the need to use another form of transport for the last stage of the journey. And invariably the ton/km costs of a short land haul are high. Take an English example.

In the movement of coal from Newcastle to London *circa* 1956, the costs of leadage on Tyneside ($0·8) and the subsequent discharge and screening ($0·6) at London represented two-thirds of the actual cost of its carriage between those two ports ($2·1). The subsequent transport of coal inland from the Albert Dock by rail had a minimum charge of 85 cents per ton, although when carried by road it was somewhat less expensive. The extent to which sea-borne coal could compete at inland markets depended essentially upon these costs in comparison with the rates for hauling coal from other coalfields overland. In the middle 1950s the pithead price of similar grades of industrial coal from the coalfields of north-east England and in the East Midlands was comparable, and transport costs were critically important in determining the effective competition of each in the London market. To the Northumberland coal there was added a 'coalfield adjustment' charge of 80 cents giving it a price of $4·3 per ton unloaded and screened at the Albert Dock. Hauled by rail, the East Midlands' coal cost $5·3 per ton at the Tottenham rail depot. At inland markets, therefore, the minimum rail charge brought the price of sea-borne coal to within 20 cents of the depot price of the Midlands fuel. However, the lower cost of road haulage extended the advantage of the former to a radius of about 12 or 13 km from the dock, and this distance was increased still further when the Midlands coal also had to be unloaded and transported to its market by lorry (Estall, 1958).

The same point can be illustrated on a larger scale by the competition of American coals in Western Europe. Basically it is the relatively low ton/km rates of ocean colliers which allows this fuel to compete so effectively against European domestic supplies. West Virginian and Pennsylvanian coal has, of course, the initial advantage of being mined at a lower cost than most European coals; but it still has to bear the cost of approximately $3 per ton rail journey from the mine to its port of export, and then a $3–4 transatlantic sea freight. Even so it is only when it carries the additional cost of both a terminal charge and a further rail journey in Western Europe that it becomes more expensive than, say, coal from the Ruhr. In the early 1960s, American steam coal at Rotterdam was priced at about $13 per ton c.i.f.; terminal charges increased its price by $1 per ton. At Utrecht the rail charges inland from Europoort (plus an import tax) still left Appalachian coal with a price advantage. Further inland, however, at Stuttgart and Duisburg, to which Ruhr coals have a very short haul, it was more economical to purchase European solid fuel.

In any discussion of energy transport by sea, some mention must be made of methane and liquefied petroleum gas tankers. By 1970 there were an increasing number of such vessels, the largest being equivalent in size to 70,000 dwt oil tankers. Clearly, they share much the same characteristics—the same advantages and the same disadvantages—as oil tankers, except that their capital costs are about twice as high, and they need rather expensive transformation (i.e. refrigeration and regasification) plants at their terminals. Methane can be transported at minus 190°C and one-sixhundredth of its volume; in contrast liquified petroleum gas is shipped at minus 32°C and as a consequence has much lower refrigeration costs. The result is that not only are the total unit costs of transporting energy by methane tanker higher than those of moving oil, but the vessels also suffer from a certain inflexibility of route (at least in these early days of relatively limited gas shipments). The relationship of transport costs to total costs varies greatly with individual circumstances. But whilst demand remains comparatively small for the vast quantities of surplus gas available at many of the world's oilfields, and the field price of gas as a consequence remains low, the cost of transport will make up the greater part of the total costs of this gas at its markets. Transport costs thus have a considerable bearing upon the competitive position of the fuel. In the shipment of methane from the Middle East to Canvey Island on lower Thamesside, the transport and processing expenses represent over 90% of the delivered price of the gas.

The broad characteristics of energy transport by inland waterway are comparable to those of sea transport, with three significant exceptions. First, route flexibility is of course limited by the availability of waterways; second, economies of scale are restricted by such factors as the depth of rivers and the capacities of locks; and, third, inland waterways are much more subject to winter freezing, and the diseconomies of capital equipment lying idle throughout part of the year. The possibilities and economics of hauling oil in bulk along inland waterways have been improved to some extent, however, by the dracone (an inflatable plastic container in which oil can be hauled by conventional vessels); and by the multiple units of pushed barges which are used along American waterways for both coal and oil. In spite of these characteristics, haulage along inland waterways is frequently cheaper than rail or road transport, a fact which has significant effects upon the geography of energy flow and consumption. Middle Appalachian coalfields are able to compete throughout a wide area of inland America mainly as a result of cheap (especially Great Lakes) water transport. Even to the west of Lake Superior, Appalachian coals can undersell the lignites of Dakota despite two breaks of bulk *en route*. And where inland waterways suffer the disadvantage of seasonal freezing, variable patterns of coal movement are sometimes developed, with the waterways being used when they are available, and railways taking over the traffic during the winter months, November to March in the American case.

Although waterways at their most competitive are inherently cheaper for energy transport than any of the alternative (inland) discontinuous media, railways sometimes respond to a loss of, an absence of, or the need for traffic by deliberately reducing their rates and undercutting barge transport. Coal shipments to the power plants of the Tennessee Valley Authority is an instance where competition is particularly fierce (Vogtle, 1956). The nature and economies of rail transport are examined in the next section.

Energy transport by rail

No other medium of energy transport is facing such a reassessment of its worth than is the railway. The child of the nineteenth century and the key to inland energy movements for so long, it is now faced with serious competition on all sides. Already in many places road transport has cut into the short and middle distance traffic in coal and oil, and the pipeline—having proved its huge advantages for the movement of oil—has issued a challenge for the middle and long distance transport of coal.

The cost to the energy industries and consumers of transporting energy by rail is rooted in the nature of railways freight-rate structures. Unlike most other media, which are used for the shipment of energy and which are usually concerned with carrying one commodity (or group of related commodities), railways are able and are required to transport almost any goods (plus, on many occasions, passengers) that are presented to them. They must, therefore, arrange their charges in such a way as to equate their total revenue with the total cost of providing all their services, and, if possible, make a profit. The charge for shipping any particular commodity, therefore, becomes inextricably involved with the economics of the railway transport system as a whole. Once the heavy capital expenses of a track, signalling equipment and the like have been sunk, railway managements must seek to maximize the use which is made of the investment, and the revenue which is derived from it. Frequently, this is achieved by quoting, for particular commodities over particular distances, rates which are sufficient to cover only the running costs of a journey plus perhaps only a small contribution to overheads. The structure of railway rates, therefore, is governed not only by the *cost* of the service to the operators but also by the *value* of the service to the shipper. Thus, in fixing their rates, railway managements make assessments of what their customers are prepared to pay, seek to measure the probable rates of any competitors, and thereby seek to encourage the maximum use of their facilities. It is partly for this reason that the ton/km rail rates for bulky, low value commodities tend to be low, whilst those for valuable and highly perishable goods tend to be high. Differences in handling costs influence this contrast as well, of course. Railway charges also vary with the regularity of shipments, with the distances involved, with the terrain being covered, with the size of the consignment and, of course, with the type of technology (both transport and management) being employed. Even the artificial stimulation of competition has been a factor in the freight rate structure of the United States.

In an American Senate document, *The Economies of Coal Traffic Flow* (1945, 60), an important point is made with reference to the importance of rail freight rates in the geography of coal production. In the United States there are both a wide blanketing of rates for the origins and destinations of coal, and differential rates between competing groups of producing centres. These characteristics—partly the consequence of administrative convenience, and partly the result of differentials in the bargaining powers of different coal producers and railway companies—have resulted in a marked disregard of distance in the costs of moving coal. For example, in 1945, the rate for hauling a ton of coal by rail from Pittsburgh to Toledo (288 km away) was $1·81; yet the same price was charged for carrying an identical freight from the McRoberts District of Kentucky (a distance of 750 km).

'The existence of rates not based upon the actual cost of transport simply means that the coal is hauled more miles than is necessary, or . . . more labour and capital are required to produce the coal than need be' (Parker, 1940, 45–6). In addition, such rate structures have important implications for the pattern of coal production and the nature of coal flows. For example it was once claimed that railway freight rates in the United States had subsidized southern (that is, Virginia, southern West Virginia and Kentucky) mines, and had given them access to markets better supplied by northern coal, since the rates were much below those justified on a distance basis. This meant that mines were opened up further from the markets than was economically justified. Subsequently the Interstate Commerce Commission came to exercise an effective regulation over railway rates and to eliminate some of the more glaring anomalies (Campbell, 1954, 44). As a result the southern coalfields have probably been exploited rather less than they would have been without Federal intervention, and with a continuance of the old rate structures. Other factors are, of course, equally or more influential in the geography of American coal exploitation. Clearly, the broad pattern of coal traffic flows is fixed by the location of production and consumption areas; however, its specific features are influenced by the character of the transport facilities, by the existing pattern of freight rates and by coal price-fixing policies. The structure of rail freight rates, in sum, is one of the major influences in the economics and the geography of the American coal industry, for it not only influences the media by which coal is transported but it also helps to determine the localities from which that fuel moves to its markets.

A multitude of factors affect the charges made for the transport of energy by rail between specific places, and inevitably unexpected rates are quoted in particular instances. The rates for coal transport in Spain, for example, are exceptionally low because the railway system is under-used and the Government is anxious to encourage its use. The low rail rates into the TVA area are a result of barge competition. Government subsidies, moreover, are not exactly unusual for railways, particularly in the more mature industrial economies, and they can have a considerable influence upon the actual rates charged. Nevertheless, certain generalizations are possible.

First, the ton/km charges for energy shipments by rail are very much lower than for most other commodities. Second, over a wide range of distances, railways are usually able to offer highly competitive rates for the haulage of coal in particular, and of oil to a lesser extent; the difference between these two fuels lies in the greater use and the considerable economies of the oil pipeline. Over very short distances (up to perhaps 40 and 50 kms in Britain), and more especially for relatively small tonnages, railway transport is usually more expensive than road haulage (Fig. 8). However, the higher operating costs of road transport mean that, although its low loading expenses gives it an initial advantage, the line-haul costs rise rapidly with increasing distance and eventually its total costs (and hence its charges) exceed those of the railways. A comparable relationship exists between railway rates and those of barges and coastal transport, which together set an upper limit to the range of effective railway competition (Fig. 9).

Many rates for rail transport are in part still based upon an historical situation, and those for the movement of coal in the economically more developed countries frequently derive from a period in which the railways were able to dominate commodity and

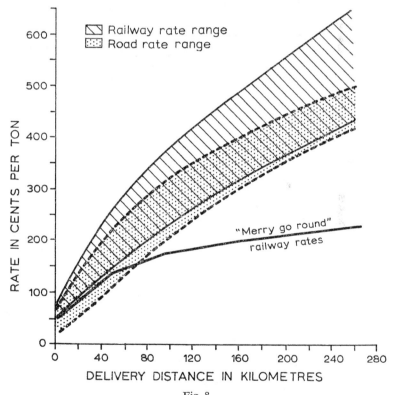

Fig. 8

Comparative rail and road rates for the transport of coal in Britain, c. 1968. (Source: Hauser, 1969, 130)

passenger movements. But with the arrival of road and air transport, they began to lose a considerable proportion of their more valuable freights, and more and more were being left only the long distance haulage of such bulky commodities as iron ore, grain, bulk chemicals and coal. Even some of these traffics were being lost as a result of increasingly efficient—and sometimes subsidized—barge transport on inland waterways, particularly in the United States; and by certain advantages offered by road transport which are noted below.

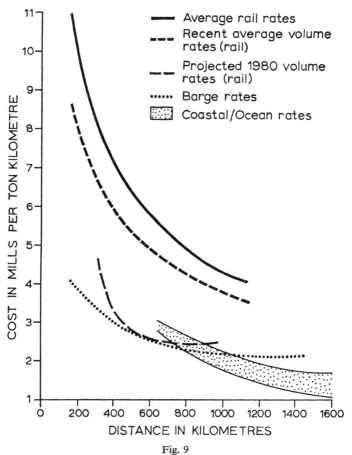

Fig. 9

Comparative rates for coal transport by various media in the United States, *c.* 1964. (Source: Federal Power Commission, 1964, *passim*)

The result has been that unless the railways have received a heavy subsidy, or some other form of protection, their remaining freights, such as coal, have had to bear an increasing share of their capital expenses. This in turn has necessitated either an increase in their ton/km rates—which in turn serves to reduce the extent of their effective competition for traffic, and in the long run accelerates their loss of custom—or a determined programme of cost reductions through the introduction of improved technologies and improved efficiency.

Advances in the methods of both haulage and handling have in fact considerably improved the competitive position of railways for the movement of energy. In Britain, for example, the use of larger locomotives and wagons (up to 100 tons each in the case of oil tank cars) plus the introduction of permanently coupled block trains, faster services and the mechanisation and concentration of handling facilities have reduced the line-haul rates by up to 50% on longer routes and considerably lowered terminal costs. For example, one North London coal depot now handles all the house coals which eight formerly received, and gets them from five pits instead of thirty-five. The transport of coal in the United States has been improved by even more radical techniques, such as the use of 110-ton hopper cars on specially strengthened ways, highly centralized automatic control systems and a high degree of mechanical handling at both ends. The so-called unit trains operate between a single mine and a single market, and with the capacity of the train increased to about 7,000–10,000 tons (and the rail cars provided by the mine) ton/km rates have been cut by 50% in many cases. On the drawing boards are the integral trains which operate for about a week without refuelling, have a capacity of 35,000 tons and travel at 80 to 100 km per hour, and could reduce rates significantly once again. The success of the railways in competing for energy traffic in the future will depend very much upon the speed with which these many new technical advances are adopted.

Energy transport by road
The last of the discontinuous means of energy transport to be considered is the lorry (Fig. 10). Its economics are based upon a relatively small proportion of capital costs in total costs, inexpensive loading and high ton/km running expenses. When relatively small quantities of energy are being transported and distances are short, road transport is invariably the most economic form of transport (see Fig. 8 and Table 8). However, with the increasing size of vehicles and the improvement of road communications, the ton/km cost

of road haulage is tending to fall, and the distances over which
lorries can effectively compete with railways is increasing. The
impact of road transport would be even greater if the rather low
average load factor in vehicle use could be increased from its present
60% to the 80% or 90% load factors which are not unknown in
connection with other transport media; or if there were not considerable taxes levied on motor fuels in many countries (taxes have been
estimated to represent between 12% and 18% of the cost of road
transport in Western Europe (Hubbard, 1960)).

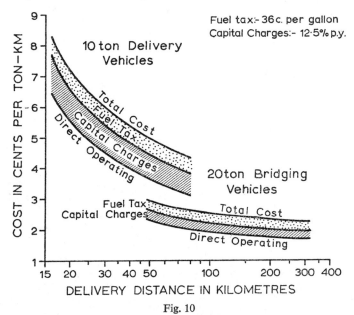

Fig. 10

Cost structure of oil transport by road in Western
Europe, c. 1967. (Source: Hubbard, 1967, 69)

In the movement of energy, of course, cost is not the only factor
which determines whether a particular form of transport is used or
not. One particular advantage of road transport is speed, for it can
often deliver energy to its markets faster than railways whose freights
are frequently delayed by terminal operations. Another advantage
is its high degree of route flexibility. By road, energy can be transported direct from a mine to a factory or from a refinery to a home.
Indeed, at the final stage of delivering energy to its market—be it for
coal, oil or liquefied petroleum gas—road transport is very often

the *only* form of transport available. The result is that road hauliers are steadily encroaching upon the traditional energy flows of the railways, as was mentioned earlier.

The degree to which road transport is used in any particular situation will depend upon a number of factors. In Pennsylvania, for example, the increasing use of road transport to haul coal appears to hinge upon two major factors. First, the age, size and nature of the mines; and, second, the location and size of the market (Deasy and Greiss, 1957). On the bituminous coalfield many old mines have railway lines and sidings already installed which provide a strong incentive to use this form of transport: the owners of new mines, in contrast, are not always prepared to invest in a branch line, and are tending to rely more upon road transport. At the same time, an investment in rail facilities offers more advantages to the larger mines than to the smaller ones, since the scale economies of rail transport are greater than those of road haulage: the result is that the small mines tend to dispatch their coal by road rather than by rail. The contrast between strip mining and deep mining also brings with it a contrast in transport preferences, for the migratory nature of the former encourages the use of lorries whilst the fixed nature of deep mining is better suited to use of a railway. In these ways the age, size and nature of mines affect transport preferences. The second group of factors affecting the Pennsylvania situation are related to the characteristics of the market, and they can be summarized as follows. Large consumers, with steady energy demands and situated adjacent to a railway line, are more conveniently supplied by rail; but small consumers, located away from a railway line and purchasing irregular quantities of coal, are more economically served by road transport.

An interesting contrast between the mining industry and its transport characteristics in northern and southern Pennsylvania results directly from these two sets of influences. In the northern part of the State, where many of the newer mines are located and where much of the mining is by large scale, strip mining techniques, road transport dominates increasingly the movements of coal. But in the older deep mining areas of southern Pennsylvania, where rail facilities already exist, road haulage on the whole has made much less impact upon the transport operations of the industry.

6

TRANSPORT (II)

Energy transport by pipeline — by transmission wire — the economics of energy transport: a summary

Energy transport by pipeline

Pipelines exhibit an obvious inflexibility in their routes, their capacities and the range of commodities which they are able to transport. This point has already been noted. But these rigidities, in effect disadvantages, are outweighed by the fact that under certain conditions pipelines offer significantly cheaper transport than nearly all their competitors. Given a large and unvarying market, the need for which will be seen below, pipelines can outcompete all other forms of land transport, and occasionally prove to be more economical than ocean transport. The actual cost of pipeline transport obviously varies with the physical conditions of the route. The cost per kilometre of laying a natural gas pipeline across the Canadian Rockies was nearly double that of the line between Texas and California; the pipes constructed through the wooded swamps of Louisiana and off the shores of that State, and those on the bed of the North Sea, were even more expensive. Further, the construction and running costs of pipelines are influenced by their size, the pressure at which energy is transmitted through them, and the efficiency with which they are used; they also vary with the rate of interest on borrowed capital, with the expense of way-leave and, if a fluid is being piped, with its viscosity. The considerable range of pipeline costs recognized, the findings of Hubbard (1967, *passim*) with reference to oil transport costs for Western Europe nevertheless serve to illustrate their highly competitive nature (Table 8; see Fig. 7).

Table 8

COMPARATIVE COSTS OF OIL TRANSPORT MEDIA,
TO AND WITHIN WESTERN EUROPE, *circa* 1967

	Capital Cost (cents per ton)	Operating Cost (cents per ton/km)
Road delivery vehicles	75–80	2·2–3·5
bridging vehicles	34–46	1·6–2·5
Canal barges	52	0·8
Coastal tankers	125–200	0·19–0·39
Pipelines (m.t.y. capacity)		
1	4.5	0·7
2	3·5	0·4
5	3·5	0·22
10	2·3	0·14
20	2·3	0·085
50	1·15	0·047
Ocean tankers (dwt)		
10,000	69	0·07
20,000	52	0·043
30,000	37	0·036
50,000	33	0·027
70,000	30	0·022
100,000	28	0·019
150,000	26	0·016

Source: Hubbard, 1967, 27.

The generally greater economies to be derived from water transport are apparent in these figures. Nevertheless there are instances when pipelines have been constructed in preference to the use of an alternative sea route. In the Middle East, for example, the voyage from the Gulf of Aden to the Eastern Mediterranean via the Suez Canal is approximately 4,800 km, whereas the pipeline from Saudi Arabia across the desert is only 1,600 kms in length (and saves any Canal dues). In this situation it was considered economic to build an oil pipeline across the desert. When it was first laid, the line was certainly competitive against the alternative tanker route. After 1957, however, for a decade the TAP line was never used to its full capacity, and served to pump only about one-half of the total quantity of oil which could have been transported through it. Although there were obvious political undertones to this situation, the explanation was basically to be found in transport economics. After the 1957 Suez crisis and the nationalization of the Canal, tanker rates began to fall, partly as a consequence of surplus shipping capacity. The transport of oil from the Gulf of Aden by pipeline, therefore, became more expensive than the use of tankers (see p. 102). After the 1967 June war, however, and the closure of the Canal, the TAP line came into its own once again—at least until the large super-tankers were built and became operational around the Cape.

Whilst pipelines clearly cannot compete with super-tankers over an equivalent distance, the largest have become competitive with the smaller 'conventional' vessels of up to, say, 25,000 dwt and for some time it was argued that a 76 cm (30 in) pipeline would be economic for the transport of oil in the rather unique American context between Texas and the Middle Atlantic seaboard. Traditionally, this considerable haul was served predominantly by small ocean-going tankers. In 1962, in fact, construction began on a 90 cm products pipeline from Houston to New York with 1,600 km of feeders to smaller markets *en route*. The profitability of this pipeline is helped by the fact that in this case, too, it transports the oil over a shorter physical distance than its ocean competitors; the straight-line distance between Port Arthur (Texas) and Philadelphia is 1,860 km, the pipeline traverses 2,240 km, but the distance by rail and sea are 2,420 km and 3,390 km respectively. In addition, the pipeline is able to compete with the alternative sea route by virtue of its size (and the economies which that will allow), by the absence of large tankers on that route, by the high cost of American coastwise transport and by a 'humped' tariff whereby users along the line will pay higher cubic metre-kilometre rates than those at the New York end of the pipe where tanker competition is obviously at its keenest.

Oil pipelines were first laid between Texas and the east coast during the war years, when the 'Big Inch' and 'Little Inch' pumped oil to such cities as New York and Philadelphia. The motive behind the construction of these pipelines, however, was more strategic than economic. After the war they were sold to two major natural gas transport companies, and provided an important basis for the expansion of the American natural gas industry. Although strategic motives are not unknown elsewhere in the laying of pipelines—for example, the Canadian government insisted that the natural gas pipe from the Prairies to Ontario should pass to the north of the Great Lakes and so remain entirely within national territory—most pipelines have an economic justification, and it is to the characteristics of their economics that we must now turn (Cookenboo, 1955; Manners, 1962a).

The first characteristic of pipeline transport is that its capital or fixed costs dominate its total cost structure. Only about 25% of the total cost of an oil product pipeline is actually running expenses. In turn this means that, granted fairly uniform physical conditions, the ton/km cost of pumping energy along a pipe tends to be almost constant with increasing distance. Thus in Table 9 it can be seen that the cost of transporting natural gas over 500 km in a 40 cm pipeline is about a third of the cost of pumping it 1,500 km. With the discontinuous media generally, the ton/km costs of transport tend to fall with increasing distance, since loading costs are spread over a greater distance and there are certain running economies which follow from the long haul. But there is little or no such variable with the continuous media.

Table 9

NATURAL GAS PIPELINE ECONOMICS IN THE
UNITED STATES, *circa* 1950
(cents/100 coal equivalent tons)

Length of line (km)	(*assuming 100% load factor*)	
	40 cm line	*60 cm line*
100	3·4	2·3
500	16·0	10·4
1,000	32·4	21·1
1,500	49·9	32·6
Load factor	*500 km/40 cm diameter line*	*500 km/60 cm diameter line*
100	16·0	10·4
80	19·7	12·8
60	26·0	16·7
40	38·4	24·4
20	75·6	47·7

Source: Kornfeld (1949).

This dominance of fixed costs in the total cost of pipelines also means that a decline in the use of a pipe below its maximum capacity results in a considerable increase in the unit costs of transport, since the greater part of the expenses incurred in the pumping operation (that is, the capital costs) still have to be met regardless of the quantities of energy actually moved. Table 9 also illustrates the way in which, in the case of natural gas, a decline in the load factor considerably increases the ton/km costs of a pipeline operation. The implications of this are twofold. First, a fairly constant market for energy is desirable if its demands are to be met economically through the use of pipeline transport. And second, if a market should exhibit daily or seasonal irregularities, considerable transport economies can be gained from the use of techniques which encourage a regular flow of energy along the pipe. In the case of oil transport, storage facilities either at the source of energy or at the market can be used to even out the flow and ensure full use of a pipeline. If such storage is not possible, then, in all probability it will be more economic to use an alternative, discontinuous form of transport. In the case of gas, the necessity of finding a means whereby the flow of energy can be made more regular is much greater than in the case of oil, since the cost of discontinuous gas transport is particularly high. In the United States, therefore, three means in particular are used to maintain a fairly regular flow of natural gas; these are the underground storage of gas near to its markets, the laying of a slightly larger diameter pipeline than the main transmission line near to the market (in order to provide pipeline storage capacity), and the manipulation of gas prices to encourage gas sales during those times when demand is normally low. These are techniques which have already been examined in some detail in Chapter 3. It is sufficient at this juncture to recognize their origin in the high proportion of capital costs in pipeline transport.

The second characteristic of pipeline transport is the exceptional economies which can be achieved through large scale transmission. These scale economies derive from the fact that the capacity of a pipeline increases more rapidly with the enlargement of a pipe's diameter than do its capital and running costs. The expense of laying and installing a pipeline does not vary significantly with its diameter, and the ton/km cost of transmission falls as the ratio of a pipeline's diameter to its capacity increases. The cost of transporting oil through a 15 cm pipeline, therefore, is twice that of a 20 cm and four times those of a 30 cm pipe. Comparable scale economies for gas pipelines can also be shown; the unit cost of pumping natural gas through a 60 cm pipeline in the United States *circa* 1950 was 33 % to 35 % lower than through a 40 cm pipe (see Table 9). Therefore, within the technological limitations to the size of pipeline which can be manufactured and through which energy can be pumped (currently rather less than 1·5 m), the larger the market and the greater the diameter of the pipe, the lower will be the ton/km cost of energy transport. The fact is illustrated in Fig. 11 which relates to the economics of crude oil pipelines in Western Europe.

As a generalization, pipeline size is more important than the load factor in the medium's economics (Stockton, et al., 1952, 180; Federal Power Commission, 1948, 263). Consequently, there is an advantage to be gained from increasing the size of an energy market even at the expense of a limited deterioration in the load factor. Table 9 shows

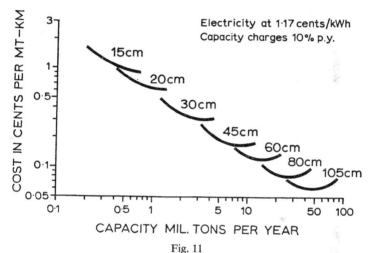

Fig. 11

Cost of oil transport by pipeline in Western Europe, *c.* 1967. (Source: Hubbard, 1967, 55)

the costs of transporting gas through a 60 cm pipeline with an 80% load factor; they are lower than those of a 40 cm pipeline with a 100% load factor—indeed, a 60 cm pipe is only slightly more expensive when it is operated with a 60% load factor. This particular aspect of pipeline costs may well be the major reason why many American gas transport companies have continued to accept further market commitments for the supply of gas in spite of their irregular demands and the load problems which they bring. There are, of course, scale economies associated with the other media of energy transport. However, their magnitude is of a somewhat smaller order than those of pipelines, and as a result the latter have become increasingly competitive for the transport of energy as large markets have developed and expanded on the face of the globe.

The final characteristic of pipeline transport is that the costs of transmission are affected by the nature of the commodity being transported. Thus, in the case of oil transport, the more viscous the crude or product, the greater are the ton/km costs of moving it. It has been estimated, for example, that the cost of pumping fuel oil through a pipeline is four to five times that of carrying crude oil through a pipe of similar diameter (Lindsey, 1954, 331). Assuming the capacity of a crude oil pipeline has an index of 100, the capacity of that same pipe has an index of about 80 for light fuel oil; the index is 60 for some heavy fuel oils, and it is as low as 10 or even 5 for others. In the case of the 32 km fuel oil pipe from Stanlow to Partington, the line has had to be fully insulated because the oil can only be handled at high temperatures. There is a limit to the distance over which such a technique can be used, and hence a limit to the range of commodities for which pipelines are a suitable mode of transport.

The importance of these three characteristics can be illustrated through a brief survey of Western European oil pipeline developments. In spite of the rapid growth of an oil market in Western Europe in the decade after 1945, there were few individual markets located some distance from good water transport facilities which were large or stable enough to justify the installation of a pipeline. London has the Thames; the Ruhr adjoins the Rhine; and both could be supplied with oil efficiently and cheaply by tanker and barge respectively. Paris was, however, an exception; and in 1953 the 'Trapil' pipeline was laid from the refineries and the ports of Rouen and Le Havre to the French capital in the face of competition from Seine barges. In more recent years, however, large inland markets for oil products, and especially for fuel oil, have grown up in such regions as the Ruhr, eastern France, southern Germany and northern Italy. In consequence, large refineries have been built there, and crude oil pipelines have been laid to feed them. To satisfy the oil product demands of Western Europe's inland markets two alternative supply strategies were available. One would have been to continue most refinery operations at or near to the coast at the ports of crude oil import, and to transport the various products inland. But since fuel oil can only be piped at high cost, and the demand for lighter products was not large enough to justify pipeline construction, such a solution would have necessitated a continued reliance upon the discontinuous transport media. The alternative supply strategy—and the one adopted by the oil industry—was to locate refineries close to their inland markets and to transport the crude oil to them. Since crude oil contains prospectively both fuel oil and the lighter petroleum products, the volume of oil which needs to be transported becomes sufficient for pipelines to be economic; and as can be seen in Fig. 8, large pipelines have a clear economic advantage over barges for crude oil shipment.

Large inland oil markets together with pipeline economics, therefore, have justified the construction of many kilometres of crude oil pipelines in Western Europe (Fig. 12). Today, the chief means of moving crude oil from the major ocean terminals on the North Sea, the Atlantic and the Mediterranean to the inland refineries is by this method. There are two major pipelines in Northern Europe, and three in the south (OECD, 1961, 16). The two northern ones are the 70 cm–385 km line from Wilhelmshaven to Cologne with an ultimate capacity of 22 million tons per year, and the 60 cm–290 km pipe from Rotterdam to the Ruhr, planned with an ultimate capacity of 20 m.t.y. These two pipelines as a result draw considerable quantities of oil through Northern European ports and serve the refineries of the lower Rhine and Ruhr region, which now has nearly half of the total West German capacity.

The southern pipelines are both larger and longer. The Southern European Pipeline, for example, is 85 cm in diameter and traverses some 770 km from Lavera to Strasbourg and Karlsruhe; with an initial capacity of 10 million tons of crude oil per year, plans exist for the addition of compressors to handle 30 m.t. This pipeline has smaller extensions into Switzerland and Bavaria. By linking several of the inland refinery complexes with the French Mediterranean coast, this pipeline has shortened the distance which oil has to travel to reach these inland markets by about 5,600 km as compared with the alternative North Sea route. It has thus had a considerable effect upon the pattern of Western European oil flows, and early calculations suggested that at its ultimate capacity it would in effect replace sixty T2 (16,000 dwt) tankers (OEC, 1961, 16). Another pipeline in Southern Europe runs 1,000 km from Genoa to Austria and Bavaria; known as the Central European Pipeline, it is capable of handling up to 18 million tons of crude oil each year. The third facility in the south, the Trans-Alpine Pipeline, carries oil from Trieste to Austria and southern Germany. This is in fact the largest pipeline in Western Europe, with a diameter of over 100 cm and it is capable of carrying some 50 million tons of oil each year. The total capacity of all these Western European pipelines in time will be in the order of 140 m.t.y. It is noteworthy that all of them have been laid for the transport of crude oil rather than refined products,

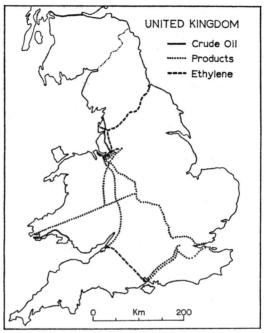

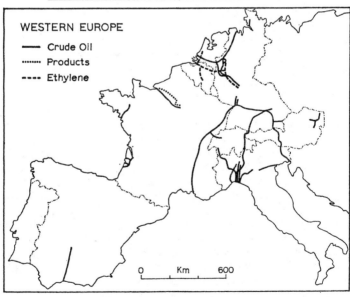

Fig. 12
Oil pipelines in Western Europe, 1970. (Source: Petroleum Information
Bureau)

and—the specialized requirements of the petrochemical industry apart, especially ethylene transfers—'Trapil' remains the only commercial product pipeline (see Fig. 12).

This Continental pattern of oil pipeline developments stands in strong contrast to the British situation in which most oil pipes have been laid to carry oil products. In Britain all the refineries have a coastal or near-coastal location, partly because many of the major markets are on or near the coast, and also because physical geography has left all parts of the country within easy reach of tidewater from which they can be easily served. Therefore, it has only been where older refineries lack nearby access to deep water facilities that crude oil pipelines have been constructed. They carry the oil however over relatively short distances. There are important pipelines from Loch Finnart to Grangemouth (90 km), from Milford Haven to Swansea (96 km) and from Tranmere to Stanlow (24 km) with a smaller extension to Heysham (110 km). Since they are each serving individual refineries these pipelines are relatively small compared with those on the Continent. The Finnart pipeline is 50 cm in diameter and was designed to carry in time 7 million tons of crude each year; the Milford pipe is 46 cm and carries 8 m.t.; the Heysham pipe is only 30 cm and carries but 2 m.t.y. All other pipelines in Britain are for the movement of refined products. Nearly 2,000 km were laid during World War II to supply airfields in the east and south-east from the ports and refineries in the west and south. Some of these pipes are still used to supply military airfields, whilst others are rented by oil companies to supply their markets or depots; Shell-Mex and BP use such a line from Stanlow to their depot at Avonmouth. In addition pipelines have been built between Walton-on-Thames in Surrey and London (Heathrow) airport, and the former depot is served by an ex-government pipeline from the BP refinery at the Isle of Grain. Other lines run from Stanlow to a distribution depot and petrochemical facilities at Partington, near Manchester. The Esso Petroleum Company pumps ethylene gas from Fawley to the Imperial Chemical Industry's complex on Severnside, and a wide range of products (including fuel oil) from Fawley to the Greater London market (including London (Heathrow) airport once again). Two further petrochemical lines run from Wilton in north Yorkshire to Runcorn and Fleetwood in Lancashire, and from Stanlow to Haydock. By far the largest product pipeline in the country, however, extends from the oil refining and storage complex on the Thames estuary to the corresponding complex on Mersey-side, serving in between the Greater London, Northampton, Notting-ham, Birmingham and Black Country markets. Extending over

500 km, and varying in diameter between 20 and 36 cm, the line is capable of carrying a wide range of oil products—motor spirit, kerosene, aviation fuels, gas oil, deisel oil and light petroleum distillates—and is the first common carrier in Britain. ('Common carrier' pipeline companies offer, indeed are required by law to offer, their facilities for general use; most pipelines in the United States are common carriers.) A second such line is proposed between the refinery complex on Milford Haven and the West Midlands and South Lancashire markets (see Fig. 12).

The contrast between British and Western European pipeline developments in recent years reflects the major factors influencing the geography of energy—physical geography, transport economies, markets and political factors. The absence of long distance crude oil pipelines in Britain stems essentially from the coastal location of the oil refineries; naturally these are supplied with crude oil by tankers (or by tankers plus a short pipeline). On the Continent, in contrast, refineries located at large inland markets can be most economically supplied with their raw material by long distance, wide-diameter pipelines from North Sea and Mediterranean ports. Although most of the refined products of British refineries are transported the relatively short distances to their markets by discontinuous media, there are a number of inland markets for oil products which are both some distance from the refineries and large enough to warrant the installation of a pipeline: the West Midlands is one example; the largest markets for chemical feed-stocks and aviation fuel are two others. On the Continent, however, 'Trapil' remains an exception, and generally speaking the markets for products not served by a local refinery are still not large enough to justify pipeline construction; an exception might have been fuel oil, but, as has been seen, this is one of the more difficult and costly products to transport in a pipeline. In both the British and Continental cases the role of political factors in pipeline construction also demands recognition. The British system of product pipelines dating from World War II has undoubtedly shaped the geography of oil distribution; and there is a comparable network of North Atlantic Treaty Organization pipes throughout the western part of the Continent. Moreover, some of the pipelines and refineries constructed in interior Western Europe are undoubtedly not without some strategic significance—certainly it has been suggested that the companies involved do not find it easy to dispose of all their refined products, notably fuel oil in Bavaria.

Most trunk pipelines for the movement of energy have been built to transport oil and natural gas. There are two exceptions, however,

which must be noted. The first is in West Germany where a long
distance pipeline system to transport reformed coke-oven gas has
been laid to serve areas as far apart as Bavaria and the north German
lowland. This pipeline distributes gas from the coke ovens and in
the steelworks of the Ruhr where a highly localized production
accounts for 80% of the country's output. It is a system which will
gradually be adapted in the 1970s for the transport of Dutch and
other supplies of natural gas (Odell, 1969). The second is the transport of coal by pipeline. Although this method of energy transport
is currently little used, in the United States a 170 km–25 cm diameter
coal pipeline was constructed between a mine and a power station
in Cleveland, Ohio, in the late 1950s. Through it one and a quarter
million tons of coal (crushed to a maximum size of 0·16 cm) was
pumped each year. The coal travelled at just under 5 km per hour
in the form of a slurry comprising 50% coal and 50% water, and
initially its costs were substantially below the rates charged by the
railroads. However, the latter quickly responded with rate reductions
and the charge per ton for hauling coal between southern and northern Ohio fell from $3·32 in 1957 to $1·88 in 1963. Simultaneously
the railroads embarked upon a more determined drive to modernize
their technology and reduce their costs. As a consequence, the Ohio
pipeline became uneconomic and was closed down, and detailed
proposals to construct yet further coal pipelines over greater distances—the 1,000 km haul between Utah and Los Angeles was
seriously studied—were quietly shelved. There can be little doubt,
however, that the very threat of more coal pipelines not only in the
United States but also in Britain has had a considerable effect upon
the performance and the rating behaviour of the railways. And it
still appears possible that coal from northeastern Arizona to a
prospective power plant in southern Nevada will be delivered by a
440 km pipeline (Landsberg and Schurr, 1968, 24).

Besides the trunk pipelines that have been laid for the long
distance movement of energy, there are many kilometres of other
pipes, in particular local gas grids and distribution systems, that are
used to move energy over relatively short distances. The grids allow
for the movement of gas in both directions, whilst the distribution
systems (like most long distance transmission pipes) are designed
to move gas in one direction only. These two types of pipelines, the
use of which has increased rapidly in recent years in most technologically advanced countries, are essential for the final stages of the
movement of gas to its markets. Yet, economically, they limit its
ability to compete there. In general, the pipes that are used for the
final distribution of gas are small in diameter, and therefore scale

economies—so important in the economics of trunk pipelines—are
absent. The result is that the unit cost of transporting gas through
a distribution system tends to be high, although the significance of
this cost varies with the type and quality of the gas being transported.
The much lower calorific value of manufactured gas (1,667 cubic
metres per coal equivalent ton) as compared with natural gas
(750 cubic metres per c.e.t.) means that the former is a much more
expensive form of energy to transport through these small pipes.
Davis (1957, 188) recounts how the change-over from manufactured
gas to natural gas in Canada in effect doubled the capacity of the
existing distribution pipelines and, in turn, nearly halved the unit
cost of gas distribution. Even with natural gas, however, the expense
of transport through local distribution systems is high; in turn this
increases the total cost of gas and reduces its competitive power.
The *Smith-Wimberley Report* suggested that 'Transport and distribution together aggregate so large a part of the total delivered price
of fuel to consumers that these elements, rather than the price of
the mine or the well, frequently are the principal determinants of the
competitive position of the fuel with respect to such consumers'
(Federal Power Commission, 1948, 335). This point is clearly made
by considering the cost of No. 2 fuel oil and natural gas in New
York City in 1955 (Table 10). Although the cost of gas was very

Table 10

COST OF FUEL OIL AND NATURAL GAS
IN NEW YORK CITY, 1955

	No. 2 Fuel oil ($ per c.e.t.)	Natural gas ($ per c.e.t.)
f.o.b. origin	16·4	3·0
Bulk transport to New York City	3·0	5·7
Price at New York City	19·4	8·7
Local distribution costs	8·7	45·6
Total cost	28·0	54·1

Source: Adelman, 1962, 70.

much lower than oil at its source, and was still less than half the
price after the bulk transport to New York City, by the time
gas had reached the small consumer, it was nearly twice the price
of an equivalent quantity of oil. The cost of local distribution in
New York City, at $46 per coal equivalent ton, was perhaps un-
usually high. But although it can be as low as $6·50 in some urban

areas, the average cost of distributing gas in American cities, $26, is still three times the cost of distributing oil in New York. To quote Adelman (1962, 72): 'Scarce fuel resources are best used if this fuel [natural gas], expensive to transport, is used to the maximum nearest its source of supply, while the transport-cheap oil moves greater distances.'

Energy transport by transmission wire
The essential characteristics of the economics of transmitting electrical energy by wire are very similar to those of pipelines. The total cost structure of the medium is dominated by capital costs; and the economies to be derived from bulk transmission are considerable.

The high proportion of fixed costs in transmission implies that, as with pipelines, the ton/km cost of transferring energy does not fall off with distance, and is graphically illustrated by a straight line— at least up to several hundred kilometres at which distance leakages and inefficiencies begin to increase the ton/km cost of transport. It also implies the necessity of maintaining a high load factor if the transmission is to be competitive. For instance, it has been estimated that the cost of transmitting electrical energy over a distance of, say, 300 km is four-fifths greater with a 50% load factor than it is with a 90% factor (Pierce and George, 1948). Since the electricity industry, unlike its gas counterpart, cannot store electricity as such to solve its load problems (except in the sense that it can make use of pumped storage schemes to store potential electricity), its principal reactions have been two-fold. First, it has distinguished between the base load and the peak load in its demands. The former represents the amount of electricity that is required without interruption throughout each day of the whole year; the peak load, superimposed upon it, varies from zero to the highest hourly demand above the base load. The industry has sought to minimize its costs by satisfying the base load with its most efficient plant, and by seeking to reduce the capital cost of the equipment used in meeting its peak loads. Second, the industry has adjusted its prices in order to encourage the consumption of energy at off-peak periods, thereby to improve the load factor. Several other solutions to this problem have already been examined in Chapter 3.

Scale economies in electrical energy transfer derive from the lower kilovolt–kilometre construction costs of the large transmission lines. A 500 kV transmission line, for example, has about four times the carrying capacity of a 275 kV line, and Phillips (1953) has shown how the cost of providing transmission equipment over a distance of 800 km can fall from $150 per kW in a 600 MW system to $90 per kW in a 3,600 MW one. Earlier it was noted that in the case of pipelines the economics of large scale transmission were generally more important than the load factor. The same cannot be said of the transmission line. Although substantial scale economies are common to both, there is a much greater problem of energy storage in the case of electricity, and the efficiency of a transmission line falls off much more rapidly with poor loads than does that of a pipeline. As a consequence, those forms of energy which can be transported by pipeline are sometimes able to compete more effectively in markets with fluctuating demands than can electricity, and the electricity industry is acutely aware of the costs of poor load factors.

In recent years technical improvements in the transmission of electrical energy have increased the optimum scale of energy transfer. In 1946 the most economic voltage for the transmission of electrical energy over *circa* 150 km (in the United States) was 287 kV, but within a decade this has increased to 330 kV. The original voltage of the British grid was 132 kV; it has since been raised to 275 kV and 400 kV and there has been discussion of the possibility of a supergrid at 700 kV later on. In the USSR trunk lines with voltage as high as 1,400 kV are planned for construction between Siberia and the Urals. The relatively lower costs of transformers and switchgear, and the proportionately greater expense of transmission lines, are the principal factors behind this trend. Together with the more efficient use of rights of way which accompanies higher voltage transmission, these economics have encouraged a gradual increase in the scale of electrical energy transfer the world over. The major restraining factor has been the limited number of load centres big enough to justify transmission on a really large scale.

But not only has the scale of transmission increased. The distances over which electrical energy can be transferred have also been lengthened. At one time it was regarded as uneconomic to move electrical energy more than about 300 km; yet today, it is occasionally transported over 1,000 km and more. In this gradual extension of the maximum possible distance for economic transmission, alternating current has been most frequently utilized. However, many authorities are of the opinion that direct current will be more important in the future. Still partly in the experimental stage, this method of energy transfer is already used for the underwater electricity cables between Sweden and Denmark, and between Britain and France. The inter-linkage of the electricity supplies of North and South Island of New Zealand is also achieved by direct current, the 250 kV cables being able to transfer 600 MW of energy. The real possibilities of direct current, however, are in long distance energy transfer. Characterized essentially by its low transmission costs and very high cost end equipment, it is clear that with increasing distance the advantages of direct current transmission multiply. An 800 kV direct current line connects the Volgograd dam (near Stalingrad) to the Donbas region, a distance of 440 km, and there are plans to utilize the technology at higher voltages and over distances of 1,000 km or more. All the evidence suggests that with further technical advances, the possible scale and range of electrical energy transfer will be increased, and the kilovolt–kilometre cost of its transport will fall.

Nevertheless, the cost of electrical energy transfer today is relatively high compared with energy transport costs generally (see Tables 4 and 5). This in turn is strongly reflected in the price of electricity at its markets, and has prevented the exploitation of many hydro-electricity resources. It is probable that one of the basic motives in the Soviet effort to reduce the cost of electrical energy transmission has been to make it possible to utilize her considerable hydro-electricity potential which until recently has been beyond the distance of economic exploitation. Moreover, as in the case of pipelines, the expense of moving electrical energy in the final stages of distribution is particularly high. Consequently, the cost of transport makes up a very large proportion of the cost of electricity to the consumer. In terms of investment, the average cost of a distribution system in a rural-urban complex has been estimated by the United Nations (1957c, 257) at between $160 and $200 per kW, or about 40% of the total costs of an electricity system. In 1967–68 the electricity supply industry in England and Wales spent nearly $163 million on the transmission and distribution of electrical energy, and over 81% of this (approximately $132 million) represented the cost of distribution. These costs vary, of course, with the size of the market. The small consumer incurs a larger percentage of distribution costs than the large consumer. Because of the highly urbanized nature of England and Wales and the economies which come in distribution to such a market, the expense of electricity is much smaller than in an agricultural country like Denmark with a scattered population. It is because of its high distribution expenses that rural electrification is invariably subsidized (see p. 45).

The economics of electrical energy transfer are not necessarily based upon transmission and distribution costs alone. At this point the distinction between transmission facilities and grids must once again be noted. The economics of a transmission system are based upon the alternative costs of moving energy between two points;

E

but the economics of a grid system are reckoned otherwise. In the latter case, besides its ability to transport energy between different places, the grid offers additional advantages such as the sharing of the same peak generating plant by several markets (as an assurance that if one power station fails another will take over its share of the load) and a much more stable distribution system. Thus the justification of, say, the transfer of electrical energy nearly 1,000 km at 380 kV from the Harspränget Power Station on the Arctic Circle to the industrial and domestic markets in the centre and south of Sweden is rooted in energy transport economics and the costs of alternative supplies. The electricity grids of the United States, on the other hand, are used mainly to transmit peak and emergency loads, and despite the development of regional interties (Sewell, 1964) and some mine-mouth generation they are only rarely used to transfer electricity over distances of more than 50 km. Their economic justification, therefore, lies in the stability and the economics of the whole system of which they form a part. In Britain, also, investment in electricity supply increasingly is directed to ensuring the stability of the constantly changing production-distribution system, rather than the transmission of large loads between different parts of the country. Any understanding of the economics of energy transmission by wire must bear this distinction in mind.

The economics of energy transport: a summary

The costs of transporting energy leave a crucial impress upon the geography of energy. They affect the expense of exploiting energy resources, and, by influencing the cost of energy at its markets, mould the competitive relationship of the several sources available there. Above all, they strongly influence the transport medium which is used for particular energy flows. Although the various means of energy transport often stand in competition against each other, it is also true that they are complementary on numerous occasions. In transporting of Middle Eastern oil to Western Europe, both tankers and pipelines have an essential role to play. And in the operations of an integrated oil company, the two can be regarded as part of a single transport system. We have seen how the optimum operating economy of a pipeline can be best achieved by working it at a high load factor; however, if the full use of a pipeline means that there is a serious underemployment of a tanker fleet, it could well be more economic to use the latter as much as possible and to use the pipeline for any additional oil transport requirements. This has happened in the past (partly for political reasons, no doubt) in the case of Aramco and the TAP line (OECD, 1961, 20).

The two media which dominate oil flows are the tanker and the pipeline, of which tankers are the more important in ton/km terms. This is partly a result of the considerable scale ecomonies which they offer, and partly a consequence of the geographical disposition of oil resources in relation to oil markets which necessitates their use. Oil tanker tonnage has risen steadily over the last fifty years. From 0·5 million dwt in 1900, the world tanker fleet had increased to nearly 56 million dwt by 1958 when it represented nearly one-third of the world's total merchant marine, and to 120 million tons a decade later. In addition, by 1968 some 8 million dwt of oil/ore and 'OBO' capacity was used by the oil industry. Moreover, measured in terms of either bulk or value, for some time oil has been by far the most important commodity entering international trade. It represents about 10 % of the world exports by value, and nearly one-half of the volume of seaborne trade. Outside the USA and the USSR at least 80 % of all oil consumed is moved by tanker and in Western Europe this figure is well over 90 %.

On the other hand, for overland transport, the inherent advantages of pipelines for oil transfers have led to their proliferation throughout the world. There were some 455,000 km of oil pipelines in operation throughout the world in 1967, and their use is rapidly increasing. No country has taken advantage of them more than the United States, where a rapid expansion of oil pipeline capacity occurred in the decade after World War II; between 1952 and 1955 alone an additional 9,000 km of crude oil pipeline above 40 cm in diameter were laid down in that country. By 1968 there were some 355,000 km of crude and product oil pipeline in the United States, and oil pipes were carrying over 20 % of the (ton/km) inter-city freight.

The importance of these two media in oil transport is endorsed by an examination of the bulk movements of oil for the American and British markets. In 1956 some 66 % of the former's oil transfers (in ton/km) was in tankers, and 92 % was in tankers and pipelines (Emerson, 1957). This particularly high figure for tankers is partly related to the fact that oil imports into the United States in that year totalled 65 million tons (14 % of total consumption), and much of the crude came 13,000 km from the Middle East. But even when consideration is given solely to oil movements within the country, water transport (including inland waterways) and pipelines still dominate the picture. By the middle 1960s three out of every four barrels of crude oil in the United States were moved by pipeline and a further 17 % by water. The transport of oil products was somewhat more diversified, but even so pipelines and water transport together accounted for nearly half of the total movement. In Britain, virtually all of the crude oil used in the refineries is handled initially by water transport in the process of being imported; subsequently over two-thirds of its movement is handled in pipelines and the other 30% by coastal carrier (Table 11). Refined products are also on average handled twice between the refinery and their markets. In the first stage, shipment to intermediate storage facilities, it is water transport which dominates the distribution system and accounts for about three-quarters of the total movement; but in the second stage road transport, handling 85% of total ton/km movements, assumes an even greater importance. The total picture is summarized in Table 11. Because of their longer average length of haul, coastal shipments account for nearly 73% of total oil product transfers in Britain, whereas road transport with an average haul of just over 40 km accounts for 11% on a ton/km basis.

World-wide, where pipelines are uneconomic and inland waterways available, a certain amount of oil is transported by barge. This form of transport makes a relatively small contribution to total oil transfers, although it is used in preference to rail and road transport when advantage can be taken of its lower ton/km rates. In the distribution of products from oil refineries and when relatively short distances and small quantities are involved, however, the lower terminal costs and the greater geographical flexibility of rail and road transport are highly advantageous. Thus for the movement of oil to the distribution depot, the garage and the individual consumer, road and rail transport predominate; and, of the two, road transport is by far the more important.

As with oil, under ideal conditions the cheapest means of moving coal is by water transport; indeed, at one time coal movements dominated the tonnage of sea transport in the way that oil has come to dominate ocean freights today. But as a result of the changed role of coal in the energy geography of the world, collier tonnage has declined both relatively and absolutely, a trend which has been counterbalanced to only a small extent by the growing use of bulk carriers. In 1965 international trade in solid fuels was some 159 million tons, compared with oil's 1,395 million tons coal equivalent. Coal exports in that year therefore represented only 10% of global trade in energy, a proportion very different from the 66% of forty years earlier. In the movement of coal, the relationship between water (including inland water) transport and the rail haulage of coal is no simple matter. But where water transport facilities are available, the market nearby and large (and the consumer not particularly discriminating about the quality of the coals which he

Table 11

OIL TRANSPORT IN THE UNITED KINGDOM, 1969

	Crude and process oils				Refined petroleum products*			
		Ton/km				*Ton/km*		
	Quantity (thousand tons)	(thousands)	(%)	*Average journey*	*Quantity* (thousand tons)	(thousands)	(%)	*Average journey*
Rail	29	6,536	0·1	225·4	15,062	2,032,550	9·6	134·9
Road	1	400	—	362·9	54,873	2,307,922	11·0	42·1
Coastwise	1,095	743,074	30·8	678·6	32,358	15,301,939	72·6	473·0
Pipeline	25,833	1,659,096	68·9	64·2	17,276	899,829	4·3	52·2
Inland waterway	—	—	—	—	8,481	528,502	2·5	62·2

* Tonnage figures in excess of inland deliveries as a result of double handling.

Source: Ministry of Technology, *Digest of Energy Statistics*, 1970

uses), sea or barge haulage is almost invariably preferred. The
greater the distances involved, the stronger becomes that preference.

However, the geographical disposition of coalfields in relation to
their markets is such that water transport frequently is not available,
and as a result railways—historically speaking and neglecting the
pipeline, the next cheapest form of transport—are used to move
considerable quantities of coal throughout the world. Before World
War II approximately one-third of American rail tonnage was
made up of coal shipments; this proportion, however, had fallen to
about one-quarter by 1965 as solid fuel became relatively less important in the American energy economy, and as alternative forms
of transport nibbled at the edges of the coal trade. Between 1945 and
1965, the proportion of coal carried by the railways fell from
85% to 75%, as barge and road transport became more attractive.
Recently in Britain, too, there has been an increase in the use of road
transport for coal, and in 1969 over 22% of all colliery disposals
left the pitheads in lorries. Nevertheless, the percentage of goods'
revenue which the railways received from the haulage of coal, and
the proportion of freight traffic which is made up by this fuel, have
continued to remain important. In 1969 British Rail received approximately 21% of its freight revenue from the haulage of coal, coke
and patent fuel, commodities which make up 60% of its total volume
of freight traffic. As the output of the National Coal Board continues
to decline, and as the average distance of coal haulage persists in
falling, however, the prospect is for a diminishing importance of
rail-borne coal in the revenues of British Rail.

Elsewhere in the world, nevertheless, the continuing importance
both of the coal industry and of solid fuel haulage by rail must not
be overlooked. Whilst coal production has been contracting or
stagnating in Western Europe and North America in recent decades,
it has experienced a notable expansion in other parts of the globe.
World-wide, coal output doubled from 1,230 million tons in 1925
to 2,261 m.t. in 1965. Especially in the USSR and in China—where
coal and lignite production reached *circa* 300 m.t. in 1965 and still
represented about 95% of the country's total energy production—
the transport of coal by rail is of steadily increasing importance.

For obvious reasons the transport of gas and electricity is invariably effected by pipeline and transmission wire. In the case of the
former source of energy, however, in recent years ocean tankers
have proved to be an economical means of bridging the considerable distances which separate the huge and wasting supplies of
natural gas in the Middle East and the Caribbean, and the energy-
hungry markets of Japan, Western Europe and North America.

At the other end of the scale, liquefied petroleum gas is of course transported by road in pressurized containers; but this is usually in the final stages of distribution where the need for geographical flexibility is paramount and can outweigh the high cubic metre–kilometre costs of such transport. Most gas, however, is transported by pipeline, and in 1967 there were an estimated 1,596,000 km of natural gas pipeline in the world, about three times the combined length of crude and product pipelines for transporting oil (Petroleum Information Bureau).

The costs of transport, then, considerably affect the geography of energy production, flows and consumption. They also influence the places at which primary sources of energy are converted into secondary and more marketable forms. The geography of oil refining is discussed in Chapter 9 (pp. 193–207). The location of gas works and power stations is the subject of the next chapter.

7

TRANSPORT (III)

Transport costs and the secondary energy industries — location principles of gas manufacture — location principles of thermal electricity generation

Fossil or 'primary', fuels are frequently used to produce an alternative, and more convenient, form of energy known as a 'secondary' source. This distinction between 'primary' and 'secondary' sources of energy is valuable in the discussion of energy problems. As with coal and oil, in the case of the primary sources of (natural) gas and (hydro) electricity, transport costs powerfully influence the cost of particular energy sources at the market, and so help to determine the extent to which a particular demand is satisfied by them. But in the case of secondary sources, not only do transport costs affect the delivered cost of energy at the market, they also influence the location of its conversion from a primary into a secondary form. This particular aspect of the importance of transport costs becomes more and more significant in the geography of energy as an increasing proportion of primary energy is used to produce secondary forms. In Western Europe the conversion of coal into patent fuel, electricity, coke and gas increased from 40% of total production in 1937 to 64% in 1959 (OEEC, 1960, 31). A decade later in Britain, secondary fuel producers consumed nearly half of total energy requirements. The importance of secondary energy production in the United States is illustrated by Fig. 13.

The contemporary patterns of gas manufacture and electricity generation are a palimpsest of historical and recent location decisions. They reflect the wide variety of factors which influence

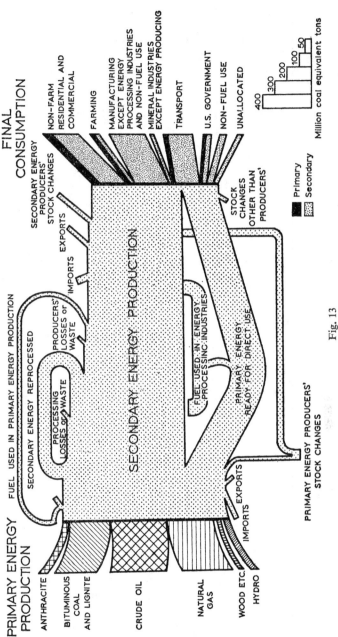

Fig. 13

Approximate structure of energy balance in the United States, 1954. (Source: Resources for the Future (1961), *Annual Report*, Washington, D.C., 54)

the location of secondary energy production. Such influences as distribution and cost of primary energy sources, the geography and costs of transport facilities, the location and size of secondary energy markets, the adequacy of water supplies for cooling and other purposes, and the availability of facilities for effluent and ash disposal all affect the location of production. And not only these factors: differences in local taxes modify the siting of secondary energy production in the United States; planning and amenity issues bedevil the industries in Britain; and everywhere such matters as the suitability of subsoil foundations, the adequacy of labour supplies and the results of diverse political influences are liable to affect a location decision. Any empirical survey of the various factors which are involved in the location of secondary energy production quickly reveals the complexity and variety of locational choice, and underlines the individuality of each case.

It is possible, however, to bypass the multifarious and at times random factors which influence the location of secondary energy production, and to single out for discussion the fundamental factors underlying its geography. Amongst these transport costs are especially important, although in technologically advanced economies they must be seen within the framework of a complex production–transmission–distribution system. Given a particular framework of raw materials sources and market centres, it is the comparative costs of energy transport which more than anything else determine —à la Weber (1957)—the *orientation* (as opposed to the exact location or siting) of production. Where a primary energy source and a market for secondary energy coincide, of course, the location issue is readily resolved. But assuming that they are geographically separate, at the simplest level the question is whether the best place for the conversion of the energy is at the source of the primary fuel, at the market or at some point between the two.

Location principles of gas manufacture

For the traditional manufacture of gas from coal, let us assume that it is possible to locate production either at a coal mine (C), or at a market for both gas and coke (M) some distance away. What, then, is the cheapest way to transfer energy from C to M? Several possible solutions to this problem are illustrated in Fig. 14 (case a). Coal can be moved from C to M by road, rail, inland waterway, pipeline or sea transport, and the gas manufactured at M. Alternatively, gas can be made at C and then piped from C to M, in which case it is also necessary to transport the coke by-product between these places by one of the discontinuous transport media. Any

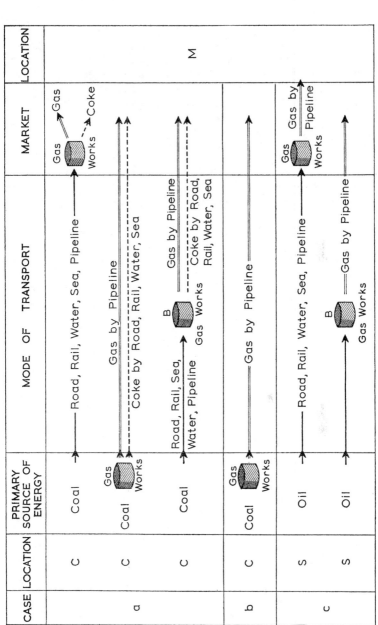

Fig. 14

Locational alternatives for gas manufacture

solution to a search for minimum transport costs is complicated by the fact that each of these modes of transport is capable of being used with different economies of scale. For example, coal and coke can be transported in wagons of different sizes, and can be hauled in either individual wagons or in complete train-loads; whichever of these alternatives is chosen will quite clearly influence the ton/km cost of transport. Similarly, the unit cost of pumping gas varies—as was seen in Chapter 6—with such factors as the diameter of the pipeline used, the cost of way-leave and the rate of interest on capital. It is important to recall once again the considerable range of variables which affects the alternative costs of transferring energy, and the impossibility of confidently analysing a particular case without a detailed study of its individual characteristics.

However, just as it was possible to generalize about the costs of transporting particular fuels by alternative media in the previous two chapters, so is it possible to generalize in this case too. Some valuable data were presented by Burns in 1958 (see Fig. 15), and it seems unlikely that their relationships have subsequently altered in any significant way. Under British conditions, for distances up to about 100 km and when small markets were being served (i.e. markets consuming up to about 100 coal equivalent tons of gas per day), at that date it was more economic to pipe gas from C to M, carrying the coke by the cheapest discontinuous media available, than it was to transport the coal and manufacture the gas at M. However, above that distance it became invariably cheaper to serve such small markets by moving the coal and producing gas at M. At one time this market orientation of gas manufacture was also applicable to larger markets. But with the improvement of pipeline techniques the distance over which gas transport was competitive gradually increased, and by the late 1950s it had become increasingly advantageous to meet the needs of more distant markets by manufacture at C. The larger the localized demand for gas (which in turn, of course, allows important scale economies in production), the greater became the advantage of coalfield sites for gas production, for with large markets the lower cubic metre–kilometre costs of pumping considerable quantities of gas outweigh the expenses of moving coke from C to M. Thus, one major factor affecting the orientation of gas manufacture is the size of the market.

There are, of course, upper distance limits to the competitive production of gas at C. Whilst there is little or no distance variable in the case of pipelines, the ton/km costs of the discontinuous media fall with increasing distance. There comes a point, therefore, where the costs of pipeline transport rise above those of the discontinuous media and the most economic place to manufacture gas once again is at M rather than C. This distance depends very much upon such factors as (once again) the size of the market, the rate of interest on capital and the exact nature of the coal transport facilities and freight rates. A distance constraint upon the pumping of gas from C economically is also imposed by the availability of water, and especially sea, transport. The costs of coal haulage recorded in Fig. 15 are for *average* British conditions in 1958. However, a more

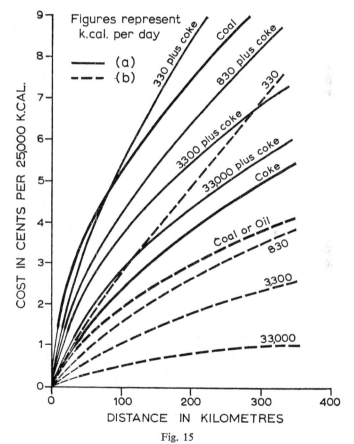

Fig. 15

Energy transport costs for the gas industry in Britain, *c.* 1958. The gas transport costs refer to (a) conventional carbonization of coal and (b) complete gasification techniques. (Source: Burns, 1958)

detailed examination of the costs of transport reveals a slightly different picture.

It has already been noted that the ton/km costs of collier transport are very low indeed. As a consequence, the least cost solution to the energy transfer problem associated with gas manufacture is to transport coal by sea from C to M for all but the smallest markets and the shortest distances. Given, therefore, a coastal coalfield and a tidewater market more than about 160 km apart, the orientation of gas production will invariably be to that market. Although pipelines have not yet been used for the long-distance transport of coal for gas production, the improvement of hydraulic techniques and the lowering of pipeline costs to a range not greatly in excess of water transport together suggest that, should this means of moving coal ever be used by the gas industry, a market orientation would again be preferred. Thus, the coal transport costs of Fig. 15 must be interpreted with care for, in fact, it was only when rail and road transport were used for the movement of coal that in 1958 C could generally be regarded as an economic location for gas production to serve markets up to rather more than 300 km away.

Where colliers and sea haulage were not feasible for the whole distance between C and M, and a change of media became necessary in order to transport coal between those two points, another solution to the location problem emerged. This was to manufacture gas at that intermediate point (B) where a change in the mode of transport and a break of bulk became necessary. Hoover (1948, 39) has shown how at such locations the total costs of transport are frequently at a minimum. The three major factors influencing the orientation of conventional gas manufacture, therefore, are the size of the market, the distance between the pithead and the market, and the range of media available for energy transport.

One of the major advances in gas technology in the late 1950s was the manufacture of gas from poorer grades of coal than had been previously used, and its complete carbonization (see Fig. 14, case b). With these techniques either less coke or no coke at all is produced as a by-product of the gas manufacturing process, and, as a consequence, the transport costs associated with gas production at C are lowered (see Fig. 15). Moreover, because the coals used in the complete carbonization plants are poorer, there is an additional incentive to manufacture gas at C, since the amount of coal required to produce a cubic metre of gas is greater, and so also is the ton/km cost of transporting a given quantity of energy as coal. The impact of these new techniques, therefore, was to reduce the spatial extent of the effective competition of coal haulage by the discontinuous media *vis-à-vis* gas transport, and to increase the distance between C and M over which a raw material orientation was preferable for gas manufacture.

There are three further factors which at times influence the orientation of gas production; these are the effects of grids interlinking a system of gas works, the implications of several widely distributed market centres, and those circumstances which make it impossible to manufacture gas at C. But since these variables are equally important in the location of secondary electricity generation, a discussion of their implications is deferred until later in this chapter. One final influence, however, must be examined. Manufactured gas can be made from oil products as well as coal. This was yet another of the technological advances which affected the industry in the late 1950s and early '60s. Since the transport of oil products in bulk is one of the most efficient means of transferring energy between two points, invariably it is more economic to move oil from its refinery source (S) to its market (see Fig. 14, case c) rather than transfer the energy in the form of gas. In some situations of course refineries are located at or near the largest markets for energy (see pp. 194 ff.), and in such cases a refinery gate location for gas production is frequently advantageous. There are also other instances where a market, without a local refinery, cannot be connected with a source of oil feedstock by a single mode of transport; in such circumstances a break-of-bulk location for the manufacture of gas is sometimes advantageous and comparable with the coal case noted earlier.

The relevance of these principles can be demonstrated by reference to a specific case. In 1968, approximately 35% of British gas was still manufactured in gas works; a further third was produced as a by-product of coke ovens and blast furnaces, and the rest was made up of North Sea and imported natural gas, colliery methane, liquefied petroleum gas and other petroleum gases. The principal consumer of coke oven gas has always been the steel industry itself, in which the gas is used at various stages of its production process, such as in the melting shops and the re-heating furnaces. But by linking coke oven gas supplies with the town gas distribution systems —as on the continent of Europe (Manners, 1961)—the much more diverse public supply markets came also to be served from the middle 1950s onwards. Over 16% of the gas distributed by the nationalized gas industry through its regional grids in 1956–57 was from coke ovens, and in that financial year the Wales, Northern and East Midlands Gas Boards purchased 80%, 62% and 61% respectively of their gas from this source. This distribution strongly reflects the major coke and steel producing areas of the country (Beaver, 1951).

At one time blast furnace gas was usually wasted; but it has come increasingly to be used extensively both for under-firing the coke ovens and in some of the furnaces of the steel industry, and for the generation of electricity. Its low calorific value results in its inability to bear high transport costs, which in turn means that it must be used near to its source. Consequently, blast furnace gas is invariably consumed on or adjacent to iron and steelworks.

Of greater interest in the context of this chapter, however, is the changing locational pattern of the town gas industry meeting domestic, industrial and commercial demands through the public supply system. Although the share of manufactured gas in total gas production began to fall rapidly from the late 1960s onwards, consequent upon the fuller exploitation of offshore deposits of natural gas, an examination of the recent geographical behaviour of the industry provides a valuable insight into the locational forces under review. Historically, the British gas industry grew in response to local demands and in the late 1940s was entirely orientated towards its markets. It manufactured joint products, coke as well as gas, which tended to reinforce this preference for a market location. The cost of railing coke was nearly as much as the cost of moving the primary source of energy (coal) and as a result any production located away from the market would have involved the expense of transporting both coke and gas there. Between 1945 and 1960, however, a series of new factors began to affect the industry some of which led to a concentration of gas manufacture at the larger market centres and others of which began to change the orientation of the industry (Manners, 1959, 1965). Basic to all these changes was the laying of the regional gas grids. Between 1949 and 1969 the length of gas mains in Britain increased from 120,000 km to over 185,000 km; the greater part of this growth stemmed from the integration of works and distribution systems, as opposed to the extension of urban distribution facilities or the laying of the natural gas trunk mains. Many advantages follow from such interconnections. For example, they safeguard the continuity of supplies; if plant at one works fails another works can help to maintain the flow of gas. When the peak demands of several markets occur at different times, and those markets are interlinked by a grid, plant for peak production can be shared between them with considerable savings in capital. The North Wales gas grid provides an example of this, for it links the industrial area in the north-east of the Principality with the resort towns along the north coast, and thereby connects markets with peak loads in the winter and summer months respectively. A third—and perhaps the most important—result of the regional grids is that they have allowed the gas industry to take full advantage of the lower unit overhead costs and the scale economies of large works sited at their most economic locations. Recent years have seen a steady increase in the operating efficiency of such larger works. Thus, whereas in 1948 the average efficiency of producing gas was 72%, the comparable figure in 1961 was 78%. A good part of this overall increase in efficiency was achieved by the closure of many of the smaller works, and the concentration of production upon fewer and larger plants in more central locations. During the first twelve years of nationalization, nearly 67% of the 1,050 gas works taken over in 1949 were closed down; and by 1969 the Gas Council made use of only 170 works. Meanwhile production had increased by about 30%.

These locational changes in gas production, which are a direct consequence of the new (grid) transport facilities, were reinforced by differential movements in the costs of transporting energy. While the real costs of moving coal and oil by rail tended to rise, the costs of pipelines steadily fell. Pipeline economics improved radically during the 1950s as a result of improved pumping techniques, a greater efficiency in the laying of mains, and the use of steel rather than cast iron pipes which allows the application of higher pressures and so lower unit costs. The result was that it became economical to pump gas over increasing distances—even allowing for the increased costs of distributing the joint-product coke. These changes not only encouraged the regional concentration of gas manufacture, but there was a time (in the middle and late 1950s) when it looked as if these differential movements in transport costs would alter the orientation of at least part of gas production in Britain. Certainly gas works of the London area and southern England—which relied upon water-borne coal from North East England—appeared likely to remain market-orientated and sited at their break-of-bulk points on lower Thames-side or on the south coast. But for markets further inland which tended to rely upon South Yorkshire and East Midlands coal, changing transport costs suggested the advantage of locating new base load carbonizing plant on the coalfield and the pumping of the gas to its centres of demand, leaving peak demands only to be satisfied from works with a market orientation.

This trend towards a coalfield orientation of town gas manufacture was reinforced by the search for cheaper fuels and new methods of production. One of the key aspects of the industry's research effort at this time was to seek out ways of using cheaper but poorer qualities of coal and to develop methods of completely carbonizing coal.

This led the industry to the German Lurgi process. With this there is no coke by-product to transport and as a result a coalfield orientation for the gas plants became clearly desirable. Two Lurgi plants were in fact built in Britain. That of the Scottish Gas Board is at Westfield, Fife, where coal is mined opencast, completely gasified, reformed to town gas standards and then pumped into a high pressure grid to serve the whole of the Central Valley of Scotland; the plant was designed to meet about one-fifth of the total Scottish demand. The second Lurgi works was located at Coleshill in the West Midlands; once again it was coalfield-orientated and its gas was fed into an extensive regional grid. The period during which transport economics suggested a coalfield orientation for gas production, however, was shortlived. Moreover it occurred at a time when the demand for gas was growing rather slowly and there was a disinclination to invest in many new plants. And before these trends could make a decisive mark upon the map of gas production in Britain, events were to overtake them.

At the beginning of the 1960s, therefore, the British gas industry remained oriented predominantly towards its largest markets. The major exceptions were, of course, those conventional gas works which were sited at coastal locations. One of the country's largest supplies of coking coal was found in the Durham coalfield; and some of the largest markets for gas are in southern England. With the haulage of coal by collier between the two relatively inexpensive, there were strong incentives to supply many of the markets within the latter region from tidewater break-of-bulk locations. In 1960–1, for example, the North Thames, South Eastern and Southern Gas Boards received 71%, 98% and 71% respectively of their coal deliveries by sea, and continued to expand their productive capacity adjacent to the ports and harbours of import. This was a pattern, however, with only a limited life.

The major problem of the British gas industry in its first nationalized decade was its uncompetitive posture in many energy markets. Its production costs were high; much of its technology was outdated. Whilst electricity sales nearly trebled in the twelve years to 1960, those of the gas industry barely increased. Of the several courses open to the industry if it was to maintain, let alone increase, its share of the total energy market, one of the most promising in the early 1960s was the import of liquefied methane (Clark, 1964). The Gas Council's first regular shipment from North Africa arrived in 1964 at Canvey Island on lower Thames-side; from there it is pumped through the national methane pipeline to eight Area Gas Boards in midland and southern England for reforming (to town gas standards) and distribution. Costings are not easy, but by 1965 the methane was probably being landed at about 2·5 cents per 10 megacalories (Mcal), and then transported through the grid and reformed for an additional 1·0 cents—a total cost of about 3·5 cents per 10 Mcal. This compares with a cost of 5 to 6 cents per 10 Mcal for gas produced by conventional methods of coal carbonization. In one respect the Lurgi plants might have worked in reasonable conjunction with these methane imports, since the former produce a lean gas which is ideal for mixing with methane to bring both in line with town gas standards. Methane has a calorific value of 7·3 kilocalories per cubic metre, whereas manufactured gas is normally sold at about 3·5 kilocalories per cubic metre; there is, therefore, a need to reform methane if it is to be used in a conventional public supply system. The costings of a joint Gas Council/National Coal Board study of Lurgi in fact quoted a delivered cost of gas (assuming a high—85%—load factor) of 3·2–3·6 cents per 10 Mcal; this is made up of 3·0 cents for the reformed Lurgi gas ex-works plus between 0·2 and 0·6 cents for transport. These figures, however, put the Lurgi technique in too glamorous a light, for other studies showed the basic cost to be rather higher, and load factors of 85% are very difficult to maintain in the gas industry. Under 1965 technology, therefore, a more realistic delivered cost for Lurgi gas was between 3·6 and 4·0 cents per 10 Mcal.

Barely had the decision to import North African methane been taken, than the costs of making gas from oil products became clearer. Oil was first used by the gas industry to produce water gas. This involved a process demanding low capital outlays and high running costs, qualities which were acceptable for satisfying peak winter loads. It was, therefore, invariably market orientated. But from the late 1950s the processes used for gas manufacture multiplied, and gas came to be produced from a wide range of oil products in a variety of different plants. The new technology was developed by the industry itself, by the oil industry, and by Imperial Chemical Industries. And with the price of oil products under downward pressure, the economic attractiveness of these processes became increasingly evident. Some of the first methods of using oil as a primary fuel were capable of making gas for about the same cost as Lurgi; but the naphtha reforming process subsequently developed by ICI brought the cost down to approximately 2·4–2·8 cents per 10 Mcal. Of course, a good deal depends upon the cost of the feedstock. On the international market, light petroleum distillate (LPD) could be purchased in 1965 on the United States seaboard at about 1·5 cents per 10 Mcal: add 0·6 cents for reforming and the total cost was 2·1 cents—well below the cost of imported methane. British LPD prices were rather higher than this, but even so the advantages of oil-based gas production became so great that even the Lurgi technique could no longer be regarded as economically attractive. As the Second Report from the Select Committee on Nationalized Industries put it, 'The Lurgi process does not point in the direction in which the gas industry is now moving.' Everywhere in Britain the Area Gas Boards began erecting oil plants and closing down their coal gas facilities as fast as possible. For not only is oil-based gas manufacture cheaper under 'optimum' conditions but also relatively more attractive under poor load conditions. A drop in the load factor from 85% to 50% increases the costs of Lurgi gas from 3·0 cents to 4·0 cents per 10 Mcal ex-works; but the increased cost in the ICI process is a mere 0·2 cents. Two further advantages of the oil processes at this time were their lower capital costs (they were about one-sixth of those of conventional carbonization plants and about one-quarter to one-fifth of those of Lurgi) and, in the medium-run at least, the fact that the price of their primary energy source appeared to be subject to downward pressures whereas the same could not be said of British coking coals.

The processes, feedstocks, and purposes of the oil-based plants are quite varied. Some use heavy oil; others use LPD; the Shell process at the Isle of Grain is 'omnivorous'. Propane, butane and refinery gases are also used by the industry. All have somewhat different transport characteristics and costs. And whilst some plants are used to satisfy base load demands, others have been built to meet the peaks. Alongside this variety, however, it is nearly always cheaper to move an oil product by water, rail or pipeline than it is to pump gas. As a result the oil-based gas industry is invariably orientated towards its regional markets. Where oil refineries are located near to a considerable regional demand for gas—as at the Isle of Grain, Fawley and Llandarcy (near Swansea), for instance—the industry has responded by locating gas plants adjacent to them; when a variety of feedstocks are used, and some of them are difficult or expensive to transport, or when refinery gases are used, there is much to commend such a location. Elsewhere oil gas manufacture has tended to be more strictly market orientated and few major centres of demand in the country failed to attract a plant. The exceptions occurred when, as at Immingham, feedstocks were moved to a regional market by water and a nearby break-of-bulk point was used for production. By 1968–9 about 83% of public gas supplies were manufactured from oil. Contrary to the predictions of the 1950s, which had forecast the emergence of a raw material based gas industry in Britain, gas manufacture thus remained until the advent of North Sea supplies of natural gas an essentially market orientated activity.

Location principles of thermal electricity generation

Secondary electricity can be generated from coal, natural gas, oil or nuclear fuel. The locational characteristics of each will be discussed in turn. Taking coal first of all, and assuming once again that generation is possible at either a coal mine (C) or at the load centre or market (M) some kilometres away, the fundamental question concerns the cheapest way to transfer energy from C to M (Manners, 1962c). The coal can be hauled between these two points by road, rail, inland waterway or collier; or it can be carried by conveyor belt or pipeline—the former is unlikely over long distances, but the latter is perhaps increasingly feasible as has been seen (p. 125). Alternatively, electrical energy can be transferred from C to M (see Fig. 16, case a).

Bearing in mind the qualifications noted in the earlier discussion of gas manufacture concerning the range of energy transfer costs using any particular medium, the British case once again provides a basis for initial generalization. In a study relating to power stations of 120 MW and 360 MW with load factors of 50% and 70%, Peterson (1952) has shown that, over a distance of 80 km or more, the cost of collier transport is significantly lower than any alternative form of coal transport (see Figs. 9 and 17). Railway costs are slightly higher than those of inland waterways. The ton/km costs of road transport are the highest of all. These alternative costs of coal haulage are already familiar. The crucial point however is that, sea transport apart, the costs of transmitting electrical energy over comparable distances and in comparable quantities is less expensive than the other forms of energy transfer. An immediate comparison can be seen between these relationships and the alternative costs of transporting energy for the manufacture of gas, with the advantages of the transmission line roughly paralleling those of the gas pipeline.

Although the details vary, these generalizations are confirmed by American studies. Comparing rail transport costs for coal with transmission costs, Phillips (1953) noted that it is cheaper to transfer electrical energy up to distances of 1,120 km under certain conditions; the parameters of his study were a 1,800 MW generating unit, an 80% load factor and three 345 kV double circuits for transmission. An earlier American study by Pierce and George (1948) is in broad agreement; they did stress, however, that the transfer of small quantities of energy is more economically performed by the

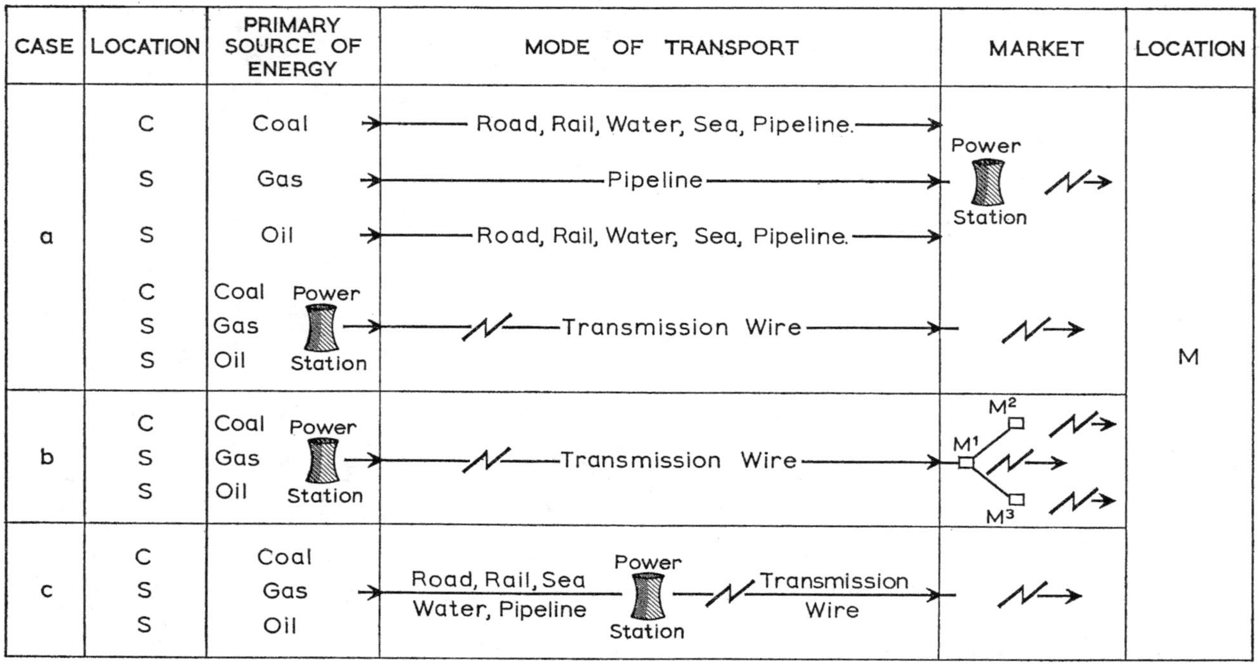

Fig. 16
Locational alternatives for power stations

haulage of coal. Of course, the variety of American ton/km rail rates must not be overlooked for charges are frequently reduced in response to competition from other transport media, including a prospective transmission line. When the Duke Power Company, for example, planned a coalfield location for one of its new plants in 1954, the railways cut their freight rates for coal and the plans were shelved in favour of a market orientated plant (Vogtle, 1956). Intense competition clearly exists between the rail transport of coal and the transmission of electrical energy by high tension line up to about 1,000 km under present technology and costs (Federal Power Commission, 1964, 149 ff.).

These first findings, then, suggest that for distances above a few kilometres and up to about 1,000 km, providing large blocks of energy are being transferred and transmission scale economics exploited, it is more economic to generate electricity at C and transmit it to M than it is to move coal between these two points. The major exception occurs when cheap water transport is available, in which case generation at M becomes the cheaper alternative. The upper and lower limits to the economic transfer of electrical energy between C and M vary from country to country and from situation to situation, but especially with the scale of energy movement.

In the British case quoted by Peterson, the transport of coal by sea for power stations of 350 MW operating at a 70% load factor was more costly than the use of a 275 kV line up to about 360 km but under no circumstance was the transmission of electrical energy economic when a smaller 120 MW power station, with a 50% load factor and using a 132 kV line, was costed (Fig. 17). This is of course a particularly small power station and transmission line by modern standards; the most recent ones in Britain are 2,000 MW units and 400 kV respectively. But it is the importance of the load factor which needs to be underlined at this point since transmission facilities, their economics dominated by high capital costs, demand a high degree of use if they are to attract the necessary investment. Where, therefore, the load factor of a market is low, it is always more economic to transfer the coal and generate at M than it is to use a transmission line—unless generation can be divided between base load and peak load stations (see below). But other factors enter into the equation also. In Belgium, for example, the electricity transmission system in the early 1950s did not exceed 150 kV, and van Mele (1952) pointed out that this low voltage—plus the existence of a good many waterways offering low cost coal transport and the relatively short distances of energy transfer in that country—meant that it was usually more economic to generate at M. In the Phillips'

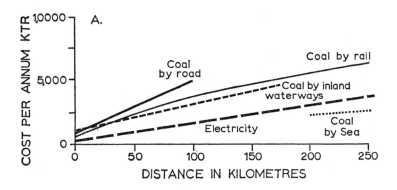

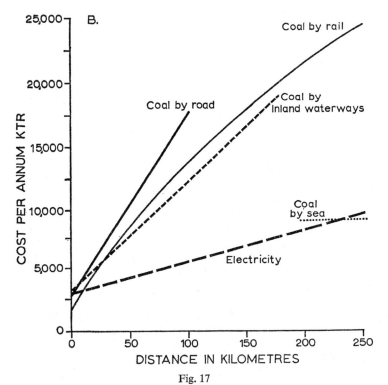

Fig. 17

Energy transport costs for the electricity generating industry in Britain, *c.* 1950. The costs of coal transport and electrical energy transmission apply to A. 132 kV for a 120 MW power station with a 50% load factor; and B. transmission at 275 kV for a 360 MW plant with a 70% load factor. N.B. Costs are expressed in KTR (kilowatt thermique de reference) per annum; this means of expressing costs of energy movement in terms of the capital costs of one kilowatt of thermal generating plant facilitates international comparison. (Source: Peterson, 1952)

study, the upper limit of economic transmission varied with the costs of capital. With a 14% charge upon fixed capital, the economic distance for the transfer of electricity was as low as 240 km; but with an 8% interest rate this distance was increased to 1,120 km. In Italy, too, the costs of capital tend to be relatively high and result in the tendency to generate electricity at M rather than C (Pedante, 1952). In these examples, several of the more important variables in the economics of electrical energy transport are thus revealed. The larger the size of the generating unit, the higher the voltage of the transmission system and load factor, and the lower the rate of interest on fixed capital, the greater is the maximum distance over which it is cheaper to transfer electrical energy rather than move coal.

Where it is possible to divide generating plant geographically into base load and peak load facilities, the former are located in accordance with the several principles already noted. Peak generating plants, however, are almost always located at M, for the obvious reason that generation elsewhere would demand the provision of expensive transmission facilities to M which would be unused or under-used for most of the time. To meet peak load demands, therefore, the use of a discontinuous form of transport plus the storage of the primary fuel at M is much to be preferred. The major exception is in the case of pumped storage schemes, where physiography can have a major influence upon their location.

There are three other variables also germane to this location problem. These are the quality of the coal, the efficiency with which coal can be converted into electricity and the prospects of new transport media. *Ceteris paribus*, the better the quality of coal, the greater becomes the distance over which coal haulage from C is economic. The utilization of low grade coals for electricity generation, such as the peat of Eire or the lignites of Australia and Poland, invariably involves generation at or near to their source. As the quality of the coal increases, so the costs of transporting a given quantity of energy in the form of coal fall, and the advantages of generating at M increase. Thus Conrad (1955) was able to contrast British and French experience in the location of thermal generating plants. In Britain during the 1960s an increasing proportion of London's energy requirements were generated in the East Midlands and then transmitted to the capital, while in France the electricity needs for Paris continued to be satisfied by transporting coal from the Nord coalfield plus the use of market orientated power stations. Conrad lists three major factors in explanation: the higher rate of interest upon fixed capital in France, the relatively low cost of coal haulage on

French railways and the rather higher calorific value of coals obtained from the Nord coalfield. Variations in boiler efficiency also affect the distance of effective competition from transmission lines, and thereby influence the location of generating plants. If the efficiency of the boilers in a power station is decreased, the maximum economic transmission distance between C and M increases accordingly; this is because more coal is required for the production of a kilowatt of electricity, the unit costs of hauling coal for generation are increased, and the effectiveness of discontinuous media is reduced. Historically, the steady improvement in power station efficiency generally has had some bearing upon the location of generating plant, as will be seen later.

The new forms of transporting energy which appear most likely prospectively to influence the location of generating plants are the pipeline and transmission by direct current. The effects of these innovations pull in opposite directions. American experience suggests that the ton/km costs of pumping considerable and regular quantities of coal for base-load power stations through a wide diameter pipeline can be of the same order as the costs of small coastal vessels. This means that in all circumstances where pipelines prove to be feasible, the generation of electricity at M will tend to be more economic. Direct transmission, on the other hand, is both lowering the unit costs of transmitting electrical energy, and extending the distance over which it is economically practicable. Its effects, therefore, are to increase the distance between C and M over which a transmission solution is preferred.

A slight variation upon the original postulate is the existence of a demand for electricity at C as well as at M. Assuming that the load at C could be most economically served by a local power station, and that comparative energy transport costs suggest the advantage of generation at M in order to meet the demand there, it may be most advantageous to build two interconnected power stations, one at C and the other at M. If, for example, the peak demands of the two regions do not coincide, the interlinkage of the two sets of generating units would allow certain economies in the provision of plant to cater for peak demands. Such an interlinkage would also create a more stable electricity supply system, making the provision of energy at both C and M more reliable. This is a simple engineering case of increased redundancy leading to greater stability, and it once again stresses the importance of distinguishing between grids and transmission systems. Once the interlinkage of C and M is established on these or other grounds, it may well then become more economic to supply some of the base load demand at M from C—in so far as the capital costs of the line have already been sunk, and such a practice would save some of the costs of coal haulage from C. As a result, a situation in which it is basically more economic to generate for M at M might well become one in which it is advantageous to generate a part of the base load for M at C and the rest at M. In this example the tendency for system economics sometimes to displace energy transfer economics can readily be seen. It is a tendency which is explored further later in this chapter.

An alternative assumption to the single load centre at M is the situation in which several geographically distinct markets for electricity are postulated. This is, in fact, a much more realistic assumption to make. Rarely punctiform, the market for energy is usually areal in character, with several foci of heavier demand. This situation can be represented by the three load centres in Fig. 16, case b, where the alternative to generating at C is three separate generating units at M_1, M_2, and M_3. Individually these three units cannot achieve the same economies of scale as a single large generating unit equalling their combined capacities. In consequence, the economic distance for the transmission of electrical energy from C becomes significantly greater than in the case of a single load centre at M; in the study of Phillips the distance increased from 368 to 528 km.

The foregoing discussion has assumed that it is possible to locate a power station at C. In many circumstances, however, this is not so, due perhaps to the absence of cooling water, to the insecurity of sub-soil conditions or to the inadequacy of provisions for ash disposal. An initial transfer of coal from the mine at C to an intermediate point B (see Fig. 16, case c) as a result becomes necessary before generation can take place. The question now arises as to whether the more economic location for a power plant is at B or at M. The advantages of transferring electrical energy from B to M are very much less than from C to M. A large proportion of coal transfer costs lies in the initial loading expenses rather than in the line-haul operation; and should generation take place at B, these loading costs have also to be carried by the energy transmitted from B to M since coal has first to be moved by rail or road from C to B. In other words, once coal is loaded into railway wagons and carried 30 or 40 km, it is usually more economic to continue the energy transfer by rail rather than to generate at B.

The forces influencing the alternative costs of energy transfer for coal-fired power stations, and hence their orientation, can therefore be summarized as follows. Within a given geography of resources, the most important factors are the distance involved in energy transfer, the type, the route and the rates of the transport media available and the characteristics—that is the size and the nature—of the market. The particular technology employed, both the scale of transport operations and the efficiency of fuel use, plus the rate of interest on capital are also especially influential in swaying the balance of advantage in one direction or another.

Two other fossil fuels, natural gas and oil, are also used to generate electricity. Assuming that supplies of these sources of energy are available (either indigenously or through import) at S, what is likely to be the orientation of electricity generation to serve a geographically distinct market at M? (See Fig. 16, case a). As in the case of coal-fired generation, different national and political situations affect individual solutions. Matters such as the size of the market at M, the efficiency of electricity generation and energy transfer, the physical geography of the region between S and M and the nature of the load all bear upon the problem. Under Western European conditions, a study by Falomo (1960) suggests that, where natural gas is to be used and the pressure at which it is found is low, it is better to generate near its source and to transmit electrical energy; if, on the other hand, the gas is found at high pressure, lower compression costs make it economic to pump the gas to M, provided that market is not more than 400 km away. This distance is based upon Italian experience and costings. Yet gas is piped for power station use from Lacq in the south-west of France to Paris—a much greater distance than 400 km—and from Texas to New York and Boston (see p. 79), suggesting that the upper distance between S and M exhibits considerable international variation. Indeed, under North American conditions as reported by Pierce and George, the transmission of electrical energy from S to M is invariably more expensive than pumping natural gas.

These contrasts have a number of roots. In the first place the size of the pipeline and the efficiency of its construction are factors of considerable importance. Larger pipes and more efficient pipe-laying techniques are to be found in the United States, making the cost of natural gas transport in that country relatively low by international standards. Second, the study by Falomo refers to electricity transfers at 380 kV, whereas the costings of the American study apply to much lower voltage transmissions. And third, it is the practice of North American pipeline companies to maintain a steady flow of gas through their facilities by the sale of very cheap 'interruptible' gas to industrial consumers (see pp. 62-3); this technique, rarely practised in Western Europe, keeps down the unit costs of gas transport. In sum, therefore, the most advantageous orientation of a power station burning natural gas is primarily influenced by the diameter of the gas pipeline and the voltage of the competing transmission line, the pressure of the natural gas at its source, and the load factor at the market, including the way in which its fluctuations are met.

As in the case of coal, but in contrast to that of natural gas, oil can be transported by several media. In this case, however, the solution to the location problem of electricity generation is relatively simple. The cheapest means of moving energy between S and M is invariably achieved by transporting oil and generating at the market. This is a direct response to the low costs of oil transport. But it does not mean that when oil is available, it will always be used to generate electricity. Its cost at S and the efficiency with which it is used, measured against the cost of alternative fuels, also need to be considered. Even in oil-rich Texas very little oil is used to generate electricity since natural gas is a much cheaper fuel at source (see pp. 79–80). When electricity is generated from oil, then, and transport costs are the major determinant of power station orientation, the transmission of electrical energy by high tension line from S to M is out of the question. System economics can, however, overrule transport costs. When an existing transmission line links S and M, or when a line needs to be provided in order to ensure the security of electricity supplies at both (and intermediate) places, the balance of advantage can swing back to S as in the coal case discussed earlier.

Similar to oil, yet even more emphatically, the generation of electricity from nuclear power is invariably performed at M because of the low unit costs of transporting nuclear fuels. Naturally, the need for solid foundations, cooling water, public safety and the like are also important and, as was seen in Chapter 2, they tend to result in nuclear power stations being sited some distance from M. In principle, however, one great advantage of nuclear power is its locational flexibility.

The transport factor, therefore, expresses itself in contradictory directions as it influences the location of power stations. For coal-fired generation, it encourages an orientation towards the source of coal as markets increase in size, as generating units become larger and as transmission voltages increase. The increasing amount of mine-mouth generation in the United States empirically substantiates this point. Further, the more dispersed the market, the poorer the quality of coal and the lower the rate of interest on capital, the stronger becomes the pull of the coalfield. The deterioration of load factors and the increase of boiler efficiencies, however, work in the opposite direction. In addition, the availability of water transport or the construction of a coal pipeline, the impossibility of generation on the coalfield, and considerable distances between C and M also encourage generation at the market. When natural gas is used as the primary fuel, the proximity of S and M and the existence of low gas pressures at its source encourage electricity generation at S; poor load factors and highly efficient pipeline operations, on the other hand, encourage market generation. In the cases of oil-fired and nuclear power stations, however, the alternative costs of transport invariably advocate a market location for electricity production. In sum, the orientation of electricity generation in so far as it depends upon transport economics is determined primarily by the type of fuel used, the distance of energy transfer, the range of transport facilities available and the characteristics of the market.

These generalizations concerning the location of secondary electricity production are particularly important in the early stages of the development of an economy's or a region's supply system. As that system matures, however, the crudeness of the assumptions become more apparent and the relevance of the analysis less immediate. Central to this shift of emphasis is the variety of roles which can be played by high voltage transmission lines. In addition to their function as a means of bulk energy transfer, they can also be used in a distribution capacity (to move energy to a load centre from the nearest available power station) and to interconnect stations to form a grid, the economics of which derive from the behaviour of the production–transfer–distribution system as a whole. Once a transmission line has been provided for one purpose, of course, it is possible to use it for the others, and the economics of the separate roles become somewhat blurred. Indeed, the single-purpose evaluation of a transmission line becomes somewhat unmeaningful.

The ability of large 2,000 MW power stations to run on base load depends heavily upon the pooling of demand over extensive areas and these areas can usually be most economically served by transmission facilities which combine the three functions noted above. Quite frequently, therefore, schemes for the bulk transfer of electrical energy are regarded as a 'graft' onto an existing grid system, with much of the (joint) costs attributed to their interconnection role. The Federal Power Commission (1964, 208) has noted, for example, that 'While multiple use loading cannot be imposed upon transmission lines without providing adequate design capacity, added capacity can usually be built into lines at relatively small additional cost and considerable economy can thus be gained through such joint utilization.' Lane and Chorlton (1966) in their study of the

British 275 kV grid assert that the facility was planned primarily for the pooling of spare plant and was fully justified economically for this purpose alone; the capacity for bulk inter-regional transfer of large blocks of energy was easily incorporated within the system. The obvious conclusion is that the economics of transmission are greatly improved if bulk transfer capacity is constructed as part of a major grid development.

Moreover, as an electricity supply system develops and becomes more complex, so the simplifying assumptions of a single centre of production and a single (or even three) foci of demand become increasingly remote; and investment in additional generating capacity as often as not demands that consideration be given not only to the best location for a power station, but also to the question of which primary fuel of the several alternatives often available will offer the lowest costs. It is this latter question which tends in fact to be answered first. Within a complex production-supply system, all the production units are listed in order of their generating costs, in Britain called the 'merit order'. As the demand for electricity increases throughout the day or year, production units start generating electricity to feed the transmission and distribution network successively in ascending order of operating costs; this feature is constrained, of course, by the capacity of the individual sections of the grid. At the peak of demand, it is the most costly generating units which satisfy the market. As each new generating unit is installed in a system, it takes its place in the merit order. If it is a nuclear power station, characterized by exceptionally low operating costs, it will be placed at the top of the merit order and meet base-load demands. If it is a coal-fired station, on the other hand, it may be that existing oil- or gas-fired stations—as well as any nuclear plant—will be given precedence should their operating costs be lower; the new coal station might then only be used when demand begins to reach the mid load phase. Some stations are designed from the start for such operation, and yet others are specifically installed to meet the peak. Obviously, the higher a new station enters the merit order the greater will be the number of other stations in the system whose position will be changed; with a change in position, they will meet a slightly different part of the load and in turn their fuel inputs and costs will be altered. The point to be noted therefore is that the economics of a new power station cannot be isolated from the total production–supply system within which it will serve.

With the development of many different types of generating plant, each with varying fixed/operating cost ratios, it has become necessary to develop new approaches towards the economic appraisal of alternative investment projects. The approach which increasingly is favoured seeks to measure the effect of the alternative new generating plants upon the whole production–supply system over the lifetime of the plant, with the objective of minimizing the present net worth of system costs (Hauser, 1971; Berrie, 1967; Cash, 1967). The capital and operating costs of each new station are calculated (and discounted to their present value) for each year of the station's expected life, and from these costs are subtracted any (discounted) savings which stem from the changed nature of the system as a whole over the same time period. The savings are particularly important in the appraisal of nuclear power stations. This approach to incremental investment in a power system demands the availability of a 'background plan'—that is an estimate of the production–supply system as a whole—for each year under consideration; this plan is obtained by an examination of possible patterns of development using different mixes of primary fuels and possible interconnection assumptions. Obviously, however, the faster demand is growing and the more rapidly the economics of different types of electricity generation change, the less accurate is the background plan likely to be and hence the poorer will be the quality of the investment appraisal.

A slightly modified approach towards such an investment appraisal is to calculate the return on any extra capital investment when one power station at a higher fixed cost is selected in preference to one with a lower capital cost (Hauser, 1971). The use of gas turbines involves a relatively small fixed cost outlay per unit of electricity; if a plant with higher capital costs, but lower operating costs, is installed and an appropriate load is available then the savings in operating expenses will yield a return on the extra capital investment. This return will be worthwhile provided the appropriate test rate of discount is met or exceeded. In such studies of investment alternatives, there is, of course, a need to make assumptions about the location of plants under consideration. The existence of a grid to serve a complex hierarchy of markets and overlapping centres of primary fuel supply is given. It is natural therefore that the investment alternatives are tested with the generating plants located as close as possible to the lowest cost centres of their respective primary fuels. It is a style of appraisal which tends as a result to encourage the location of generating plant as near as possible to the source of its primary fuel.

The validity of all these principles can be seen by examining the changing distribution of conventional electricity generation in Britain. The first electricity stations were built just over ninety years ago. Because demands were small in the first instance and because transmission was technically difficult over any significant distance, power stations were built as near as siting conditions would allow to the centre of their loads, with coal being transported to them. Although the industry was liberated in the technical sense from this urban base in the inter-war years, it nevertheless remained market-orientated. By then, however, it was regional rather than a local markets which attracted the industry. Whereas the gas industry had to wait until the late 1940s and early '50s for its first major grid facilities, those of the electricity industry were first installed some twenty years earlier. Between 1930 and 1936 a national electricity grid system was built in Britain at 132 kV and allowed two developments to take place. First, many of the smaller and less efficient works were either closed down or were relegated to meet regional peak load demands. And, second, the exchange of electricity between those markets where the incidence of peak market demands differed allowed considerable savings in the provision of peak generating capacity. Although advocates of electrical energy transfer from the coalfields to the larger markets in southern England were to be found during the inter-war years, the long distance transmission of energy did not in fact take place. Many factors contributed to this situation (Rawstron, 1955).

In terms of alternative transport costs, some advantage appeared likely to be gained by base load transfers between certain parts of the country. Admittedly, the transmission of electrical energy was not economic when it was competing with the transport of coal by sea; it was, therefore, out of the question as far as energy transfers from the coalfields of North East England and South Wales to London were concerned. But for the movement of base load electrical energy in bulk from the East Midlands and Yorkshire to London, transmission was competitive with all other forms of land transport above a distance of about 80 km. (It was not, of course, economic to transfer mid loads or peak loads over that distance.) Progress in plant design, however, more than anything else prevented the development of such a long distance base load transmission. The rapidly increasing efficiency of the turbo-generator was such that the attention of the industry's management was focussed particularly upon this source of savings rather than upon any possible location economy. This was not unreasonable since nearly 70% of the costs of the industry were composed of generation costs. Moreover, the growth of demand plus the rapid rate of obsolescence of generating plants in such circumstances were such that any one generator did not remain on the base load for more than a few years. The much greater effici-

F

ency and lower operating costs of newer plants soon relegated it to
mid and peak load working, a phase of generation which was pre-
ferably market orientated. In other words, certain short term advantages in generating on the coalfields were foregone as a consequence
of the knowledge that in the longer run plants built at or near the
market would be efficiently located to meet non-base load demands.
Thus, electricity generation remained essentially market orientated
in Britain until after World War II.

Following nationalization in 1947 a change in the industry's
location policy came about. It was anticipated at that time that
substantial improvements in the efficiency of generation were at an
end. In turn this focussed the attention of management upon a
search for the best locations for electricity generation, and a desire
to minimize transport costs as a means of gaining yet further economies (Conrad, 1955). An initial decision was taken to improve the
efficiency and lower the cost of energy transmission by superim-
posing upon the 132 kV grid a new 275 kV grid which could serve
in a bulk transfer as well as an interconnection capacity (see Fig. 19).
The new grid meant that there emerged clear economic advantages
to be derived from locating new power stations on the coalfields—
at least in certain geographical circumstances. The economy of
water-borne coal transport from the coalfield in North East England
to the energy deficient markets in South East England remained. Mid
and peak load stations, especially designed to operate as such, were
also built in the major market areas away from the coalfields. But
as far as the inland markets of southern England and Lancashire
were concerned, markets whose electricity at that time was generated
from low cost East Midlands' and South Yorkshire coal, the case
for coalfield generation and base load transmission was very strong
indeed. As a result, a decision was made to build a series of new,
large power stations along the rivers Trent, Aire and Calder, designed to meet the base load electricity demands of southern England
and Lancashire for many years.

As a result of this new location policy of the electricity generating
industry, the map of energy flow in Britain began rapidly to change
(Fig. 18). Whereas as late as 1955 the greater part of the energy
movement from the coalfields of eastern and North East England for
or after the generation of electricity was in the form of coal, transported by rail or collier, and a mere 0·8 million coal equivalent tons
travelled by wire, by 1960 the figure was nearly 5 million c.e.t. By
1965 the bulk of these transfers took place along the transmission
wires of the Central Electricity Generating Board (CEGB), especially
energy flows from the East Midlands; and by 1970 about 10 million

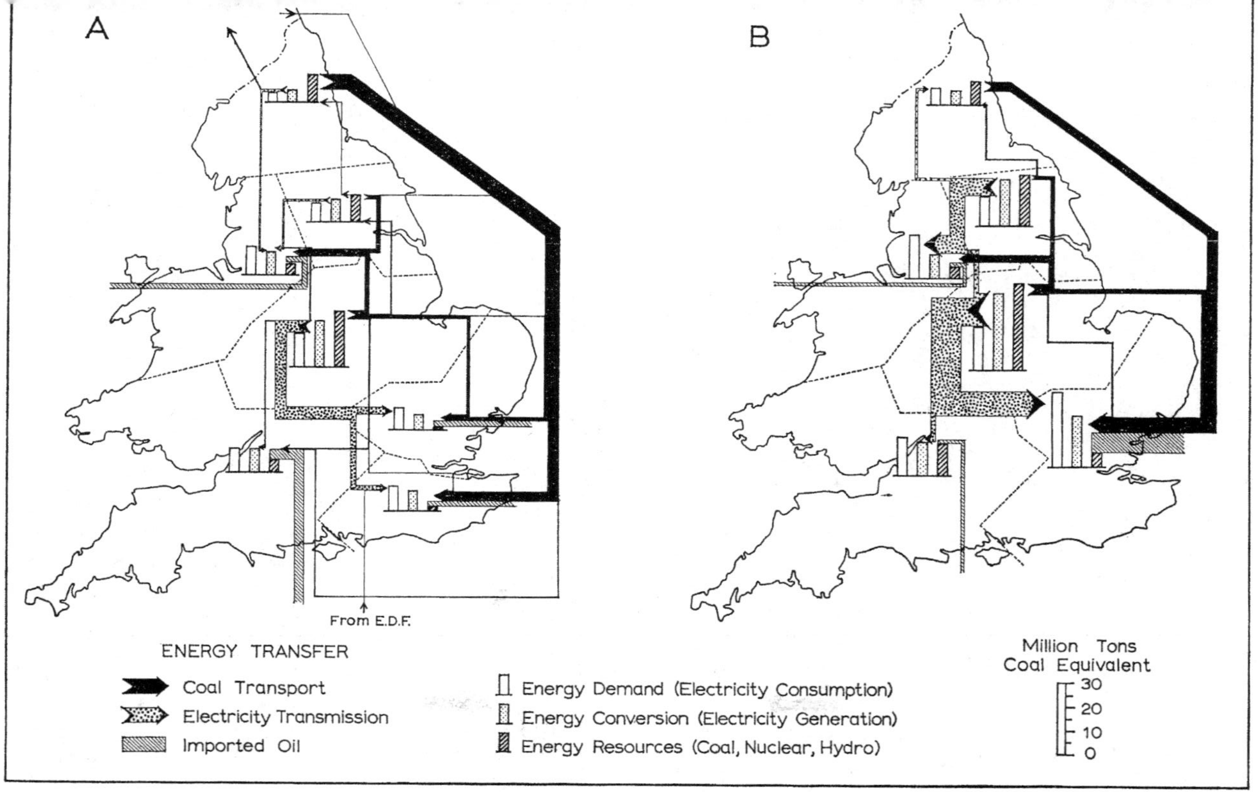
A
B
From E.D.F.
ENERGY TRANSFER
Coal Transport
Electricity Transmission
Imported Oil
Energy Demand (Electricity Consumption)
Energy Conversion (Electricity Generation)
Energy Resources (Coal, Nuclear, Hydro)
Million Tons
Coal Equivalent
30
20
10
0

Fig. 18

Energy transfers of the Central Electricity Generating Board, *c.* 1960 and 1970. (Source: CEGB)

c.e.t. of electrical energy was transmitted into South East England. Similarly, the movement of energy into southern Lancashire in 1955 was dominated by rail-borne coal, whereas by 1970 this coal flow had in large measure been replaced by the transmission of electrical energy. The growth of electricity demand in south-western England in the same period was also met largely by transmission rather than by transfer of coal (Clark, 1962).

This pattern of energy transfers, however, essentially reflects decisions taken by the electricity authorities in the late 1940s and early '50s. Since then, many of the assumptions underlying the policy have demanded careful re-examination, and by the middle 1960s the justification of a coalfield orientation for a significant part of electricity generation in Britain began to look questionable. To start with, the basic characteristics of the national energy market have been transformed several times. The country emerged from the war with rather traditional assumptions concerning her energy supplies, in particular the proposition that the economy would continue to be powered largely by coal. By the middle 1950s, however, it became only too clear that the country in general, and the CEGB in particular, would not in the future be able to rely upon domestic sources of energy, for the National Coal Board simply could not guarantee the electricity authority all the coal which it seemed likely to require in the foreseeable future. The immediate reaction by the government to this state of affairs was a rejection of one obvious alternative, oil. At that time the magnitude of the world's oil resources was grossly underestimated, and there was a political reluctance to allow the country to develop too heavy a reliance upon oil imports. Some power stations were converted from coal to oil firing as a short term measure to bridge the energy gap, but it was decided that the long term solution should be sought through harnessing atomic power. The programme and its fluctuating fortunes were discussed in Chapter 2 (pp. 37–42).

By 1960, however, the situation had changed again. A period of energy surpluses was at hand. The vast oil wealth of the Middle East and North Africa had been proved; and, through a loss of markets to oil, there was more domestic coal available for the electricity generating industry. In addition, the improved efficiency of generation by conventional techniques had left the costs of nuclear power still above those of coal-fired and oil-fired stations. The use of oil for British electricity generation has had a somewhat checkered history. Adopted because of earlier forecasts of coal shortages, its use was deliberately curtailed five years later as a result of a growing surplus of British coal. Stations which had been

converted to oil-firing were reconverted to coal at the expense of
the National Coal Board. After about 1962 in Scotland, and 1964–5
in England and Wales—the years when oil, despite a tax of £0·10
per ton, began to display a marginal cost advantage over coal in
many locations—the use of oil in British power stations began to
rise once again and for the first time stations were designed and built
from the outset to burn oil and satisfy base load demands. By mid-
1969 oil was the primary fuel for about 14% of the country's electricity. In that year there were fifteen power stations burning heavy
fuel oil, and a further four large ones were under construction.
Shortly afterwards, in the wake of further coal shortages, permission
was given by the Minister of Power to convert several existing stations to burn oil and two to burn natural gas, and the CEGB had
announced plans for the construction of additional new oil-fired
plants (Manners, 1971, 176). Like the manufactured gas industry,
therefore, by 1970 the British electricity industry was no longer
based solely upon coal. In contrast with gas, however, it was a
four-fuel rather than a two-fuel industry.

To return to the location theme, nuclear power stations are characterized by their regional mobility. They are most competitive where
coal has to bear high transport costs, and as a result the first generation of stations, and most in the second programme, were located
in those parts of the country which had considerable energy demands
and yet were deficient in local coal (p. 39 ff.). The nuclear stations,
therefore, are oriented to their markets—although clearly siting
and safety factors have precluded their construction *at* their markets.
It is in these same 'domestic energy deficient' markets that oil-fired
generation appeared in the first instance—partly because of the
higher cost of coal there and partly because it is in these parts of the
country that the refineries are located. In the 1970s the bulk of
British refining capacity will be on lower Thames-side, Southampton
Water, Milford Haven, Merseyside and Humberside; the major oil-
fired power stations, existing and proposed, have a similar geography.
There is, therefore, a tendency for new, large, non-coal based power
stations to be located in the south and west of the country. These
stations, it should be noted, are the ones with the lowest operating
costs (nuclear because of the nature of their cost structure; oil
because of their competitive primary fuel costs) and by the
early 1970s, the number of stations in this category will be large
enough to supply a large share of the base load of the whole British
system. By that time, therefore, grid economics will begin to demand
an off-peak transfer of energy from what is domestically an energy
deficient zone in the south of the country to an energy surplus zone

in the north, since it is those stations with the lowest operating costs which are always given preference to satisfy base load demands. This in itself is an upset for post-war location policy. But the economics of locating coal-fired stations has also changed.

The post-war policy of the CEGB was based upon the assumption that there would be no further major developments in the technology of electricity generation and that the large new power stations on the coalfields would be able to generate on base load for many years to come. However, the 1960s in fact have seen considerable improvements in the efficiency of power stations. In the early 1950s a thermal efficiency of about 30 % was thought to be the technical maximum but by 1970 efficiencies of over 38 % were being obtained in the newest stations. Likewise, the cost of generating capacity fell dramatically: stations planned in 1955 had a capital cost of £55 per kW, whereas those under construction in the late 1960s cost only £40 per kW. In other words, some of the units built deliberately to generate base load from East Midland and South Yorkshire sites within a decade were relatively inefficient and high cost. As a consequence they were shifted to middle and peak load working much sooner than was expected. Moreover, 1964 saw a significant reversal of the long term trend in energy transport costs in Britain. Until then, transmission costs had persistently tended to fall relative to rail freights. But the agreement in that year between the CEGB and British Railways (and the adoption of unit or block trains, 32-ton hopper cars and automatic loading and discharge) led to a significant reduction in coal freight rates to several new coal-fired power stations. The new ton/km rate over a long haul represented a 50 % reduction on the old ones. This development finally undermined the rationale of the CEGB's immediate post-war thinking. That same policy of building coalfield orientated base load plants for the energy deficient markets of southern England was meeting another snag in any case—the problem of finding sites with adequate supplies of water—and therefore it could be argued that the new rail freight agreements simply gave the Board greater flexibility to do what it would increasingly have had to do in any case, namely, generate further away from the coalfields and nearer to the markets for electricity.

There is one more new location factor to consider. This is the effects of the grid (Fig. 19) which was up-graded to 400 kV from the middle 1960s onwards and which was the result of a complex interplay of both economic forces and amenity considerations (Dreyfus, 1964; Hauser, 1971). The grid was justified in the first instance by the additional stability which it gave to the whole of the electricity supply system, by the facility it offered for a greater sharing of peak capacity, and by the fact that it allowed the large modern 2,000 MW stations to generate to their full capacity immediately they were built. Once such a grid was in existence, its geography—rather than that of markets or raw material sources—became the

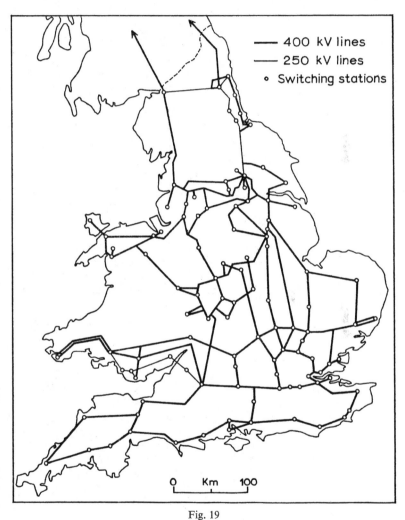

Fig. 19

250 kV and 400 kV grid of the Central Electricity Generating Board, 1970. (Source: CEGB)

starting point for power station location decisions. If a suitable site is found close to the grid and if a primary source of energy can be transported to that site at a competitive delivered price, the case for generating there becomes strong indeed. This is not to argue that once you have a grid superimposed upon a hierarchy of markets, locational choice within the network becomes irrelevant. There is a limit to the amount of electrical energy which can be transferred between any two regions of the country—only about 8,000 MW can be moved between the East Midlands and the south of England, for example. But it *does* mean that the existence of the 400 kV grid has substantially widened the market area within which a power station can be satisfactorily located. It also means that the locational issue becomes geographically less clearly defined than in the past and that other factors (cooling water, pollution, amenity issues and the like) can play a more important part in location decisions than was once the case. Even more important, grid or system economics has meant that the locational issue has ceased to be a central concern of the authorities, and that their attention has come to be more persistently focussed upon the questions of choice between different types of generating plant. It is following these decisions that the greatest savings can be made today for the production and transmission phase of the electricity industry. It has even been suggested that in the future the grid system of England and Wales might be divided into two or more parts, each with a balanced load and generating capacity, and with only limited interconnection between them (Dreyfus, 1964).

With the advent of nuclear power and oil-fired power stations, following the steady improvement in the efficiency of electricity generation and as a result of grid economics, the raw material orientation of part of the country's base load electricity production has become increasingly difficult to justify. Rather like the manufactured gas industry, therefore, power stations are clearly in the process of becoming wholly market orientated once again. But whereas twenty years ago the markets to which it was drawn were local, today it is the large regional market, geographically extended by the existence of the high voltage grid, which is drawing the new investment of the electricity generating industry.

8

POLITICAL FACTORS (I)

Regulation of production, transport, prices and consumption – stimulation and protection – participation in energy industries

As in so much of economic life, 'the invisible hand' of Adam Smith has been playing a diminishing role in energy geography in recent years. At all scales, from the international oil business of the Western world to the state-owned energy industries of the Soviet Union, and from the regional power authorities of the United States to the local utility company operating under the watchful eye of a public authority, the impress of political decisions is clear. This chapter and the next seek to make explicit some of the more important aspects of this political factor. They consider the way in which governments and their agencies regulate, stimulate, protect and participate in energy production and consumption. National and international energy policies are also considered, and, in passing, consideration is given to the motives which underlie these political actions.

Regulation of production
The international regulation of energy production is a rare but not unknown phenomenon. One of the better examples is provided by the European Coal and Steel Community (ECSC) which is attempting to bring about a common energy market for its member countries. More than anything else this has involved adjusting the coal industries of some member countries to a shrinking market and, with the removal of tariffs, to each other. In West Germany and France pits have been closed down and production deliberately

F*

curtailed; but the biggest problem for the Authority has been in Belgium. In 1957 the coal industry there accounted for 12% of the value of that country's industrial production, 10% of its industrial workers and a considerable quantity of purchases from the Belgian economy. Its importance in the regional economies of the Borinage and Centre coalfields was even greater, for 62% of the industrial workers on the former and 38% of the workers on the latter were engaged in mining. Yet these coalfields suffer from geological difficulties, old pits, outworn investment and worked-out seams. Both the prices and the output of the Belgian coal industry in the middle 1950s were hopelessly ill-adapted to the contemporary European energy market, a situation exacerbated by the fact that the industry had been supported by government subsidy for a long time.

During the last fifteen years or so, some adjustments have been made. From having 143 pits in 1952, to 120 in 1957, 74 in 1960 and 32 in 1969, the Belgian industry has contracted in size, and reduced its labour force substantially. An output of *circa* 39 million tons in 1952 was simultaneously reduced by more than 50%. The effects of this contraction and the pit closures upon both local mining villages and upon the country as a whole were offset to some extent by the payment of compensation by the High Authority and by the temporary continuation of the government subsidy. Further, the Authority advised, and the Belgian Government legislated, that in order to ease the impact of this programme, coal imports into Belgium should be restricted and destocking by coal merchants should be limited to 20% in any one year. This policy of the High Authority led to the contraction of production in the less efficient mines at a faster pace than had essentially nationalist policies prevailed, but more slowly than if a free market in energy supplies had suddenly been created.

By 1970 it was clear that the Organization of Petroleum Exporting States (OPEC), founded a decade earlier, had become not only a means whereby the underdeveloped oil-producing States could present a reasonably common front to the international oil companies in price and tax negotiations, but also a possible means of regulating the production of crude oil on the international scale. Certainly, many of the member States of OPEC remain hopeful that during periods of oil surplus a system of quotas might be instituted between themselves in order to stablize or even increase prices in real terms, and to reduce some of the 'waste' often associated with a free international market for oil. For these countries some form of international 'prorationing' is a very attractive idea, although its qualified effectiveness within the United States does not guarantee its success when national sovereignties are involved.

The exploitation of oil within the United States has traditionally operated within the legal framework of the 'rule of capture', by which any person is able to exploit the mineral resources under his own land, and—in the case of the oil and natural gas industries—under anyone else's land for that matter, since oil belongs to anyone who can bring it to the surface. This tradition and law—which has embarrassed conservationists and liberals for generations—has been responsible for a considerable wastage of oil in the past, since it is obviously advantageous for any single producer to recover as much oil as possible from a field before some other producer takes it. As a consequence most American oilfields (the new Alaska field is a notable exception) are characterized by an over-investment in pumping facilities, and it was inevitable that some form of control over exploitation should become necessary.

The regulation of the oil industry, piecemeal in the first instance, really began with the work of the Interstate Oil Compact Commission (IOCC), founded in 1935. With no legal authority, it sought to provide a forum for the interchange of ideas and information concerning the exploitation of oil reserves between States, and to encourage conservation practices. The word conservation is used here in the sense of preventing waste. Through the IOCC most oil-producing States came to accept prorationing, by which each producing area is given a quota of oil as its maximum output for each month. This quota is based upon estimates of demand made by the Bureau of Mines, and the States allot output between themselves and their producing areas (Resources for the Future, 1968, 31 ff.). Not all the States are willing to conform to the system; Illinois, for example, still places no restrictions upon its domestic oil producers, and in other States compliance with prorationing is voluntary rather than compulsory. There are in addition in most producing areas a number of 'stripper wells', representing the last stage in the exploitation of an oil pool, over which there is no State control whatsoever. However, the overall effect of these quota arrangements has been enormous. Throughout most of the 1950s and '60s, for example, spare pumping capacity which was 'shut in' for the lack of a market could have produced an extra 2 million tons of oil each week, an equivalent of about 30% of actual oil production; and, on average, American oilfields are today pumping oil on only about nine or ten days in each month.

Without these controls, consumers in the United States might have had relatively cheap oil in the short run; but there would have been considerable physical waste also and the cost and price of domestic oil would inevitably have soared in the longer term. 'Each producer, operating under the traditional rule of capture, would be forced to withdraw oil from his well as quickly as possible--before his neighbour drained it from under his land—and the result would be above ground and below ground waste of this irreplaceable natural resource' (Joint Economic Committee, 1960, 581). Prorationing was, and is, of course, enlightened self-interest on the part of the oil producers, for one of the major motives behind its institution (in spite of the passionate disclaimers to the contrary) was not so much an ideal of conservation, but rather a desire to maintain and stabilize the price of oil. As Watkins (1944) put it: 'Price stablization is a thinly veiled objective of the institution of prorationing, and, in fact, as it has developed in the several State jurisdictions, it may be stated unreservedly to have been everywhere the dominant consideration.'

Attempts have also been made after the wasteful extravagances of the early years of oil production in the United States to encourage, through State conservation officials, as complete a use of each oil-well and oilfield as possible—rather than allow the exploitation of the most accessible oil and then the abandonment of the rest. In particular, natural gas and steam have been used to maintain the pressure in oil pools, and have allowed a fuller use of many fields. Strategic arguments, in particular the need to conserve domestic oil supplies for emergencies and war, have been used in discussions aimed at offsetting the excesses of 'market' priorities.

Such State bodies as the Railroad Commission of Texas and the Department of Conservation of the State of Louisiana, therefore, have come to exercise a very powerful and necessary control over the United States domestic oil industry. They have limited the quantities of oil available in place and time; they have influenced both the price of oil and the intensity of oil competition in energy markets; and hence, they have helped to mould the geography of oil production.

The regulation of oil production in the United States has its counterpart in most producing countries where controls over oil exploitation seek to ensure the rational development of oil deposits and appropriate resource conservation. In Canada, for example, a system of quotas is administered by the Provinces. In Venezuela, the government, owning all exploration rights, insists upon specified conservation practices and a control over the distribution and the spacing of wells; it also demands the maintenance of certain oil-gas ratios. Whether or not there is a 'natural' tendency for it to produce surpluses, experience has shown that the oil industry tends to alternate between periods of surpluses and periods of deficiencies;

as Frankel once put it, 'There is always too little or too much.' In times of over-production, therefore, few would deny that the basic health of the industry demands some form of regulation which can prevent a rapid fall in the price of oil and the wasteful use of resources. Reluctant though the international oil industry might have been to negotiate with OPEC in 1970–1, these points were not lost on them after more than a decade of weakening market prices for oil.

Regulation of transport, prices and consumption
To the extent that the geography of energy is shaped by the differential costs which separate competing sources of power from the markets which they might serve, governmental influences upon the efficiency and the costs of energy transport are clearly of considerable significance. In many Western European countries, for example, for some time railway operations have to a greater or lesser degree been subsidized by the State; since the greater part of the coal produced there is moved to its markets by rail, its competitive position is as a result somewhat enhanced by the existence of such transport policies. Again, as amenity considerations assume a greater importance in the considerations of physical planning authorities, and as the electricity industry is required increasingly to underground or re-route its transmission and grid facilities, costs are imposed upon that industry which are bound ultimately to be reflected in its size as well as its geography.

In the United States also the importance of public regulation in the operation of the energy transport system is everywhere apparent. The Inter-State Commerce Commission, for example, supervises the rates charged for the rail movements of energy and, it can be claimed, has tended to delay somewhat the response of the coal industry to the competitive challenges of alternative fuels. The Jones Act of 1920 still requires that coastwise shipments of energy be carried in American vessels, built in American yards and manned by American crews; the relatively high cost (by international standards) of such a law not only has encouraged the use of pipelines for oil transport, but also has weakened the competitive position of water-borne oil and coal in relation to alternative sources of energy. Pipelines, too, are subject to public regulation in the United States. Those which operate in inter-state commerce are regulated by the Federal Power Commission (FPC) in regard to their rates and services under the Natural Gas Act of 1938. New pipelines, and extensions and abandonments of existing pipelines, have to be certified by the Commission on the basis of their gas supply, markets, projected revenues and costs. This Federal regulation of sale prices and services was introduced as an extension to the supervision of utility companies exercised by the States, and was designed essentially to protect consumers from the monopoly powers of the pipeline companies beyond the reach of the state regulatory bodies. As in public utility regulation generally, the earnings of pipelines are limited to a specific annual rate of return on a technically defined capital value, which in recent years has been in the range of 6·0–6·5%. Such public activities naturally leave their impress upon the outcome of inter-fuel competition, and hence the geography of energy.

It was noted in Chapter 4 that when, from a technical point of view, there is a high elasticity of substitution among different forms of energy, price is a decisive factor in determining the use of energy. Through influence, regulations, instructions and a variety of other devices, such as price control and rationing, governments can play a key role in this matter even though they do not enter directly into the production, transport or marketing process. They can reduce the flexibility with which supply and demand factors determine the price level, and hence modify the size of the market for a particular source of energy. For example, in the period 1965–7 the British Government strongly influenced the outcome of the lengthy negotiations between the explorer-producer companies and the Gas Council in regard to the beach price of North Sea natural gas, and thereby ensured the prospect of a fairly rapid substitution of that fuel for coal and to a lesser extent oil in the early 1970s. In the United States, the regulation of the field price of natural gas has a very much longer history.

At one time in America (as still frequently happens on many of the oil- and gas-fields of the developing world today) any natural gas which could not be sold locally, or could not be used for the pressure maintenance programmes of the oil industry, was simply flared off and wasted. After 1938, however, the FPC came to assume a general surveillance over almost every aspect of the industry. The transport implications of this role have already been noted. But perhaps the most important aspect of this Federal control over the industry relates to the field price of natural gas. Up to 1954 prices were decided largely by the market opportunities for that fuel; but since then the Commission has assumed an important control over them (Resources for the Future, 1968, 56 ff.). Initially reflecting consumer interests, it sought to keep gas prices as low as possible, and regulated them in such a way as to reflect ascertainable historical costs plus a 'fair rate of return' on the investment—a procedure derived from its earlier supervision of the gas transport companies.

But it made no reference in its pricing policy to the costs of explora-tion or field development; nor, and this is more important, did it take note of the increasing demand for gas. The industry itself naturally resented this utility-like control, and the pricing policies of the FPC. It claimed that the regulation of the industry within the States was not the intent of the Natural Gas Act (although a Supreme Court ruling in 1954 was the basis of the Commission's actions), and that the return to producers was too low to justify the industry engaging in further exploration and development. The difficulties inherent in this method of fixing prices in any case led to its aban-donment and since 1960 the FPC has been working on a new pro-gramme to establish prices in relation to the average costs of produ-cing gas in particular areas. Their first decision, in 1965, related to the Permian Basin in south-west Texas. Other contracts, meanwhile, are being kept 'in line' with prevailing prices and so limiting the effect of upward pressures on gas prices.

As a consequence of the FPC's pricing policy, it has been argued that in effect the oil industry is being left to carry the exploration and development costs of the natural gas industry. Yet it is, of course, quite unrealistic to talk about the exploration costs of oil and natural gas as if they could be separated. These two industries are prime examples of joint cost industries, since it is impossible to allot costs to either of the fuels individually, when they are so frequently found in association with each other, or to any one field as opposed to another. Oil is, of course, frequently found without gas; and there are many dry gas-fields. Nevertheless exploration costs are still invariably shared between the two fuels. Moreover, Adelman (1962, 25 ff.) has noticed that an increasing proportion of exploration for hydro-carbons in the United States is primarily inspired by a search for gas rather than oil. This suggests that many of the com-plaints of the gas industry are stimulated as much by the existence of government regulation as by the nature of that regulation, and that the FPC policy might be more appropriately questioned in terms of whether or not it is encouraging the best use of the limited energy raw materials in the American economy. Be this as it may, the important point to note is that the 'cheap gas policy' of the FPC with-out doubt continues to depress the price of gas below its market level.

This has many implications. First, the wasteful consumption of gas in 'inferior' uses continues, and full advantage cannot be taken of those outstanding qualities of cleanliness and ease of control in heating which gas offers. Second, the policy undoubtedly helps at the margin to preserve an older pattern of industrial location, and especially the importance of the Manufacturing Belt which initially obtained its energy from the Appalachian coalfields. But by far the most important result of the FPC's policy of low field prices for gas is to make an already attractive fuel even more attractive, and to enlarge (in both quantitative and spatial terms) an already enormous market. One estimate in the early 1960s suggested that natural gas was cutting into the traditional markets of oil to the extent of some three million tons of oil each week, a formidable problem for the United States oil industry.

Comparable regulation of energy prices and consumption is also found at the regional and local scales. The best examples are provided by the secondary energy industries, for in their case a combination of technical and economic considerations together make local monopoly the most satisfactory type of organization at the distribution phase in particular. Since monopoly can rarely be left without some form of public control, the pricing policies and the market areas of both gas and electricity undertakings generally come under some form of public supervision. This, in turn, influences the size and the location of secondary energy production. There can be little doubt that had England and Wales been divided between three or four generation authorities at nationalization, the pattern of electricity production and flows would have been radically different from that developed under the CEGB. By the same token the geography of electricity in the United States is powerfully influenced by the spatial subdivision of the market between different utility companies (Church, 1960, *passim*).

Stimulation and protection
Governments often influence the geography of energy, of course, in a more decisive way than simply the regulation of production, transport, prices and consumption. By the judicious use of cheap loans, subsidies, tariffs, quotas and taxes, they can more positively affect the fate of a particular energy industry. Directly or indirectly, they can stimulate its initial development, protect it from competition and quicken or restrain its rate of growth. The decision of an economically advanced country to help others less favourably placed is a modern commonplace. Through the United Nations and its agencies, or through direct inter-governmental negotiations, considerable sums of public money from North America and Europe have been invested in the poorer economies of Africa, Asia and Latin America in recent years (United Nations, 1957c, Annex 10). A significant share of this money has been used for the development of energy resources and the provision of energy supplies, whilst much of the rest has stimulated new demands for fuel and power. Thus

the Kariba, the Aswan and the Volta River dams in Africa, and many of the river-basin schemes of South East Asia, are all in large measure the result of deliberate international attempts to stimulate the economies in general and the electricity industries in particular of the poorer parts of the world. Although the motives may range from pure altruism to a calculated self-interest within the context of international politics, the effects are the same, and the geography of energy is modified. Already existing on a significant scale, the stimulation of energy industries through international cooperation seems likely to be even more important in the future.

Within countries the stimulation of energy industries for political reasons springs from two different sets of motives, one economic and the other strategic. Many governments help in the development of their natural energy resources simply in order to increase their gross national product and, particularly in the case of oil, to increase their revenue from taxes. In this matter, the basic attitude of a country to foreign capital is crucial, especially as it expresses itself in legislation concerning the exploitation of minerals. The contrast between Venezuela and Columbia illustrates this point. In Venezuela, although the taxes on oil have risen in recent years and government control over the industry has increased, the law of the country nevertheless remains that 'any person, national or foreigner . . . may freely explore and carry on geological or geophysical investigations . . . in national territory' (Pratt and Goode, 1950, 73–4). Columbia, on the other hand, offers no such courteous invitation, and this goes a long way to explain the different stages of development in the oil industries of these two countries.

Sometimes governments negotiate with foreign companies in order to speed up the development of their resources. For example, the Thai Government in 1960, anxious to ascertain the extent of its oil resources and to develop any which could be found, signed an agreement with the Standard Oil Company of Indiana. In this Standard Oil were given the sole right to explore and develop the oil resources of Thailand for a number of years in return for a temporary monopoly of the Thai market. Similarly, in the late 1950s, foreign companies were invited to explore for and/or develop oil resources in the Argentine with the firm promise that any oil produced would be guaranteed a market and a price equal to the cheapest crude imported from overseas (Odell, 1970, 149–52).

Associated with such desires to increase national wealth is the need to save foreign currency which might otherwise be spent on energy imports. In the post-war years, Japan created an agency concerned with accelerating the development of her hydro-electricity sources having particularly in mind her shortage of foreign currency. Where private capital has been reluctant to invest in certain hydro-electricity sites, this agency—with over one-half of its capital provided by the government—has financed their development. The more familiar case of Western Europe's search for alternative sources of oil supply and the construction of oil refineries to save dollars in the 1940s and early '50s will be discussed later (pp. 205–6). Although many motives have been imputed to the flow of Soviet oil into markets outside COMECON, one of the major reasons for its availability is undoubtedly the Soviet desire to earn 'hard' foreign exchange in order to pay for the imports of the Eastern Bloc. There is a world demand for energy; the Russians have ample supplies of hydrocarbons to meet their domestic needs; we have seen (p. 90 ff.) how oil travels easier and cheaper than natural gas; the search for oil markets outside Russia, therefore, is not unnatural. Since Soviet oil bears no royalties, and is produced jointly with natural gas, however, it is impossible to say where the lower limit of a 'fair price' ends and where dumping begins.

A shortage of foreign currency can also influence the emphasis of developments in a country's energy economy. In Brazil, for example, it was realised in the late 1950s that within a decade imports of fuel could be absorbing 18·6% of the country's foreign exchange, whilst equipment purchases would be taking a further 9·5%. (These figures might have been increased even further if the production targets for domestic oil were not reached.) In such a situation, there was clearly a long term advantage for Brazil to produce and refine all her own petroleum requirements. Yet the capital and foreign exchange requirements of such a scheme made it quite impracticable. In developing economies generally, unskilled labour costs are low and sometimes scarce foreign currency can be saved by encouraging the construction of hydro-electricity rather than thermal power stations. In the former, civil engineering works make up a much larger part of total costs and can be built with an extensive use of domestic resources; the same is not true, however, for thermal power stations whose costs are dominated by expensive machinery, much of which has to be imported. Nuclear power is at an even greater disadvantage on this score, for its capital expenditure per kilowatt of capacity is even greater than for conventional power plants. However, although nuclear plants necessitate a heavy capital expenditure in the first instance, they can possibly be more advantageous in those countries where the construction of a conventional power station would involve the continued and heavy foreign expenditure on imported primary fuels.

Strategic motives can also lie at the root of a government's action in stimulating particular domestic energy industries. The scale of the German brown coal industry in the 1950s owed much to Hitler's desires to see the Third Reich self-sufficient in its basic military needs. It was from this resource that Germany was able, through the Fischer–Tropsch process, to produce one-third of the country's petrol requirements at the peak of her war effort, and in the process a new industrial region with a considerable capacity for electricity generation and a wide range of chemical industries was created in Saxony. The French, too, were spurred largely by strategic motives in their exploration and development of the Saharan oil- and gas-fields at Hassi-Messaoud and Edjele. In this particular case the strategic advantage of lessening France's dependence upon the somewhat vulnerable supplies of the Middle East crude was considered of greater importance than the world surplus of crude oil from the late 1950s onwards and the somewhat imappropriate qualities of the Saharan reserves for Western European markets (see above, pp. 69, 71).

The stimulation of energy industries can also have a regional expression. One of the most famous cases is the Tennessee Valley Authority. The original motive behind the creation of this Authority was to revitalize an area and a people which had become physically and economically run down to the point of exhaustion. As part of an all-embracing programme started in 1933 to encourage the proper use, the conservation and development of the natural resources of the Tennessee River Basin, both hydro-electric and thermal power stations were built in the area. It is true, of course, that the social aims of the Tennessee Valley Authority had to be furthered behind legislation connected with inter-state commerce, but it is the ends rather than the means which must concern us here. By the middle 1960s the total generating capacity of the Authority was $14\frac{1}{2}$ million kilowatts as compared with a mere 800,000 in 1933, and the region's consumption of electricity has risen at more than twice the national average rate since its creation. All the evidence points to the fact that without the intervention of the Federal Government in the region's economy this growth would not have taken place. Its success, in fact, has meant that the TVA has become the archetype of river-basin development the world over.

At all scales, then, political action can be invoked to stimulate the growth of particular energy industries. Another side of the coin is the fact that governments can protect industries which are already established and so deny market access or further market penetration to their competitors. A case in point is the United States' domestic oil industry which shields behind both an import duty on petroleum and, more important, a quota on the import of crude and refined oil. The American industry is finding it increasingly difficult to compete with many overseas sources of oil, and without this protection would have to contract its production significantly. Similarly, the coal-mining industry of Nova Scotia has sheltered behind a sizeable transport subsidy for about forty years in its struggle to compete with United States' coal in Canada's east coast markets. The British coal industry too is heavily protected, likewise, by a substantial tax on fuel oil. And the use of peat for the generation of electricity in Eire can in no sense be regarded as cheaper than oil—although it does bring other economic gains such as the improvment of the agricultural value of the land from which the peat is cut, a stimulus to local industry and a reduction of underemployment which a national policy must take into account.

Political action can also be used, of course, to prevent or to restrain the exploitation of an energy resource in particular places. In Maine, for example, the export of electrical energy has been prohibited for many years now. This policy is rooted in the Fernald Law, which may be unconstitutional but which has yet to be challenged in the courts. Its effect has been to retard the development of that State's water resources, for only a very small electricity market exists locally—in contrast with the nearby southern New England demands, some of which might otherwise have been met from Maine. Similarly, in Canada the considerable hydro-electricity potential at Grand Falls in Labrador has been neglected whilst poorer sites in Quebec have been developed as a direct consequence of political priorities and fears.

Such political restraints upon the development of energy resources need not, of course, be deliberate. Some commentators have ascribed the slow rate of growth of Canada's oil industry in recent years in part to the absence of a positive energy policy by the Federal Government. Although the potential production of the Prairies would allow Canada to supply all her own needs and export at least half her present output (57 million tons in 1968) as well, in fact she imports 50% of her requirements, 32 m.t. out of a total demand for 64 m.t. in 1968. However, the Montreal refineries, which handle most of the imported crude, and the Canadian oilfields are both in the hands of international oil companies for whom economic considerations tend to outweigh national sentiments and national economic aspirations. They may occasionally consider the latter in their reckonings, but their priority will tend to be low in the absence of strong political pressures. It is a fair argument, therefore, that a more decisive stance by the Federal Government could alter these priorities, and raise the level of Canadian self-sufficiency in oil. The full cost of such a policy, however, is not easy to assess.

Participation in energy industries

Attempts to control many a game from the touchline are frequently both ineffective and frustrating. So, too, are political efforts to regulate and influence the geography of energy. It is not unnatural, therefore, that governments should often wish to participate directly in the production, transport and marketing of energy. The oil industry provides a good example of the way in which governments, for many years concerned only indirectly with energy operations, are now coming to play a more direct role in them. In most countries (the United States is a partial exception) the concessions for exploiting oil deposits are vested in the hands of their governments, many of which rely heavily (and increasingly) upon the incomes which they derive from these concessions. In the Middle East, where 'Politics and oil are mixed together in a dangerous whirl' (Pratt and Goode, 1950, 339), oil revenues rose from $200 million to $1,300 million per year between 1950 and 1960. By 1969 the Middle East (excluding Iran) plus Libya and Algeria secured well over $3,000 million in oil revenues. The oil-producing States are, of course, constantly seeking to increase their revenue from oil. Throughout the 1950s and '60s the general basis for agreement in the Middle East was that the 'host' government should receive as tax 50% on the profits on the posted prices of oil sold from its territory; but this was slowly beginning to change. The discounts given by the oil companies on their posted prices were being carried by the companies alone, with the result that the oil states received in effect more than 50% of the profits obtained from the sale of oil. Over time also additional payments have had to be offered by companies anxious to secure concessions in the face of many competitors. In 1960 no fewer than eight companies applied for the Kuwait off-shore concession, for example, and the successful Shell group offered terms which included production bonuses, an agreement to permit Kuwaiti capital participation and other benefits to the government (Odell, 1963, 198); other bids offering the Kuwait Government the equivalent of nearly 80% on net profit were unsuccessful. The step from 70% or 80% to 100% is not very long, and the next logical move is for the host governments to engage directly in the oil production, refining and marketing business themselves. And this has, indeed, already happened in India, Brazil, Peru and Mexico, amongst other countries.

The participation of a government in an energy industry can, of course, have quite dramatic results upon the geography of energy. The expropriation of oil company property in Mexico, for example, and the formation in 1938 of *Petróleos Mexicanos* (Pemex), started a chain reaction of events which considerably influenced the size and the spatial relationships of that country's oil industry. Output fell as a result of the boycott of Mexican oil by the expropriated companies; expansion was hampered as a result of poor transport facilities both within the country and to overseas markets; and for many years American capital was reluctant to move into the Mexican industry. As a result, oil production in Mexico for many years remained much smaller than it would have been if it had remained the child of the American companies. Again, the nationalization of the Iraq industry under Mossadeq in 1951 not only disrupted supplies overnight but it also left a legacy in the attitudes of international oil interests in their subsequent dealings with that country. The Iraq Petroleum Company, in which five major international companies have an interest, has periodically had to cut back production levels in the last twenty years and to revise its investment plans in response to subsequent political difficulties, and there have been times when the oilfields have been completely closed down. There can be little doubt that Iraq oil would today be playing a much larger role in the satisfaction of world demands today but for this turbulent political history.

Whilst 'host' governments have become increasingly involved both indirectly and directly in the oil business, the governments of the oil-deficient countries, especially those of Western Europe, have also elected to intervene more regularly in the decisions of the industry. Recognising that their economies were becoming increasingly dependent upon oil, they have also sought to safeguard their supplies by using the whole range of their political armoury, from threats to favours, from agreements to bribes. In addition these governments too have gradually become directly concerned with an increasing share of the oil business, either through the ownership of shares in private companies (the British Government, for example, owns 49% of the ordinary shares of British Petroleum), or through the outright ownership of oil operations (such as the state-owned refinery company in Finland). In Italy, Ente Nazionale Idrocarburi (ENI) is state controlled and the government insists that all refineries must hold in reserve capacity equal to 30% of their normal operations, one-third of which in any case has to be devoted to export operations. The French Government is a part-owner of the Compagnie Française des Petroles (CFP), and hence has international production, refining and distribution interests. Something of the wider importance of political factors in refinery location is noted in the next chapter. One of the best examples of increasing government involvement with the oil business with essentially consumer interests is afforded by Japan. The government decision in 1950 to allow the major international oil companies to supply the market through local refining companies was a response to acute post-war foreign exchange shortages and was uncharacteristic of the Japanese. Since then, the government has been increasingly concerned with exerting greater control over the situation. The most recent being the 1967 inauguration of a Petroleum Development Public Corporation with the object of raising the Japanese-owned share of oil provision to 30% by 1985 (Odell, 1970, 127–8).

In order to guard against the dangers of expropriation and the loss of supplies—as well as to increase their bargaining power in oil royalty and tax discussions—the governments of many oil deficient countries have encouraged the diversification of their supplies in order to avoid too heavily a reliance upon a single source of oil. In the development of the world's oilfields, therefore, petroleum needs have not always been met from the lowest-cost production areas. If, by chance, they had then a small number of oilfields (mainly in the Middle East) would gradually have come to dominate world petroleum supplies, many American fields would have been abandoned, and supplies would have been highly vulnerable to political disruption. In diversifying their supplies of oil, governments and oil companies alike have had to balance their desire for the lowest cost oil against policies designed to ensure the continuity of supply. Such policies of diversification have been stimulated not only by the political uncertainties in the producing countries, but also by the nature of governments along their lines of supply. Thus, after the Suez crisis in 1956, when the Canal was blocked and the Syrian pipelines were damaged, the international oil companies set about discovering alternative sources of oil to the west of Suez; the result was an acceleration of the development of new fields in North and West Africa, Libya especially, and a decade in which there was a considerable surplus of crude oil world-wide. When the Canal was closed for a second time just over a decade later those fields received a further boost, although the industry also responded to the crisis by having built a large number of super-tankers to transport Gulf oil cheaply via the Cape of Good Hope.

As Levy (1961) has noted, already 'No industry is more world wide in its ramifications, is more essential to the world economy or is more entangled in world politics than oil.' But with the increasing involvement of governments in the industry, particularly their direct participation, there is a possibility and a real danger that 'Every oil problem, commercial or otherwise, will become an inter-governmental affair, or subject to a tug-of-war between political blocks, or an issue of the east-west struggle.' Something of this tendency could once again be seen in the confrontation between the OPEC countries and the representatives of the international oil industry at Teheran in 1971.

Government influence upon the geography of energy through its participation in energy production can be noted at the national as well as the international scale, and illustrated by reference to one of Britain's nationalized energy industries. For the last twenty-five years the British coal-mining industry has been protected against foreign coals by a government ban (lifted only in 1970) upon imported solid fuels; and for the last decade it has been protected against its major competitor—oil—by a tax of £2 per ton on fuel oil. However, it is especially at the regional level that the full impact of political decisions has been felt, for the higher cost pits and coalfields of the country have been persistently protected both by the pricing policies adopted by the National Coal Board and by certain prerogatives vested in the Minister of Power. The prices of industrial coals in Britain are based upon their quality rather than their costs of production; and domestic coals are sold within a system of 'zone-delivered prices', their prices being determined by the place of consumption and (once again) irrespective of the mines in which they are won. The Board has taken the view that prices should reflect the *average* cost of producing and transporting coal to the consumer; that the relative prices of different coals should reflect their quality; and that (regardless of its origin) coal of the same quality in the same market should sell at the same price. Of necessity these are crude ideas, for rarely will prices reflecting quality at the same time match the average costs of their production and transport. Beacham (1958, 153) has argued that, 'The present price structure appears to be rigid and artificial, and one suspects that it might be "rigged" in order to preserve the existing balance of production between coalfields and their spheres of interest in tradition markets.' In 1962 in fact the Board's pricing system was modified slightly to take more account of the regional differences in the costs of winning coal. And in 1966 the differentials were widened yet again. Nevertheless, these policies have meant that for many years the less efficient pits and coalfields of Britain have been subsidized by the industry as a whole, and it still remains broadly the case that the more efficient East Midlands and South Yorkshire pits carry the interest charges of the industry as a whole, on top of their own operating expenses, while many other divisions and coalfields find it recurrently impossible to cover even their working costs.

At the same time, the Minister of Power has had a (little used) prerogative to determine from which coalfield the supplies for any of the major coal markets (such as the London power market) should come. Obviously the Ministry had to recognize the costs of supplying these markets, but social factors could also be taken into consideration before a decision was reached. In essence, this authority stemmed from the quota system of the inter-war years, which sought to distribute the demand for coal between the several coalfields of the country in part regardless of the relative costs of production and distribution. More important, however, is the supervision exercised by the Minister over the investment plans for the Central Electricity Generating Board, and his interventions in favour of coal. Ministerial approval is required before a new power station can be constructed, or the primary fuel of an existing station changed. As a result, for most of the 1960s the Board was required to burn many tons of coal which was not strictly in its own economic interest, and only in the later years did it receive compensation from the Exchequer. Such a policy, once again, served primarily to limit the contraction and stabilize the geography of British coal production. By the time of the Coal Industry Act of 1967, however, the government had come to accept the need for, and the inevitability of, a reduction in the size and a shift in the geography of the industry (Manners, 1971, 170 ff.). As a result, some £415 million of capital 'assets' were written off and public money was provided to assist those communities which would be worst hit through the closure of mines. Nevertheless, attempts still continued to be made to maintain as large a market for coal as possible, by granting the industry preferential treatment in government contracts and by making arrangements with the secondary energy producers to maximize their use of solid fuel.

Thus, as a consequence of both pricing policies and more direct government influences, the worst social and economic ills which undoubtedly would have resulted from the operation of a freer market have been avoided for many British coalfield communities. Whilst markets for coal mined in Wales, Scotland, Durham and Cumberland have to some extent been artificially maintained, the production on the East Midlands and Yorkshire fields has been deliberately restrained, possibly to their long term detriment. The relationships between governments and their nationalized industries are subject to considerable variation, and they are not always easy to define. In the history of the National Coal Board, however, it is easy to see how public policies are capable of decisive expression and can considerably modify the geography of an energy industry.

9

POLITICAL FACTORS (II)

National and international energy policies – location of oil refining

National and international energy policies

The complexities of political involvement in the energy industries—through regulations, stimulation and protection, and direct participation—are such that not infrequently contradictory policies come to be pursued within the same country and economy. In Britain, for example, the coal industry is protected from oil on the one hand, but its markets in the long run are threatened by the development of a nuclear power technology which is heavily underwritten by government funds. The coal industry (in its production phase, at least), the gas and the electricity industries are nationalized and are responsible ultimately to parliament through the Minister of Power; the oil industry, in contrast, remains within the private sector. Government policies in many fields—fields such as taxation, imports, land use, clean air legislation, and distribution of industry policies—affect the several fuel industries, and yet it was 1965 before a Minister of Power had the courage to produce a White Paper on *Fuel Policy*.

In the United States also, contradictory policies can be seen. For example, the domestic oil industry is protected from foreign competition by import duties and quotas at the same time as the pricing policies of the Federal Power Commission are exposing it to unnecessary competition at home from cheap natural gas; and whilst oil imports are restricted, natural gas imports from Canada, Mexico and now Algeria steadily rise. Such apparent inconsistencies underline the case for some form of national energy policy. In 1961 the United

States' Committee on Interior and Insular Affairs was authorized to make a study which would lead to a better coordinated, and more effective, national policy towards the country's energy resources and industries. Neither the detailed study of the nation's energy position, nor the advocacy of the need for a coordinated policy, was, of course, new. In 1939, for example, the National Resources Committee recommended that 'Energy resources . . . lie at the foundation of our industrial civilization . . . (and) it appears beyond doubt that the nation's patrimony should be safeguarded, and that a sound national policy must be concerned with the conservation and prudent utilization of these basic resources'. Again, in 1952, the Paley Commission after a very thorough survey of the United States' energy resources advocated that 'The hydra-heads of energy policy must be reined together. This can be accomplished only if all the parties concerned—the President and Congress, the State and Federal agencies, and the energy industries—work from a common base of understanding of the total energy outlook, the interrelations within the energy field, and the relations between energy and the rest of the economy'.

Yet in spite of these and many other authoritative recommendations nothing was done in the 1950s to develop a comprehensive national programme of energy production and use. It was not surprising, therefore, that John F. Kennedy, as Senator from Massachusetts, should have argued that 'The time has come to put some common sense and consistency into the way this country handles its vital fuel supplies', and that in his second year of office as President a new Committee was appointed to study the matter again. But 'common sense and consistency' and political expediency proved once again to be uneasy bedfellows. Just as 'prorationing' in the United States oil industry originally stemmed from roots of self-interest, so did the reactions to the proposal of the country's several energy industries and interests reflect comparable priorities (Joint Economic Committee, 1960, *passim*). The natural gas industry and the major oil companies, for example, whose operations are already considerably influenced and constrained by government regulations and agencies, fought strongly against the possibilities of a coordinated policy. The coal industry and the domestic oil industry, on the other hand, both in somewhat precarious economic positions, tended to welcome and encourage any political moves in this direction on the assumption that their positions would thereby be improved. In other words, the reaction of the energy industries to the possibility of an American energy policy has tended to take the form of an elaborate defence of industrial (and regional) vested interests.

188 The Geography of Energy

Any attempt which might be made to reconcile contradictory public policies in the energy sector will have to be as mindful of these interests as it is of the criteria for a rational policy.

What, then, are the legitimate bases upon which a national energy policy can be formulated? The discussion in this context is best related to long term policy criteria only; other aspects of energy policy, such as short run problems or the efficiency of fuel utilization, are not considered in the discussion which follows. It has already been established that an energy policy should seek to remove any inconsistencies that exist within an already existing pattern of government action affecting the energy industries. There are, however, much more substantial considerations as well. The exploitation of fossil fuels involves the use of non-renewable natural resources, and it is by maximizing their long-term utility that the best interests of a country will be served. But in a free market the demands of consumers—be they individuals or firms—are not always the most effective means of ensuring that the best use is made of these resources, for consumers are essentially interested in short term gains and tend to neglect the importance of the long term. The flaring of natural gas on the oilfields of the developing world is an extreme example of this situation. With the future thus undervalued in a free market, it follows that some form of public action should try to reconcile immediate demands with the longer term goals of conservation by, at the very least, preventing if possible the sheer waste of natural resources. It is, of course, easier said than done. Nevertheless, this objective should be the corner stone of a national energy policy.

A third, and more controversial, criterion in the formulation of an energy policy arises from a set of strategic questions. Assuming a variety of options to be open, to what extent should a country allow itself to become dependent upon foreign sources of energy? Should it seek to provide at least a minimum proportion of its energy needs from its own resources and regardless of cost, rather than come to rely entirely upon cheaper imported supplies? If so, what proportion is reasonable? The degree to which different Western European countries in the late 1950s depended upon foreign sources of energy ranged from 100% in the case of Luxembourg to 9% in the case of West Germany (OEEC, 1960, 73 ff.). Since some countries depend heavily upon energy imports out of necessity, on what grounds can others with (relatively expensive) domestic resources justify a restriction of imports? Military and strategic arguments have been used. Yet their logic is suspect. If a country becomes involved in a limited war of the 'bush-fire' variety, there is undoubtedly a chance that one or possibly two of its sources of energy might be lost or cut off; but this is a justification for a diversity of overseas energy suppliers—plus a certain amount of energy storage and a ready-to-hand rationing scheme—rather than a reason for restricting energy imports. If, on the other hand, the world ever became involved in an atomic holocaust, the energy distributing and energy consuming facilities of all the major economies would disappear as rapidly as their energy supplies; on these grounds too, military reasons for a high level of national self-sufficiency in energy supplies carry only a limited conviction (McClesky, 1960, *passim*).

There is, however, an economic argument which can be employed to justify a degree of national self-sufficiency in energy supplies. It is related to the balance of payments and it has been touched upon earlier. It is sometimes reasoned that energy imports must be limited to ensure the availability of foreign exchange for those needs of an economy which can only be imported or which are relatively more expensive to import. The strength of the reasoning clearly depends upon the economic circumstances facing individual countries. For some developing countries the argument carries much weight, and there are occasions in developed countries, particularly at times of economic dislocation (for example, in Western Europe after World War II), when it also holds. But for the developed economies generally the argument is less tenable, since the cost of energy represents such a small part of the total value added in the production of most goods, and the foreign exchange earnings from the export of manufactures produced with imported energy more than cover its delivered costs.

If an energy policy is going to place some importance upon consumer choice as a means of indicating the relative efficiency of different supplies, then a further criterion must be to ensure that the costs of the several energy industries are reflected reasonably in their prices. This task is not so simple as it may at first appear, for at different times and in different places the energy industries price their products quite legitimately in response to somewhat different yardsticks. Sometimes it is their marginal costs; other times it is average costs. Sometimes a price is determined by the value of energy in the market; on other occasions it is priced f.o.b. and a transfer charge has to be added. The costs of producing some forms of energy can be reckoned simply; the costs of producing other forms of energy are shared with other products. Some industries incur social costs, by requiring major infrastructure investments or causing atmospheric pollution, whereas others do not. The problems involved in attempting to monitor the energy industries' costs in relation to their prices must not be minimized. Nevertheless, the greater the reliance placed by the community upon the market, the more vigorously must the task be pursued.

The final criterion for a national energy policy concerns not so much the final objectives of a policy, but rather the means of achieving it. Changing economics, shifting demands and new techniques mean that energy geography is in a constant state of transformation. This can lead to localized economic dislocation and social distress in the energy industries: unemployment on the coalfields of Western Europe is a good case in point. As a result, a strong case exists for ameliorating such situations, not by supporting a 'dying' industry or region indefinitely, but by instituting policies which are designed to limit the speed of change and so minimize the degree of social upheaval during the period of adjustment.

A national energy policy, therefore, must seek to remove the conflicts within, and the inconsistencies of, existing governmental policies towards the energy industries. It must seek to provide the necessary political reconciliation between the extravagances of the market and the needs of conservation. It must weigh the validity of strategic and economic arguments for the restriction of energy imports. It must monitor the relationship between energy costs and prices. It must seek to ameliorate (if necessary) localized social distress resulting from change in the energy economy. And it must operate from a base of existing energy industries and vested interests. The difficulties in the precise formulation of a policy are clearly enormous; but the nature of economic life is such that political decisions have to be taken with regard to the energy industries, and they are the normal and inevitable framework within which a country's energy geography evolves. It is well that they should be both consistent and in the long term national interest.

But are national energy policies enough? The European Coal and Steel Community (ECSC) was charged with setting in motion a common coal market for its members. Clearly, in the 1950s, when it embarked upon this task, there were many vested interests to be reconciled. A number of Western European countries were inclined to stabilize the coal sector of their energy markets, and to continue the protection of their coal industries. Others preferred to leave the energy market as free as possible. West Germany and Italy epitomized these two conflicting positions. All, however, were agreed on the need to check excessive competition which might have resulted in costly changes not in line with the long term trend. In other words, they were not prepared over a five or ten year period to let Western European coal-mining contract, as a result of a temporary fall in the price of oil or a temporary abundance of low cost natural gas, knowing that at the end of that period the full capacity of their coal industries would be required to meet their energy needs. It was, of course, relatively easy to agree upon such a short term objective. Its longer term counterparts, however, present many more difficulties (OEEC, 1960, 73 ff.). In particular broader issues relating to all the energy industries are raised, and these are matters which can only be discussed adequately within the context of a total energy policy and are the concern of the European Economic Community (EEC).

For a number of years now attempts have been made to agree upon the basis for a common energy market for the EEC—but all have failed. The early protectionist Lapie proposals of 1960 were torpedoed by the energy importing countries, Italy and the Netherlands, while opposition from the major energy producers, France, West Germany and Belgium, prevented acceptance of the more liberal Marjolin proposals two years later. The failure of these frontal attacks on the problem persuaded the Commission initially to agree upon more limited objectives. The year 1965 saw the formal recognition of the need for coal-mining subsidies. A policy for oil and gas was revealed in the following year. Although the member countries of the EEC are still some way from agreement on a completely unified approach to their energy industries and problems, three general principles do appear to have gained fairly widespread recognition. The first is that the most economic flow of energy supplies should be encouraged throughout Western Europe. The second is that when a single energy market is established—and possibly before—it will require international coordination of investment. And the third is that an energy policy should seek to ensure a security of supplies, and that there should be a dependable minimum quantity of energy requirements always available from within the Community. Under these three banners, it is anticipated that the Western European energy market will continue to be led on an orderly retreat from coal.

Underlying the policy considerations of both the British Government and the EEC—and, indeed, basic to the energy policy suggestions of the Robinson Report to the wider Organization for European Economic Cooperation (OEEC) in 1960, and of the report produced by the yet further enlarged Organization for Economic Cooperation and Development in 1966—is an assumption that the security of extra-continental energy supplies can be secured by the diversification of sources from which they are imported. To quote from the OEEC Report: 'Most of us [members of the Commission] do not think that the required security [of energy supplies] is best provided by greater self-sufficiency. It can be equally well, and in our view more cheaply, provided by a wider diversification of supplies than existing at the time of the Suez crisis.' This attitude contrasts vividly with the official United States' view on oil imports. The special committee to investigate crude oil imports, appointed by the President in 1955, stated that: 'The cost of imported oil is attractive . . . [but] Imported supplies could be cut off in an emergency and might well be diminished by events beyond our control. . . . It is therefore believed that the best interests of domestic consumers, as well as of national security, will be served if a reasonable balance is maintained between domestic and foreign supplies.' These conflicting assessments of the security problem have an important set of implications.

As Schurr (1960) has pointed out, Western European policies are in part based upon an assumption that present American attitudes towards energy imports (and especially oil imports) will continue. In its assessment of strategic oil reserves, it would appear that Western Europeans take for granted the continuing existence of excess productive capacity in the United States; and, even though at the time of the Suez Crisis American oil producers were not especially cooperative, it continues to be assumed that this reserve can be relied upon in an emergency. Yet this excess production capacity depends to a considerable extent upon the protection of the United States' industry behind a tariff and quota wall. Remove that wall (and Western Europe generally argues for a reduction of such trade barriers), and it is certain that the current level of investment in the domestic oil industry in the United States would fall. As a result part of Western Europe's strategic oil capacity would be lost. The relatively liberal oil import policy in Western Europe, in other words, depends in part upon an American protectionist attitude towards its oil imports. Amongst other reasons, this suggests the desirability for some form of consultation between North America and Western Europe on energy matters, not to ensure that their policies are necessarily identical, but rather to reach agreement about the assumptions upon which they are based. The OECD is one institution through which such consultation is possible.

But the limitation of such consultative procedures to the industrially advanced, energy deficient, countries would not only exacerbate suspicions in the developing, energy surplus, nations; it would also neglect an important opportunity for international cooperation —or at least consultation—on a yet larger scale. The interests of the developing energy producers on the one hand and the highly developed energy consumers on the other are by no means totally antagonistic. The relative stability of the posted prices of oil during the 1960s—notwithstanding the increasing size and number of discounts given on posted prices—are a reflection of this. The major reason for posted oil price stability in spite of the over-investment in, and the excess capacity of, the world's oilfields undoubtedly lies in the fact that the governments of neither the major oil-producing nor the largest oil-consuming countries really want to see a fall in the price of oil. The countries rich in oil reserves naturally want to maximize their revenues; and with the world market for oil relatively inelastic for political if not for economic reasons, they clearly prefer oil prices to remain as high as possible. At the same time the governments of many of the oil-deficient countries have no strong desire for a fall in the price of oil; on the contrary, their interests too are generally best served by relatively stable oil prices. The government of the United States would have greater difficulties maintaining its quota on oil imports if the gap between the domestic and international prices for oil widened further. Again, the governments of Britain, France and West Germany would have even greater problems in seeking to ameliorate economic and social distress in their contracting coal industries if competition from oil were intensified. Granted there are countries like Italy or Switzerland which have no coal industries to protect, and a preference for a fall in oil prices; but their interests are no match for the pressures of the rest. In sum, attempts to formulate energy policies either nationally or through such bodies as the ECSC, the EEC or the OECD need not be inherently opposed to the aims of, say, the Arab Petroleum Conference or OPEC.

The arguments for, and the advantages of, a world consultative forum for energy policies need not detain us here. But two points have to be made. First, such a body is the natural extension of the present interest in, and gropings towards, national energy policies. And, second, policy decisions taken by supra-national organizations, and subsequently observed by the member governments, are providing a new political framework within which other factors and influences mould the details of energy geography.

A final example—the location of oil refining

To illustrate the importance of the three factors to which the greater part of this book has been devoted, it is appropriate to conclude this study of the geography of energy with a brief examination of the location of oil refineries (Alexandersson, 1957; Frankel and Newton, 1961; Odell, 1963, 109 ff.).

Some of the largest refineries in the world today are oriented towards their crude oil input. In the Middle East, for example,

G

there are large refineries in such places as Abadan (21·5 million tons annual capacity in 1970), on Bahrein Island (10·3 m.t.), at Mina al Ahmadi, Kuwait (12·5 m.t.), and at Ras Tanura (12·8 m.t.). Similarly, in the Caribbean there is a considerable refinery capacity at Aruba (22 m.t.), Curaçao (15 m.t.), Pointe-à-Pierre, Trinidad (17·5 m.t.) and at Amuay Bay on the Gulf of Maracaibo (26 m.t.). And amongst the largest refineries in the United States are those at Baton Rouge, Louisiana (21 m.t.), Port Arthur, Texas (16·5 m.t.), Beaumont, Texas (15·8 m.t.), and Bay Town, Texas (17·3 m.t.). Although a number of small refineries are located actually at the well-head (the so-called 'tea kettles'), most of these 'raw material oriented' refineries are in fact sited at natural trans-shipment points *en route* to the markets for oil.

At one time all refineries had a raw material orientation. But over the years others sited at or near to their markets in total have come to have an even greater importance—although individually they tend to be somewhat smaller. In North America they are located along the north-east seaboard at such places as Philadelphia (8 m.t.), Bayway, New Jersey (7·5 m.t.), and Marcus Hook, Pennsylvania (7·9 m.t.); in the Mid-West there is considerable capacity in the Chicago region, such as the plants at Whiting, Indiana (14·0 m.t.), and Lamont, Illinois (12·3 m.t.). Similarly, in Western Europe large refineries have been built on the Thames estuary at the Isle of Grain (12 m.t.) and Shellhaven (10 m.t.), on Southampton Water (16·3 m.t.), at Antwerp (15 m.t.), at Gonfreville on the lower Seine (16·3 m.t.) and near Rotterdam where three large refineries in 1970 had a combined capacity of 46·3 m.t. In Japan, too, many large refineries have been built—for example the 11 m.t. plant at Negishi, Yokohama, and the 9·4 m.t. facility at Wakayama. In fact, the largest centres of population and industry in most countries now have a local refinery. Once again, as in the case of their raw material counterparts, 'market oriented' refineries are frequently located not exactly at the market, but rather near to it *en route* from the oilfields and at natural trans-shipment points.

There has also emerged an 'intermediate' category of refinery location where the operations take place at a natural trans-shipment point some distance from both their major markets and their raw materials. The plants at Naples (5·8 m.t.), at Augusta in Sicily (13·8 m.t.), at Aden (8·9 m.t.) and at Singapore (6 m.t.) are in this category.

Such a generic classification of refinery location is, of course, to some extent arbitrary. Part of the refinery capacity in Britain and the Netherlands, for example, is used to meet demands outside those countries, and might reasonably be regarded as 'intermediate' in category. Moreover, the listing of a refinery within one of these three groups does not necessarily mean that it will always be there. Many refineries have been located near to crude oil in the first instance, but the growth of local demand has subsequently absorbed all their output and made them equally market oriented. This has happened in the case of the Burmese and Mexican refineries, as well as some of the refining capacity of the Gulf Coast of the United States. Similarly, it is conceivable for a refinery to 'shift' categories in the other direction. If Argentine oil production should increase to the point where that country becomes a net exporter of oil, some of her refineries, at present market oriented, would then become raw material oriented. With these qualifications in mind, it remains clear that an increasing proportion of the world's refineries have been located away from the oilfields in recent years. How can this change be explained?

The factors influencing refinery location are too complex to be analysed effectively at an abstract level alone. As in the study of gas works and power station locations, each situation tends to have its own individuality and needs to be studied on its own merits. At the root of this complexity lies the considerable variety of crude oils, refinery schedules and oil products, and the fact that the cost of any given refinery operation *per se* tends to vary significantly from place to place. In the United States, for example, the oilfields offer economies as far as fuel, power and steam are concerned (largely as a result of cheap natural gas found in association with the oil); but these same areas, many of them located in semi-arid conditions, have very high water costs. Again, the costs of capital, housing, local transport, skilled labour, and water supplies are lower in Western Europe, whereas the costs of energy and unskilled labour are cheaper in the Middle East. In spite of the range of such local and regional variations in the costs of refinery operations, it is nevertheless possible to generalize about the location of refineries and to single out the major forces which mould the oil industry's decisions.

Of all the factors which influence the advantages and disadvantages of particular locations for refinery operations, those associated with comparative transport costs are amongst the more important. All other things being equal, the least cost location for a refinery is clearly where the costs of getting crude oil from its source to the refinery, and then the products from the refinery to their markets, are at a minimum. At one time, primitive techniques meant that considerable quantities of oil were lost in the course of distillation and the volume of oil fell during the process by some 25% or even

50%; and before the development of oil cracking techniques 5 tons of crude oil were required to produce one ton of petrol. In the early days of the industry, therefore, the much lower transport costs on the significantly smaller volume of oil products was a major reason for the raw material orientation of the industry. Technology, however, has now been improved to the point where only a 4–8% reduction in volume is normally associated with refinery operations. As a result, although a greater volume of oil is still transported to a refinery than from it, the additional volume is very small compared with the past. In fact, for twenty years or so—and in a widening number of circumstances—comparative transport costs have actually encouraged a market location for oil refining, since the average transport cost per ton for crude oil tends to be lower than that for refined products taken as a whole. There are three main reasons for this.

First, there are considerable savings in the bulk movement of crude oil which are denied to the wide variety of products produced in a refinery. Tankers over about 40,000 dwt are only rarely used for the transport of oil products since either their markets are too small to justify a larger vessel or there are draught limitations at the ports of discharge. Crude oil, in contrast, can be moved in much larger vessels—now over 300,000 dwt—the economic advantages of which were noted in Chapter 5. Again, where pipeline transport is utilized, the smaller markets for oil products prevent advantage being taken of the large diameter pipes which are used for pumping crude oil. Moreover, there are limits to the range of products which can be transported economically by pipeline. Heavy fuel oil, for example, flows so slowly, particularly in low temperatures, that its movement over long distances is very costly if not technically impossible; and, even though lighter oils can be pumped over considerable distances, mixing occurs if different grades are transported successively down the line. Certain scale economies, therefore, which are available for crude oil transport, are denied to the movement of products.

A second reason for the lower ton/km cost of transporting crude oil compared with products results from its handling characteristics. For both tankers and pipelines, it is technically easier to transport crude oil than some of the heavier oil products. Crude oil is regarded as a 'clean' cargo in the tanker trade, whereas some oil products are classified as 'dirty' and charged a higher rate. In the case of pipeline transport, once again, the ton/km cost of moving oil products on average is somewhat greater than the cost of moving crude oil—although particular products, such as petrol, are cheaper to pipe than crude oil. The unit cost of transporting light products by pipeline from West Texas to Chicago, for example, is lower than that of crude oil; but the high ton/km cost of moving residual oil by rail and barge means that the total expense of moving all the products is higher than the costs of transporting crude oil (Table 12).

Table 12

OIL TRANSPORT RATES FROM TEXAS TO CHICAGO,
circa 1956

Route	Type of oil	Mode of transport	Distance (km)	Rate (cent per ton/ 100 km)
W. Texas–Chicago	Crude	Pipeline	1616	8·4
W. Texas–Chicago	Petrol	Pipeline	1616	7·4
W. Texas–Chicago	Other products	Pipeline	1616	8·0
W. Texas–Memphis	Residual oil	Rail	1099	120·3
Memphis–Chicago	Residual oil	Barge	1282	12·0
W. Texas–Chicago	Residual oil	Rail and barge	2381	132·3

Source: Lindsey, 1956, 313.

The result is a strong disincentive to refining oil for the Chicago market in Texas.

A third advantage to be derived from transporting crude oil is the flexibility which it affords in the source of refinery inputs. Thus, Philadelphia refineries can economically draw upon crude oil from the Gulf Coast, Venezuela and the Middle East, taking advantage of the differences in their qualities and costs through space and time; a refinery in the Persian Gulf on the other hand generally finds it uneconomic to refine anything other than local oil, since the subsequent shipments of the products to the markets of perhaps Western Europe or Japan would in part involve a reverse-haul and unnecessary transport expenses.

Oil transport costs today therefore tend to encourage a market location for refinery operations. The major exception arises where the demand for individual products is large, where low cost transport is available for the movement of products, and where local circumstances prevent full advantage being taken of the economies associated with the bulk movement of crude oil. The land-locked markest of the West Midlands and the Paris Basin provide two examples of this situation.

The market itself, however, is also a decisive factor in refinery location decisions. Its size, location and nature are all-important. The nature of refinery operations are such that considerable economies of scale can be obtained from large production units. Assuming that the capital cost per ton of throughput in a 1 million ton per year plant is 100, the cost indices for 5 million and 10 million ton units are 65 and 55 respectively. Larger refineries similarly afford considerable operating cost economies. It is clear that, in smaller refineries particularly, economies of scale are a major consideration in total production costs; in larger plants, in contrast, the advantages of size are relatively small compared with other costs, and can easily be offset by other factors. For these reasons alone, refineries all over the world have been getting larger. In 1947, amongst the refineries owned by the 20 largest companies in the United States, there were 67 which had an annual capacity of less than $\frac{3}{4}$ million tons. By 1959, however, 43 of these were not operating, 2 more had increased their capacity to over $2\frac{1}{2}$ million tons, and the rest continued production in isolated locations largely as a result of a decided transport cost advantage (Livingston, 1959). Whilst the aggregate capacity of United States refineries has increased considerably, since 1940, the actual number of plants had fallen from 459 to less than 300 by 1958; and by that year over 45% of the country's refinery capacity was to be found in 24 plants, each with a throughput of more than 5 million tons per year. The same tendency towards larger and larger refineries can also be seen throughout the rest of the world.

The implication is that if an oil company wishes to take advantage of economies of scale in its refinery operations it must have access to a large market. The market orientation of operations suggested by relative transport costs, therefore, is limited to large markets. If a market is not large enough to allow a local refinery to exploit scale economies which exceed lower refining costs elsewhere plus the higher transport charges on their products, then the operation is 'thrown back' either to the source of the crude oil or to an intermediate (break of bulk) point having access to a larger market. Refineries located away from their markets, however, have the disadvantage of being relatively slow to adjust their schedules and satisfy their markets after rapid changes in demand. For example, the first (unpredictable) frost along the north-east seaboard of the United States brings with it a sudden rise in the demand for heating fuels and a fall in the demand for petrol. A local refinery can quickly change its schedule to meet such demands but there is an inevitable time-lag (equal occasionally to the time taken by a product tanker to travel between, say, Houston and New York) before a distant refinery can adjust its schedule to meet them. The cost of storage at the market to meet such demand fluctuations has to be added to the cost of refining elsewhere (in this case on the Gulf Coast).

The price of both crude oil and oil products increases with distance from the world's major oilfields. It is, therefore, generally uneconomic to ship products against the general direction of oil flows. If a market oriented refinery is to be economic, it must be able to adjust its schedule to the needs of either that market alone, or that market plus other demands further away from the sources of oil. Only occasionally can the back-haul and movement of products towards major centres of oil production be economically justified. The nature of Western European oil demands until 1939 created only a very small market for fuel oil, and the only available sources of crude oil were in the Western Hemisphere; consequently, only a few (and then rather small) refineries could be economically located in Western Europe, since the oil companies would otherwise have had to reverse-haul their surplus fuel oil back to the United States. After 1947, however, the Western European oil market was completely changed. Requirements for fuel oil increased six-fold between 1939 and 1956, and the more balanced demand for oil products (as well as the post-war changes in the major sources of oil for Western Europe—the shift to the Middle East and later North Africa) encouraged the location of an increasing number of market oriented refineries. By the 1960s, in fact, a major problem of Western European refinery operators was to find sufficient outlets for lighter petroleum products. In Italy, for example, fuel oil in 1960 made up 61% of total oil sales, whilst petrol accounted for only 12% of the market. This imbalance could well limit the rate of Western European refinery expansion in the future, and encourage more 'intermediate' refinery construction nearer to the oilfields of the Middle East and North Africa.

The increasing complexity of oil product demands in different countries throughout the world encourages this prediction. The nature of the market in many developing countries is such that, with present techniques, it is impossible for one refinery or group of (market oriented) refineries to meet market demands without producing some surplus products. Once again, therefore, at least part of the refinery operations for these markets tend to be thrown back towards the sources of crude oil. Indeed, new techniques of double refining reinforce this trend. If the emphasis of Western Europen demands remains biased towards fuel oil and that of South East Asia towards the lighter ends, an economic solution for refinery operations might be for the fuel oil to be removed from the crude in the Persian Gulf for the Western European market, and for the de-fuelled crude oil to be shipped for further refining to South East Asia (Mock, 1961).

In short, there are three advantages of refining oil at or near an oilfield: several markets can be served and full advantage can be taken of the scale economies of refining; the demands for the differing proportions of products in several markets can be balanced and met more economically; and the possibility occasionally exists of a saving in transport costs as a result of refinery losses, or if the movement of crude oil is relatively inefficient. The advantages of a market location are also threefold: generally speaking, the ton/km costs of transport operations is lower; crude oil from several sources can be processed, and full advantage can be taken of its alternative qualities and costs; and, within certain limits and under certain circumstances, refinery schedules can be readily adjusted to the precise changing needs of the market.

The interplay of transport costs and market forces, therefore, sometimes pulls refinery operations in one direction, sometimes in another: and the actual pattern of refinery location is generally a compromise between the advantages of these alternative orientations. How have they worked out in reality? In the United States (Lindsey, 1954, 1956; Alexandersson, 1967, 113 ff.), refineries are to be found on the Gulf Coast, Mid-Continent, Appalachian and Mid-West and Californian oilfields, at the major markets along the north-east Megalopolis coast, the Mid-West and California, and at a number of scattered and isolated locations in the west (Fig. 20). The pattern results from both past as well as more recent location decisions.

The Gulf Coast, the Mid-Continent and the Appalachian and Mid-West oilfields are clearly the most suitable location at which to refine those products needed for their growing local and regional markets. But refineries based upon the Gulf Coast oilfield—and they still represent about one-third of the total refining capacity in the United States—also supply products to the large and highly diversified markets of the industrial north-east. The continued ability of the Gulf Coast refiners to serve these markets economically is the result of several factors. First, the lower cost of refinery operations on the Gulf, particularly as a result of the availability of cheap power from natural gas; second, the huge investment already sunk into refinery operations in that region, which allows capacity to be expanded more economically than the development of new sites on the east coast; third, the (small) loss of weight in processing; and fourth, the fact that the scale economies of crude oil transport have not been fully exploited. As a result of the conservatism of the coastwise tanker trade, which is protected against foreign competition

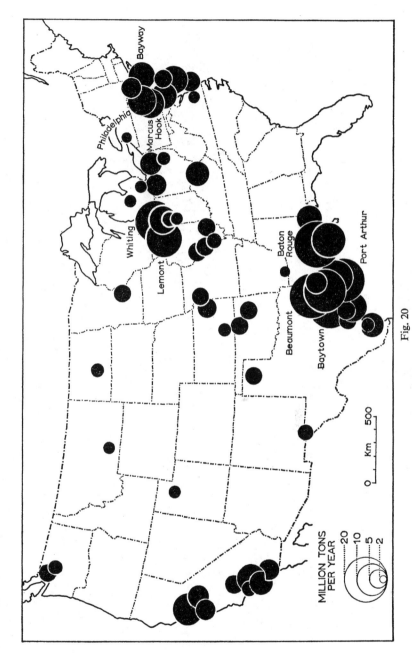

Fig. 20

Oil refineries in the United States, 1970. (Source: *Oil and Gas Journal*)

MILLION TONS
PER YEAR

20
10
5
2

0   Km   500

by the Jones Act, the vessels used to move crude oil between, say, Galveston and Philadelphia are relatively small and certainly high cost by contemporary international standards; oil from the Gulf moving coastwise in the early 1960s, for example, had to bear a transport charge which was $1·05 to $1·75 more than oil hauled from the Caribbean. Moreover, there is no large diameter crude oil pipeline connecting the Gulf Coast oilfields directly with the north-east seaboard to act as a spur to competition and efficiency. On the other hand, a large diameter pipe to transport oil products has linked these two regions since the middle 1960s, and has served to consolidate an existing pattern of refinery location. This is not to argue that Gulf crude cannot be refined economically on the north-east coast; it is simply explains why, generally speaking, the most economic refinery location for supplying Megalopolis with products refined from Gulf Coast crude continues to be on or near the oilfield.

However, when crude oil from the Caribbean or the Middle East is used to satisfy the energy demands of the Atlantic seaboard, the advantage swings heavily in favour of a market location. The greater insensitivity to changes of demand, together with the rather higher costs of (skilled) labour, water and chemicals at overseas refineries, are the major economic reasons behind this, together with the transport cost advantage of a market orientation; in this case, crude oil can be transported in large super-tankers, often flying flags of convenience and offering a highly competitive freight rate. And to these reasons are added the political uncertainties surrounding many refinery operations overseas. Within about 160 km of Philadelphia there is to be found about 15% of the refining capacity of the United States, and imported crude and residential fuel oil represents between 40% and 50% of the total consumption of oil in the huge urban market Boston and Washington, even with the quota on imports.

The Mid-West market in general is also most economically served by locally refined oil products. Some are produced from Appalachian or local crude oils. But the region also relies heavily upon inter-regional and international imports, especially from the Mid-Continent and Gulf Coast fields, but also from Wyoming and several Canadian Provinces. The reason for this market orientation is once again to be found principally in relative transport costs, and especially the high costs of moving fuel oil and other heavy products. Refineries located on the oilfields could, and indeed sometimes do, pipe their lighter products to market, but they also have to ship (at considerable expense) their heavier products either in rail tank cars to the Mississippi River system and then by barge, or alternatively all the way by rail, to their markets. It is therefore generally very much more economic to pump the crude oil to the market and to refine it there; in consequence large diameter trunk pipelines carry huge quantities of crude oil into the Mid-West each year. However, in so far as the markets on or near to the oilfields also generate considerable demands for products and local refineries have been built to serve them, it is sometimes found to be advantageous for particular companies to meet some of the Mid-West's lighter product requirements from oilfield refineries. To handle this movement, several product pipelines have been constructed from the Gulf and Mid-Continent fields to such centres as Cincinnati and Chicago, to Kansas City, St Louis and Minneapolis.

The third major market area, California, is in some senses an anomaly. Its demands are considerable, but they are heavily biased towards the lighter oil fractions. Part of this market can be satisfied from local supplies of crude oil, and a number of refineries are located on or near to the Californian oilfields. These sources however are increasingly inadequate to meet the region's burgeoning demands, and an increasing proportion of its crude oil requirements have to be imported. Exempt from the oil import quotas applicable to the rest of the country, the options before the Californian oil industry are two-fold. One is to import crude from the Middle and Far East; in this case, a market orientation is clearly preferred for refinery operations on both transport cost and political grounds. The other is to make use of Gulf and Mid-Continent oil. Some of this is piped to southern California for refining in Los Angeles (in the same way as Canadian crude oil, on a smaller scale, is pumped to Puget Sound further north for refining). But there is also a possibility in the southern Californian case that, at some time in the future, products will also cross the mountain west to satisfy some of the west coast's requirements. At the heart of this issue lies the 'skewed' nature of demand in California which at present results in surplus heavy oils being shipped to the east coast. With refineries located on the interior oilfields, the cost of a reverse-haul of the heavy products could be avoided. One of the main reasons why this option has not been adopted to date is that the 'export' oil simply is not available at a competitive price from the interior fields; it could well be that only with the development of the oil shale deposits in Wyoming will a resource based refining industry emerge to satisfy part of the west coast's needs. Meanwhile refinery activities for the Californian market tend increasingly to be a market oriented, with the largest facilities located in Los Angeles and San Francisco. Together with the other refineries in the State these now represent over 13% of total capacity in the United States.

The trends in refinery location in the United States, therefore, reflect quite contrasting tendencies. Taking an over-view of the industry since 1920, the spatial emphasis has undoubtedly moved from the oilfields to market, and this for four principal reasons. First, the increasing efficiency of refinery operations has meant that the difference in the volume of products and crude oil from which they are refined has lessened; no longer, therefore, does a major transport cost advantage accrue to oilfield locations, and other factors now play a larger role in the geography of oil refining. Second, the growth of the north-east coast markets to a size capable of absorbing all the products of large refineries, and the increasing volume of crude oil imports from overseas, have given the Atlantic seaboard a considerable advantage for many refinery operations. Third, the growth of large inland markets in the Mid-West, and the expense which would be involved in transporting heavy oils from the oilfields to them, has encouraged yet another group of market oriented refineries. And, finally, the Californian market, having out-grown the capacity of local resources, has come to be supplied increasingly from inter-regional and international imports which are in large measure locally refined. But for the peculiar transport economics of the Gulf Coast to Megalopolis seaboard route, the swing away from oilfield locations would have been even greater. The continuation of this trend into the future will depend as much upon government policy with regard to oil imports and the exploitation of the shale oil resources of the West—and also the degree to which advantage is taken of the economies of crude oil coastwise transport in bulk—as it will upon the fundamental economics of refinery location.

An increasing number of market oriented refineries are also to be found outside the United States. In Western Europe, for example, which had only a few small refineries before 1939, drastic changes in both the pattern and nature of oil flows have taken place since 1945. Besides those which have been constructed near to domestic sources of oil (such as the Bordeaux refinery built to handle crude from the Parentis field), most of the new Western European refineries have an essentially market orientation. Transport costs are heavily in favour of this; and the larger and better balanced the market, the stronger are the attractions for refinery operations at or near the market. However, there remains a general reluctance to locate refineries where the demand is large yet unbalanced—unless they are nearer to the oilfields than other markets which might absorb their surplus products. The contrast between Norway and Italy illustrates this point. In both countries the requirements for heavy and middle distillates are strikingly greater than the demand for petrol; yet Italy in 1967 exported 18 million tons net of oil products whilst Norway (with her first large refinery constructed only in 1960) imported 2·6 million tons net. In terms of Western European demands, the large refineries on or near to the world's oilfields are today 'fossil refineries' dating from the time when, because of the rather low density of oil markets in Europe, refining at source was the most economic means of serving them. For this reason, therefore, refineries in the Middle East and the Caribbean have tended to expand rather slowly in recent years—and then primarily to satisfy a growing bunker market. The emerging pattern of refineries to meet Western European demands would appear to be units of about 2 to 4 million tons per year centred upon important regional markets, and supplemented by a few really big *entrepôt* refineries such as those at Southampton and Rotterdam, Antwerp and Marseilles, which can handle the crude imports with exceptional efficiency; the latter serve to balance out the quantity and quality needs of the regional markets, and export to those areas with a substantial deficiency of refining capacity such as Scandinavia and Switzerland.

The most rapidly expanding complex of market oriented refineries, of course, is in Japan, where oil demands in recent years have been growing by *circa* 20% per annum, and where crude oil imports in 1968 had reached a level in excess of 120 million tons. And despite its completely contrasting political economy, the USSR has also witnessed a shift in the location of its refineries from the producing regions to its major market areas. In 1950 the average length of crude oil pipeline there was only about 236 km, whereas fifteen years later it had increased to 660 km (Campbell, 1968, 141–2).

But it is not only economics which enters into decisions about the location of oil refineries. Politics play their part too. As early as 1928 France insisted on building her first refinery against the dictates of economics and for essentially strategic reasons; Italy followed suit in 1934; and Britain enlarged her (small) refining capacity during the war years, although in this case the new capacity was obtained by persuading the oil companies of its desirability rather than through legislation and tariff protection such as were used on the Continent. Again, in the immediate post-war years, most governments in Western Europe encouraged the construction of refineries on their soil. One of the more pressing reasons was, in fact, economic. At that time, when each was experiencing an acute shortage of foreign (especially dollar) exchange, one of the quickest ways of reducing dollar expenditure was by refinery construction in order to reduce oil product imports from the Western Hemisphere. Together with the growth of Western European oil markets and the changing economics of refinery location, this initiative spearheaded a rapid expansion of Western European refinery capacity—from 26 million tons annual capacity in 1949 to over 600 m.t. in 1969. In effect these political forces, which also encouraged the shift of Western Europe's oil supplies away from dollar sources and towards the Middle East, served to accelerate a tendency which was beginning to emerge in any case for purely economic reasons (Melamid, 1955; Mendershausen, 1950).

Elsewhere in the world, however, the effects of political forces have generally been to encourage the construction of refineries in economically marginal locations. On the one hand, there have been political pressures to construct refineries near to the sources of oil. By 1960 the Venezuelan Hydrocarbons Act (of 1943) had helped to multiply tenfold the country's annual refinery throughput by comparison with pre-war years by insisting upon a minimum proportion of national oil output being refined at source. Saudi Arabian concessions agreements with Japan have stipulated the quantities of oil which must be refined there if and when oil is found and production commences. On the other hand, there are political pressures to build refineries in the consuming countries, no matter how small their markets might be. For reasons of national pride, a refinery has become almost an essential ingredient in national economic self-esteem in many of the developing countries of the world, with the result that there has recently emerged a world-wide scatter of small, marginally economic, 'patriotic' refineries. The countries in Central America afford a case in point. The first refinery there, built on the Caribbean coast of Guatemala, was opened in 1963; six years later each of the other Central American republics had a plant, and Guatemala was having a second one built on its Pacific coast. The six refineries—each with a capacity of less than 750,000 —not only suffer the high costs of small scale operations, but the additional penalty of under-utilization for their combined capacity of 4 million tons exceeds the local market by 1 million tons.

The protection required by these and similar refineries is, of course, considerable, and it tends to take one of two forms. Either high tariff walls are erected against the import of oil products—sometimes they rise to as much as 40% of import parity in Africa and Central America—or, alternatively, the government bargains with an oil company offering a monopoly of part or all of its market in return for a refinery. The first of such refineries was built in Portugal;

comparable arrangements have subsequently been concluded in many developing countries such as Tunisia, Morocco and Ghana. The marketing of oil globally is sufficiently competitive to make this sort of bargaining feasible—for any one oil company cannot afford to be without marketing outlets in all such economies and (from its viewpoint) the cost of such a refinery is simply the price that has to be paid in order to ensure for itself a minimum market in the 'third world' in the future.

The oil refinery industry, in brief, has experienced quite extensive changes in its location patterns over the last forty or so years, and especially since 1945. These changes are rooted essentially in technological change and the way in which it has modified the economics of refinery operations, the alternative methods of transporting oil, and the nature of the market requiring oil products. The rapid growth of oil demands and their distribution throughout the world, however, is also important; and with it must be ranked political considerations, whose impress upon the world pattern of refinery location, although sometimes eluding precise definition, without doubt is steadily growing. It will be variations of these same factors which undoubtedly will be primarily responsible for the essential changes and characteristics of the geography of oil refining in the future.

BIBLIOGRAPHY

Adelman, M. A. (1962), *The Supply of Natural Gas,* Oxford: Journal of Industrial Economics Supplement.
——(1964a), The world oil outlook, in Clawson, M. (Ed.), *Natural Resources and International Development,* Baltimore.
——(1964b), Efficiency of resource use in crude petroleum, *Southern Economic Journal,* **31,** 101.
——(1964c), Oil prices in the long run (1963–75), *Journal of Business of the University of Chicago,* **37,** 143.
——(1966), American coal in Western Europe, *Journal of Industrial Economics,* **14,** 199.
——(1969), Significance of shifts in world oil supplies, paper presented to 20th Alaska Science Conference, University of Alaska, Fairbanks.
Alexandersson, G. (1957), The Oil Refineries of the World—A Case Study, *Proceedings of the International Geographical Union Regional Conference in Japan,* 260.
——(1967), *Geography of Manufacturing,* Englewood Cliffs, New Jersey.
Balestra, P. (1967), *The Demand for Natural Gas in the United States,* Amsterdam.
Ballert, A. G. (1948), The Coal Trade of the Great Lakes and the Port of Toledo, *Geographical Review,* **38,** 194.
——(1953), The Great Lakes Coal Trade; Present and Future, *Economic Geography,* **29,** 48.
Beaver, S. H. (1951), Coke Manufacture in Great Britain, *Transactions and Papers, 1951,* The Institute of British Geographers, 142.
Beecham, A. (1958), The Coal Industry, in Burn, D. (Ed.), *The Structure of British Industry,* vol. 1, Cambridge.
Berrie, T. W. (1967), The economics of system planning in bulk electricity supply, in Turvey, R. (Ed.), *Public Enterprise,* London.
Booth, E. S. (1967), *Power Supply for 1970,* London: CEGB.

Bradley, P. G. (1967), *The Economics of Crude Petroleum Production*, Amsterdam.

British Railways Board (1963), *The Reshaping of British Railways*, London.

Brunner, C. T. (1962), Productivity in oil distribution in Britain, *Institute of Petroleum Review, 5.*

Burn, D. (1967), *The Political Economy of Nuclear Energy,* London: Institute of Economic Affairs.

Burns, J. (1958), Presidential Address, *Publications No. 521, Institution of Gas Engineers,* London.

Campbell, R. W. (1968), *The Economics of Soviet Oil and Gas,* Baltimore.

Campbell, T. C. (1954), *The Bituminous Coal Freight Rate Structure—An Economic Appraisal,* Morganstown, West Virginia.

Cash, P. W. (1967), *Expansion of the British supply system with particular reference to reliability and economic evaluation,* paper presented to Latin American Electrical Energy Seminar on Electric Systems Planning, Lima.

Chandler, G., and Priddle, R. (1960), The Influence of Economic Fluctuations on the Demand for Energy, *World Power Conference,* Madrid, IB/16.

Chapman, J. D. (1961), A Geography of Energy: An Emerging Field of Study, *The Canadian Geographer, 5, 10.*

Chardonnet, J. (1962), *Géographie Industrielle,* tome 1, *Les Sources d'Énergie,* Paris.

Christenson, C. L. (1962), *Economic Redevelopment in Bituminous Coal,* Cambridge, Massachusetts.

Church, M. (1960), *The Spatial Organisation of Electric Power Territories in Massachusetts,* Chicago.

Clark, D., Littler, D. J., and Scott, E. C. (1962), The Design and Operation of the Grid System of England and Wales, *World Power Conference,* Melbourne, III 0/11.

Clark, L. J. (1964), *Gas production development in Great Britain,* paper read to 9th International Gas Conference, The Hague.

Committee on Interior and Insular Affairs, United States Senate (1962), *Report of the National Fuels and Energy Study Group,* Washington, D.C.

Conrad, R. (1955), Economic Comparison between the Transport of Coal and the Transmission of Electricity, *International Union of Producers and Distributors of Electrical Energy,* London, III/2.

Cookenboo, L. (1953), *Economies of Scale in the Operation of Crude Oil Pipelines,* unpublished Ph.D. Thesis, Massachusetts Institute of Technology.

——(1955), *Crude Oil Pipelines,* Cambridge, Massachusetts.

Dales, J. H. (1953), Fuel, Power and Industrial Development in Central Canada, *Papers and Proceedings, American Economic Review, 43,* 181.

Darmstadter, J., et al. (in press), *Energy in the World Economy,* Baltimore.

Davis, J. (1957), *Canadian Energy Prospects,* Ottawa.

Deasy, G. F., and Greiss, P. R. (1957), Geographical Significance of Recent Changes in Mining in the Bituminous Coalfield of Pennsylvania, *Economic Geography*, **33**, 283.

——(1960), Factors influencing distribution of steam-electric generating plants, *Professional Geographer*, 12.

Dreyfus, H. B. (1964), The growth of the CEGB transmission system, *Electrical Times*, 26 March, 499.

Economic Commission for Europe (1955), *The Price of Oil in Western Europe*, Geneva.

——(1966), *The Comparative Economics of Transport and Storage Operations for Different Forms of Energy*, Geneva.

Edwards, R. S., and Clark, D. (1962), Planning for expansion in electricity supply, paper read to the British Electrical Power Convention.

Egerton, A. C. (1951), *Civilization and the Use of Energy*, Paris: UNESCO.

Emerson, H. N. (1957), Oil Transportation Preferences—Their Bases *Proceedings, American Petroleum Institute 1957*, sect. 5, New York.

Estall, R. C. (1958), The London Coal Trade, *Geography*, **43**, 75.

Estall, R. C., and Buchanan, R. O. (1961), *Industrial Activity and Economic Geography*, London.

Falomo, G. (1960), Economics of Long-Distance Fuel Transportation and Electric Transmission, *World Power Conference*, Madrid, III/2.

Federal Power Commission (1948), *Natural Gas Investigation*, Washington, D.C.: Docket no. G-580, Report of Smith, N. L., and Wimberley, H.

——(1964), *National Power Survey*, Washington, D.C.

——(1969, *A Staff Report on National Gas Supply and Demand*, Washington, D.C.

Forster, C. I. K., and Whiting, I. J. (1968), An integrated mathematical model of the fuel economy, *Statistical News*, 3, 3.1.

Frank, H. J. (1966), *Crude Oil Prices in the Middle East*, New York.

Frankel, P. H. (1946), *Essentials of Petroleum: A Key to Oil Economics*, London.

——(1962), *Oil: the Facts of Life*, London.

Frankel, P. H., and Newton, W. L. (1961), The Location of Refineries, *Institute of Petroleum Review*, 197.

Fritz, W. G., and Veenstra, T. A. (1935), *Regional Shifts in the Bituminous Coal Industry*, Pittsburgh.

Fulton, A. A., et al. (1962), The Application of Low Load Factor Hydro and Pumped Storage Plants in Great Britain, *World Power Conference*, Melbourne, III/I_1/II.

George, K. D. (1960), Economics of Nuclear and Conventional Coal-Fired Stations in the United Kingdom, *Oxford Economics Papers*, **12**, 294.

George, P. (1950), *Géographie de l'Énergie*, Paris.

Grigg, V. H. (1954), *International Price Structure of Crude Oil*, unpublished Ph.D. Thesis, Massachusetts Institute of Technology.

Guyol, N. B. (1960), Energy Consumption and Economic Development, in Ginsberg, N. (Ed.), *Essays in Geography and Economic Development*, Chicago.

Hallett, G., and Randall, P. (1970), *Maritime Industry and Port Development in South Wales*, Cardiff.

Hartley, H. (1962), Transportation Costs of Energy as a Factor in the Changing Pattern of Power, *World Power Conference*, Melbourne, III/9.

Hartshorne, J. E. (1962), *Oil Companies and Governments*, London.

Hauser, D. P. (1969), *Postwar power station location and interregional fuel and electricity flows in England and Wales*, unpublished Ph.D. thesis, University of Cambridge.

——(1971), System costs and the location of new generating plant in England and Wales, *Institute of British Geographers Transactions*, **54**.

Hawkins, E. K. (1953), Competition between the Nationalized Electricity and Gas Industries, *Journal of Industrial Economics*, **1** (1952/3), 155.

Henderson, J., and Allan, C. L. C. (1958), Economic Integration of Coal-Fired, Nuclear and Hydraulic Generation of Electricity with Special Reference to Scotland, *World Power Conference*, Montreal, A/4.

——(1960), Energy Resources and Growth of Consumption in Scotland, *World Power Conference*, Madrid, IA/4.

Henderson, J. M., and Wood, A. J. (1956), An Economic Study of High Voltage Transmission, *Power Apparatus and Systems*, 695.

Hirst, D. (1966), *Oil and Public Opinion in the Middle East*, London.

Hoover, E. M. (1948), *The Location of Economic Activity*, London.

Hubbard, M. E. (1960), Pipelines in Relation to Other Forms of Transport, *World Power Conference*, Madrid, IIIA/8.

——(1963), Productivity in the petroleum industry—the sources of some of its improvements, *Journal of the Institute of Petroleum*, **49**, 29.

Hubbard, M. (1967), *The Economics of Transporting Oil to and within Europe*, London.

Hunter, A. (1966), The Indonesian Oil Industry, *Australian Economic Papers*, **5**.

Issawi, C., and Yeganeh, M. (1962), *The Economics of Middle Eastern Oil*, New York.

Jensen, J. E. (1967), Crude oil: capacity, supply schedules and imports policy, *Land Economics*, **43**.

Jensen, W. G. (1967), *Energy in Europe, 1945–1980*, London.

Joint Economic Committee (1960), *Energy Resources and Government*, Washington, D.C.

Joint Committee on Atomic Energy (1964), *Nuclear Power Economics—Analysis and Comments—1964*, Washington, D.C.

Kornfeld, J. A. (1949), *Natural Gas Economics*, Dallas.

Landsberg, H. H., and Schurr, S. H. (1968), *Energy in the United States: Sources, Uses and Policy Issues*, New York.

Lane, F. J., and Chorlton, A. (1966), The 400 kV system in England and Wales, *Proceedings, American Power Conference*, **28**, 897.

Lenczowski, G. (1960), *Oil and State in the Middle East*, Ithica, New York.

Levy, W. (1961), World Oil in Transition, *The Economist*, 19 August, 723.

Lindsay, J. R. (1954), *The Location of Oil Refining in the United States*, unpublished Ph.D. Thesis, Harvard University.

——(1956), Regional Advantage in Oil Refining, *Papers and Proceedings of the Regional Science Association*, **2**, 304.

Little, I. M. D. (1953), *The Price of Fuel*, Oxford.

Livingston, S. M. (1959), Economics of Refinery Location in the United States, *Fifth World Petroleum Congress*, IX/9.

Longrigg, S. H. (1968), *Oil in the Middle East*, Oxford.

Lovejoy, W. F., and Homan, P. T. (1967), *Economic Aspects of Oil Conservation and Regulation*, Washington, D.C.

Lubell, H. (1962), *Middle East Oil Crises and Western Europe's Energy Supplies*, Baltimore: Rand Research Study.

Lufti, A. (1968), *OPEC Oil*, Beirut, Lebanon.

MacAvoy, P. (1962), *Price Formation in Natural Gas Fields*, New Haven.

MacAvoy, P., and Sloss, J. (1966), *Regulation of Transport Innovation: the ICC and Unit Coal Trains to the East Coast*, New York.

McCleskey, H. C. (1960), *Petroleum, Conservation and National Defense*, unpublished Ph.D. Thesis, Harvard University.

McClean, J. G., and Haigh, R. W. (1954), *The Growth of Integrated Oil Companies*, Boston.

Manchester Joint Research Council (1960), *Economic Aspects of Fuel and Power in British Industry*, Manchester.

Manley, G. (1957), Climatic Fluctuations and Fuel Requirements, *Scottish Geographical Magazine*, **73**, 19.

Manners, G. (1959), Recent Changes in the British Gas Industry, *Transactions and Papers 1959*, The Institute of British Geographers, 153.

——(1961a), Thermal Electricity Generation in the United States, *Tijdschrift voor Economische en Sociale Geografie*, 291.

——(1961b), The Gas Industry in Europe, *The Canadian Geographer*, **5**, 30.

——(1961c), Natural Gas in the USA, *Gas and Coke*, 181.

——(1962a), The Pipeline Revolution, *Geography*, **47**, 154.

——(1962b), Fuel and Energy Policy in the USA, *Gas and Coke*, 96.

——(1962c), Some Location Principles of Thermal Electricity Generation, *Journal of Industrial Economics*, **10**, 218.

——(1965), The changing location of secondary energy production in Britain, *Land Economics*, **41**, 317.

——(1968), Latter-day leviathans for bulk transport, *Optima*, 164.

——(1971), Some economic and spatial characteristics of the British energy market in Chisholm, M. D. I., and Manners, G. (Eds.), *Spatial Policy Problems of the British Economy*, Cambridge.

Marjolin, R. J. (1961), Co-ordination des Politiques de l'Énergie, *Bulletin d'Association Française de Techniciens du Petrole*, 13.

Melamid, A. (1955), Geographical Distribution of Petroleum Refining Capacity: A Study of the European Refinery Programme, *Economic Geography*, **31**, 168.

——(1968), Geography of the Nigerian Petroleum Industry, *Economic Geography*, 44.

Mele, R. van (1952), Cost Comparisons between Coal Transport and Electric Power Transmission, *International Union of Producers and Distributors of Electrical Energy*, Rome, IV/4.

Menderhausen, H. (1950), *Dollar Shortage and Oil Supplies in 1948–50*, Princeton: Essays in International Finance no. 11.

Ministry of Power (1965), *Fuel Policy* (Cmnd. 2798), London.

——(1967), *Fuel Policy* (Cmnd. 3438), London.

Mock, G. B. (1961), The Market Orientated Refinery and the Challenge it Poses, *Oil and Gas International*, 1/4, 20.

Mounfield, P. R. (1961), The Location of Nuclear Power Stations in the United Kingdom, *Geography*, **46**, 139.

——(1967), Nuclear power in the United Kingdom: a new phase, *Geography*, **52**, 310.

Naess, E. D. (1965), *The Tanker Industry: Problems and Prospects*, Bergen Institute for Shipping Research.

Nagler, K. B. (1960), The Transportation and the Storage of Gaseous Fuels, *World Power Conference*, Madrid, III/A/5.

Nash, G. D. (1968), *United States Oil Policy, 1890–1964*, Pittsburgh.

National Board for Prices and Incomes (1969), *Gas Prices* (Cmnd. 3924), London.

O'Connor, H. (1955), *The Empire of Oil,* London.

Odell, P. R. (1963), *An Economic Geography of Oil,* London.

——(1965), *Oil: the New Commanding Height*, London: Fabian Research Series 251.

——(1968), The British Gas Industry: Review, *Geographical Journal*, **134**, 81.

——(1969), *Natural Gas in Western Europe*, Haarlem.

——(1970), *Oil and World Power*, London.

O'Loughlin, C. (1967), *The Economics of Sea Transport*, Oxford.

Organization for Economic Cooperation and Development (1961), *Pipelines and Tankers*, Paris.

——(1964), *Oil Today (1964)*, Paris.

——(1966), *Energy Policy, Problems and Objectives*, Paris.

——(1969), *Pipelines in the US and Europe*, Paris.

Organization for European Economic Cooperation (1960), *Gas in Europe*, Paris.

——(1960), *Towards a New Energy Pattern in Europe,* Paris.

Parker, G. L. (1940), *The Coal Industry,* Washington, D.C.

Parsons, J. J. (1958), The Natural Gas Supply of California, *Land Economics*, **34**, 23.

Pask, V. A. (1950), Modern Trends in the Design and Location of Electrical Generating Stations, *World Power Conference*, London, 8.

Pedante, R. (1952), Étude Comparative des Différentes Formes de Transport d'Énergie, *International Union of Producers and Distributors of Electrical Energy*, Rome, IV/12.

Penrose, E. T. (1968), *The Large International Firm in Developing Countries*, London.

PEP (1963), *An Energy Policy for EEC?*, London.

PEP (1966), *A Fuel Policy for Britain*, London.

Peterson, G. R. (1952), Comparisons du Coût de Transport de l'Énergie Electrique et du Charbon pour le Choix de l'Emplacement des Centrales, *International Union of Producers and Distributors of Electrical Energy*, Rome, IV/13.

Phillips, C. N. (1953), Economics and Development to Expect in Transporting Energy, *Edison Electric Institute Bulletin*, **21**, 271.

Pierce, R. E., and George, E. E. (1948), Economics of Long Distance Energy Transmission, *American Institute of Electrical Engineers*, **67**, 1090.

Polach, J. (1964), *Euratom, its Background, Issues and Economic Implications*, New York.

Polanyi, G. (1967), *The Price of North Sea Gas*, London: Institute of Economic Affairs.

Pratt, W. E., and Goode, D. (1950), *World Geography of Petroleum*, New York.

Pratten, C., and Dean, R. M. (1965, *The Economics of Large-Scale Production in British Industry*, Cambridge.

Priddle, R. (1961), The Effect of Fluctuations in Economic Activity on the Demand for Energy, *Economia Internazionale Delle Fonti de Energia*, 5/4.

Pugh, J. C. (1962), The floating power stations of Scandinavia, 1959–1961, *Geography*, **47**, 270.

Putnam, P. C. (1954), *Energy in the Future*, London.

Rawstron, E. M. (1955), The Salient Geographical Features of Electricity Production in Great Britain, *Advancement of Science*, **12**, 73.

Resources for the Future (1968), *US Energy Policies, an Agenda for Research*, Washington, D.C.

Robinson, C. (1969), *A Policy for Fuel?*, London: Institute of Economic Affairs.

Schurr, S. H. (1960), Foreign Trade Policies Affecting Mineral Fuels in the United States and Western Europe, paper presented to the American Association for the Advancement of Science, New York.

——(1963), *Some Observations on the Economics of Atomic Power*, Washington, D.C.

Schurr, S. H., et al. (1960), *Energy in the American Economy, 1850–1975*, Baltimore.

Schurr, S. H., and Homan, P. T. (1971), *Middle Eastern Oil and the Western World: Prospects and Problems*, Baltimore.

Scottish Development Department (1962), *Electricity in Scotland* (Cmnd. 1859), Edinburgh.

Sewell, W. R. (1964), The role of regional interties in postwar energy resource development, *Annals of the Association of American Geographers,* **64,** 566.

Shaffer, E. H. (1968), *The Oil Import Program of the United States: an Evaluation,* New York.

Simpson, E. S. (1966), *Coal and the Power Industries in Postwar Britain,* London.

Sorre, M. (1948), *Fondements de la Géographie Humaine,* tome IIi, Paris.

Stockton, J. R., Henshaw, R. C., and Graves, R. W. (1952), *Economics of Natural Gas in Texas,* Austin, Texas.

Sub-Committee on Automation and Energy Resources (1959), *Energy Resources and Technology,* Washington, D.C.

United Nations, (1957a), *Economic Applications of Atomic Energy,* New York.

——(1957b), *Proceedings of the International Conference on the Peaceful Uses of Atomic Energy,* **1,** 112.

——(1957c), *Energy Development in Latin America,* Geneva.

——(1967), *Small-Scale Power Generation,* New York.

United States Senate (1945), *The Economics of Coal Traffic Flow* (Document no. 82, 78th Congress), Washington, D.C.

Van Der Tak, H. G. (1966), *The Economic Choice between Hydroelectric and Thermal Power Development,* Baltimore.

Vogtle, A. W. (1956), Impact of Freight Rates on the Distribution of Coal, *Proceedings of the American Power Conference,* **18,** Chicago, 192.

Warren, H. V. (1961), Some Pertinent Factors in Energy Studies, *The Canadian Geographer,* **5,** 16.

Watkins, N. (1944), Scarce Raw Materials: an Analysis and a Proposal, *American Economic Review,* **34,** 254.

Weber, A. (1957), *Theory of the Location of Industries,* Chicago: English trans. by Friedrich, C. J.

Wigley, K. (1968), *The Demand for Fuel 1948–1975,* London.

Williamson, H. F., et al. (1959), *The American Petroleum Industry, 1899–1959,* Evanston, Illinois.

Winger, J. G., et al. (1968), *Outlook for Energy in the United States,* New York: Chase Manhattan Bank.

Zannetos, Z. S. (1959), *The Theory of Oil Tankship Rates,* unpublished Ph.D. Thesis, Massachusetts Institute of Technology.

INDEX